CAUGHT IN THE CROSSFIRE

THE INSIDE STORY OF PAKISTAN'S SECRET SERVICES

Naseem Akhtar Khan

Pen & Sword
MILITARY
AN IMPRINT OF PEN & SWORD BOOKS LTD.
YORKSHIRE - PHILADELPHIA

First published in Great Britain in 2024 by
PEN AND SWORD MILITARY
An imprint of
Pen & Sword Books Limited
Yorkshire – Philadelphia

Copyright © Naseem Akhtar Khan, 2024

ISBN 978 1 03610 507 5

The right of Naseem Akhtar Khan to be identified as Author of this work has been asserted by him in accordance with the Copyright, Designs and Patents Act 1988.

A CIP catalogue record for this book is available from the British Library.

All rights reserved. No part of this book may be reproduced or transmitted in any form or by any means, electronic or mechanical including photocopying, recording or by any information storage and retrieval system, without permission from the Publisher in writing.

Typeset in Times New Roman 10.5/13.5 by
SJmagic DESIGN SERVICES, India.
Printed and bound in the UK by CPI Group (UK) Ltd.

Pen & Sword Books Limited incorporates the imprints of Atlas, Archaeology, Aviation, Discovery, Family History, Fiction, History, Maritime, Military, Military Classics, Politics, Select, Transport, True Crime, Air World, Frontline Publishing, Leo Cooper, Remember When, Seaforth Publishing, The Praetorian Press, Wharncliffe Local History, Wharncliffe Transport, Wharncliffe True Crime and White Owl.

For a complete list of Pen & Sword titles please contact
PEN & SWORD BOOKS LIMITED
George House, Units 12 & 13, Beevor Street, Off Pontefract Road,
Barnsley, South Yorkshire, S71 1HN, England
E-mail: enquiries@pen-and-sword.co.uk
Website: www.pen-and-sword.co.uk

or

PEN AND SWORD BOOKS
1950 Lawrence Rd, Havertown, PA 19083, USA
E-mail: uspen-and-sword@casematepublishers.com
Website: www.penandswordbooks.com

BOOK REVIEWS

Lieutenant General (Retd) Amjad Shuaib, HI (M)
(Ex-adjutant General Pakistan Army and a leading defence analyst/vlogger)

The book, *Caught in the Crossfire: An Inside Story of Pakistan's Secret Services* (in the Khakis), presents the crux of Brig Naseem's decades-long experiences with the Pakistan Army and Inter-Services Intelligence Agency (ISI), by skilfully moving readers like a tourist guide through his memory lane. As a result, the narration of events in this book makes it quite absorbing to read.

Being an eyewitness to some important geo-strategic and geopolitical developments in our region and within the country, having far-reaching consequences for Pakistan's national security, he has tried to raise the curtain from many hidden aspects of the military history of our region, that are not generally known. His personal involvement in successfully handling many treacherous and complex situations makes the narrative an eye-opening account of the conspiracies that Pakistan security forces had to confront over the years to safeguard our national security. The book should be a very beneficial read for those who wish to ponder history through realistic interpretation of the events.

In his book, Naseem has also very rightly brought out some of the inadequacies among our domestic socio-political environments adversely affecting the system of governance in place. Unfortunately, the net result is our failure to counter the brutal anti-Pakistan malice spread around by our adversaries.

Brig Naseem's views on international and regional security manoeuvrings and emerging scenarios with reference to Pakistan, augmented through a strong premise, must attract the attention of readers within and abroad, to understand the intricacies that shape Pakistan's national security paradigm.

This book is a very valuable addition to the personal experience-based literature. I must commend Brig Naseem for his truthfulness and great sense of purpose with which he has penned down his memoirs. I have found this book to be an excellent choice for personal and public libraries.

Lieutenant General (Retd) Ghulam Mustafa, HI(M), Tbt
(Ex-Director General of Pakistan Army's Strategic Division)

Being of the same vintage, I too, am witness to the tumultuous moments in Pakistan's exciting history which form the backdrop of Brig Naseem's book. Our personal experiences may differ, but the context does not. That is what makes this book very interesting for me. I am sure it will also be a stimulating read for everyone else, interested to know what makes the Pakistan Army the bedrock of Pakistan's national security and therefore, the ultimate objective of all our enemies, within as well as without. The chain of conspiracies to disrupt our unity and cohesion has been continuous, as history tells us time and time again. History is also witness to the fact that we as a nation, armed forces fully backed by our great people, have defeated most of their malicious designs very effectively.

Is it any wonder then that 'Khakis' are increasingly being subjected to an offensive of another kind? That is the nature of fifth G going on to sixth G Warfare; destroy the strong glue bonding people with their armed forces and within the forces, create mistrust between rank and file and their senior leadership. God forbid, if that were to happen even halfway through, our enemies would stand victorious much before guns, tanks, and missiles come into action. This is the central theme of the book as I understand it.

Brig Naseem has done justice to the subject. I am almost jealous of him for having taken this much-needed lead to apprise our people of the most dangerous attack on Pakistan.

My felicitations to Brig Naseem for having authored this wonderful book. Wish him all the very best in his further endeavours aimed at helping the world at large understand Pakistan, its people, and its armed forces, better.

Air Marshal (Retd) Masood Akhtar, HI (M), SI(M), Tbt
(Ex-Pakistan Air Force)

Brigadier Naseem's book *Caught in the Crossfire: An Inside Story of Pakistan's Secret Services (in the Khakis)* is a delightful guide full of important information on the Pakistan Army, explicitly highlighting the salient aspects of its strengths;

its make-up, mentoring process, and final delivery of its obligations to the country. Daunting security challenges faced by the army and by Pakistan have been thoughtfully highlighted.

Though I have known Brigadier Naseem since 1987, I came to know more about him as an intelligence operative after I did some work with one of his mentored officers in the ISI. That is when I found out about some very fine work accomplished by him in that organization. His book is a true reflection of his dedication and hard work over the decades and should serve as authentic study material for military historians to ponder.

I strongly recommend this book be placed in all national and international libraries. I also wish this to be published by the book clubs at home and abroad.

Colonel (Retd) Azam Qadri
(Ex-Pakistan Army and military historian/biographer)

The punch lines of the book read, 'Every Soldier has a story, and every story deserves to be told'. How apt? He has done exactly that and done it so articulately. Being a soldier myself and a writer, not only can I truly sense and feel his vibes but feel the same flavour, because I have been a victim of a similar experience as him when it comes to writing 'Nothing but the whole truth'.

The book mostly covers the military history of the 70s, 80s, and 90s all the way through to date, with particular reference to our region and Pakistan. Military historians will bear me out that all these years have seen some extremely fateful developments in our region with far-reaching consequences. Naseem takes the readers on a misty, twisted, and eye-opening journey into the perilous world of the military expeditioners, with a matching bumpy and piercing tone in the book. He has truly unravelled his journey literally from his life in the cradle to this day and how articulately he has done this, is highly appreciable.

I had an opportunity to glean through this book, during its evolutionary stage and I am fully aware of his dedication, hard work, and passion to see the journey be completed. It has virtually come out to be a book of great substance and candid exposition of events of historic values based on his first-hand information and experiences.

I will recommend this not only to my comrades in the army but to everyone fond of reading and reading biographies and military history must give this book a read.

Captain (Retired) Mohammad Ahsan ur Rahim T I (M) (Ex-Pakistan Navy)

I came to know Brig Naseem a couple of years back in Dubai and our common armed forces background, brought us closer to regularly sharing information of common interest and discussing important developments in Pakistan and internationally. Reading his articles in print media in Pakistan and abroad, describing varying security hypotheses in the region and sharing his thoughts on various other administrative and security-related issues within the country, always fascinated me to know more about his work.

Close interaction helped me to know more about him as an intelligence operative and the highly valuable work accomplished by him during his decades-long service with the Pakistan Army. It was then that I came to know of him writing his book.

I found the book an excellent work to highlight the emerging security patterns in the region, endangering our national security and some prudent methodologies needed to counter these threats. It should help people to know more about our armed forces and the sacrifices they make towards the security of our country. It should particularly help the strategic institutions within the country and abroad, as authentic study material to contemplate the military history of our region in its correct perspective.

Major (Retired) Farooq Malik
(Ex-Professor of English Literature, University of Central Punjab, Pakistan)

Being his ex-colleague in the 16 Self-propelled (SP) Regiment, I had not the least doubt that Naseem Khan had the will and the steel to undertake any venture and see it to its befitting fulfilment, unawed by the odds; yet one area that I thought was a minefield for him, was producing a book. This was a surprise to me that never entered the remotest corner of my brain!

The book is an eventful and absorbing account from the front-line observer that deserves reading and understanding. The story of a patriot and a soldier. It is told from the heart with no clever after-touches. A lot many of us, especially the ones who had the distinction of wearing a uniform, might find themselves donning in the same boots.

It is a worth reading account to see the momentum of life at close quarters. Best of luck, my friend n buddy, Naseem Khan.

Brigadier (Retired) Khalid Afridi
(Colonel of the Regiment, 16 SP Regiment, Pakistan Army)

Brigadier Naseem A. Khan is a dedicated and die-hard parental officer of 'The Dashing Sixteen' and commanded the unit for nearly three and a half years. Under his able command, the unit changed its outlook and made strides in all spheres of regimental activities; operational, training, sports, and administration. Raised in May 1956, the unit grew in high military traditions and culture due to its valiant and chivalrous officers and men and holds a protuberant name in the Pakistan Army. Brigadier Naseem has always been amongst the front-line runners in all such pursuits.

Besides a comprehensive analysis of national and international security issues, the book carries a detailed account of our great unit which explicitly defines the martial passion and the virtues of honour, discipline, loyalty, and superb response to the call of duty amongst all ranks of the unit. We feel indebted to Brigadier Naseem for having done so, most proficiently.

May-Britt V. R. Ronnebro
(Ambassador for United Nations Sustainable Development Goals)

Caught in the Crossfire: An Inside Story of Pakistan's Secret Services, will give you an insight into living military life as an intelligence operative and a comprehensive understanding of the Pakistan Army. Facing security and counterintelligence issues in this region of the world with its challenges is an experience which is shared by the author and worth reflecting on. This book would be a valuable read for those who cherish wider knowledge and encourage the new generation to protect their country's security, borders, and institutions with the aim of safeguarding democracy.

Doctor Samih Teymur
(Ex-First-Class Police Chief, Turkish National Police)

This book is Brigadier Naseem's memoir of his forty years of military experience in the Pakistan Army and its elite intelligence agency ISI, starting from lower ranks to the top. His continuation in the private security industry in

Dubai after his retirement from the army has equally been very fulfilling. I am personally aware of some of his very fruitful ventures in this field.

The book is an excellent narration of his adventures in his military career and will be a precious resource for those who want to study the Pakistan Army and read a first-hand narration of a very eventful military history of South Asia during the last four decades. Should be a very interesting read for students of military history and strategic studies.

ACKNOWLEDGEMENT

The book *Caught in the Crossfire: An Inside Story of Pakistan's Secret Services* was initially, intended to be titled 'In the Khakis'. The words 'Khakis', referred to the colour of Pakistan's army uniform and it is commonly used in Pakistan while referring to the army. However, to make the title more relevant to its content and easily comprehensible for international circulation, subsequently, it was changed to the current book title.

It has been tough going reaching so far and being able to compile the book into its final shape. However, sense of purpose, determination, and total commitment to the cause, made it possible for me to take on this challenging task to its logical end. The unwavering support from my family, friends, and mentors has been the key to its successful ending.

I wish to take this opportunity to say 'thank you' to all who have been an outstanding inspiration and a great help to me in writing this book. My wife and children have been at the forefront among these persuaders who practically joined me to bring this project to a successful end. I cannot help but mention my eldest daughter Maryia who sat by my side at the writing desk for long hours, helped me align my thought processes, edited the script, and consumed more than half of the share of Panadol tablets that we both had to consume to fight against headaches due to prolong sittings in front of the laptop, for about the last year and a half.

My special thanks to some of my mentors at home and abroad, who continuously encouraged me to undertake this project and were kind enough to pen down their thoughts on this book. I want to make a special mention of Major General Bruce M. Lawlor, ex-US Army, a person whom I met for the first time in Dubai a few years back. Since then, he has been a great friend and I always found him forthcoming to render any kind of guidance or support that I was looking for during the writing of this book. He was amongst a few of my close associates who initially persuaded me to write a memoir, based on my personal experiences as a soldier, having been an important part of the action-packed military history of this region during the last four decades. His encouragement and timely guidance during the process of publishing this book, have been unprecedented.

Another person that I cannot miss mentioning is Col Azam Qadri, my ex-instructor in the School of Armour. He too has been a great support to me during the process of writing this book. He was always forthcoming to render any kind of support that was needed to complete this project and went out of the way to get the procedural formalities completed from Pakistan Army Headquarters, enabling me to publish this book.

I have no words to thank the prestigious institution of the Pakistan Army and ISI for having given me so much in life to share with people who may wish to benefit from this read.

I cherish the support from my family, my mentors, and the great institutions I have been part of, and I wish to dedicate this book in their names.

CONTENTS

FOREWORD – I   xvi
FOREWORD – II   xviii
PREFACE   xxi

PART 1: THE ARC OF MY LEARNING CURVE

CHAPTER 1: THE OPENING SHOT   2
- The Spotlight   2
- Flashback   4
- The Storyline   7

CHAPTER 2: AT 'RED-CLAY CASTLE'   10
- The Guardian Angels   10
- My Comrades   12
- The 'Taat' School   15
- The Breeze at the Dawn   16

CHAPTER 3: THE GAME CHANGER   20
- In a Different World   20
- The Formative Process   22
- Narrow Escape   24
- Thank You, CCH   25

PART 2: IN THE KHAKIS

CHAPTER 4: THE BRIDGEHEAD OPERATION	28
Assault Across	28
The Bridgehead Battle	31
CHAPTER 5: THE BREAKOUT MANOEUVRES AND THE MENTORS	36
The Dasher's Way	37
Battling in the Silent War Zone – Part 1	47
Back to the 'Dasher's Den'	55
An Exposure to Martial Law Duties	56
Becoming Wiser than an Owl	59
On the Line of Control	60
'Hannibal' of Murree Hills	62
Leading the 'Dashers'	63
At Army General Headquarters	70
Battling in the Silent War Zone – Part 2	71
Exposure To International Diplomacy	76
Battling in the Silent War Zone – Part 3	78
CHAPTER 6: IN THE KHAKIS: AN INFINITE BLESSING	82
A Personal Treasure	82
The Army Values of a Pakistani Soldier	84

PART 3: JOURNEY THROUGH THE CHANGING WORLD ORDER

CHAPTER 7: DIRECTION AND INTENSITY OF THE CROSSFIRE	88
Crossfire from Across the Borders	89
The Enemies Within	120
A Treasonous Interplay with Staggering Consequences	137

CONTENTS

CHAPTER 8: EMERGING SECURITY CHALLENGES AND THE WAY FORWARD — 138

- An Overview of Regional Security Challenges — 138
- Major Security Concerns for Pakistan — 139
- Role of Pakistan Armed Forces — 141
- The Way Forward — 143

PART 4: FAREWELL TO ARMS AND POST-RETIREMENT VENTURES

CHAPTER 9: RETIREMENT FROM ARMY AND A JERKY RE-START — 152

- Transition to Civvies — 152
- The Close Circuit Routine — 153
- Soldiering Through a Patch of Turbulence — 154

CHAPTER 10: QUESTIONING LIFE IS NEVER AN OPTION — 157

- Getting into Warrior's Mode — 157
- The Fightback — 158
- Lessons Learnt — 159
- Private Security Sector: My New Playground — 163

CHAPTER 11: GLOBAL SECURITY PATTERNS: TRENDS RESHAPING PRIVATE SECURITY PROTOCOLS — 165

- The Prevailing Security Framework — 166
- Emerging Trends in Private Security — 167
- Expanding Horizons for the Security Professionals — 168

CHAPTER 12: BEYOND THE FRONTLINES: A SILENT TRIUMPH — 171

- The Base of Fire — 171
- The Infinite Gain — 173
- Bridging the Realms: From Guns to Books — 175

CONCLUSION — 176
THANK YOU NOTE — 180
GLOSSARY — 181
INDEX — 187

FOREWORD - I

General Ehsan ul Haq NI(M), HI(M)

(Ex-Chairman Joint Chiefs of Staff Committee – Pakistan Armed Forces)

Owing to its presence on the global fault lines, both in the context of geo-strategic location as well as other security-related issues, Pakistan has continued to figure out prominently on the international scene. The regional dynamic and strategic stability in South Asia remain tenuous and predominantly influenced by the differences between Pakistan and India. A history of conflicts, unresolved disputes, particularly the Jammu and Kashmir dispute, India's relentless arms built up in pursuit of its hegemonic ambitions and great power status, aggravated by the rise of Hindutva, continue to haunt Indo-Pakistan relations.

The emergence of neighbouring China, as a global power, has unfolded a new paradigm, shifting the geopolitical centre of gravity of Asia Pacific and triggering strategic realignments. The tri-polar dynamic between the US, China and Russia is evoking concerns of a new Cold War and directly impacting the co-relation of forces in Asia. The US focus on India-Pacific and US- Indian strategic alliance projects India as a regional net security provider with immediate and momentous consequences for the balance of power in South Asia, particularly Pakistan. Emboldened by its economic growth and the patronage of the Indo-US strategic partnership, Indian ambitions in the region and against Pakistan, have been magnified, and have received a particular boost with the ruling Bharatiya Janata Party (BJP) extremist/fascist ideology of Hindutva.

The existential threat from India and its inexorable quest to dominate the neighbourhood has been a dominant factor in shaping Pakistan's security and foreign policy. It also impacts its domestic debate, thrusting Pakistan's armed forces, as a bulwark against India, into a high-profile role in national decision-making, with a huge impact on the economy and socio-cultural environments.

FOREWORD – I

The people of Pakistan have traditionally honoured soldiering, reposed trust, and displayed great respect for the armed forces. Military service is a popular and coveted profession in Pakistani society that takes pride in the fact that it has one of the largest, highly disciplined, well-trained, volunteer armed forces.

The role and influence of the armed forces, in Pakistan's national life, over the last seventy-five years, has been momentous and crucial. It has witnessed martial laws as well as close collaboration of military leadership, in support of political parties and civil society, to restore and consolidate a functional democracy in the country. An objective and dispassionate assessment of our national experiences is essential to draw lessons for the future. It is particularly important that those who directly participated in, or witnessed these events at close quarters, come forth to record their views and experiences.

Let me commend Naseem Khan for his courageous endeavour which is not only a readable compilation of his memoirs and experiences but also a valuable account of current history. The more than three decades of military and intelligence service of the author spans a crucial period in Pakistan's history.

Brigadier Naseem held senior assignments in the Pakistan Army and is among a few military officers with an extended tenure in our elite national intelligence agency ISI. He participated in many operations. His first-hand knowledge of events, developments, and important personalities gives an incisive insight into history at close quarters. The conceptual clarity that he expounds as a consequence of his extensive experience will be of enormous benefit to professionals seeking advancement in their military/intelligence careers. Moreover, his narration of pure military/intelligence matters in an understandable manner makes it intelligible to those with no military background.

Brigadier Naseem Khan's book *Caught in the Crossfire: An Inside Story of Pakistan's Secret Services (In the Khakis)* is very timely on several accounts. As we witness the end of the post-9/11 phase, and the withdrawal of US/NATO forces from Afghanistan, there have been deliberate attempts to malign Pakistan and its armed forces. In addition to derogating Pakistan's enormous contribution and sacrifices in support of international efforts to stabilize Afghanistan and in the struggle against terrorism, it scapegoats it for the US/NATO failure. Pakistan, particularly its armed forces, has been a target and victim of the Indian Fifth Generation Warfare. The informed insight into the role, history and working of the Pakistan Army, from a highly experienced professional, will be an effective counter to these noxious narratives.

FOREWORD - II

Major General (Retired) Bruce M. Lawlor

(Ex-US Army)

Brigadier Naseem Khan set out to tell people about Pakistan's army and the ISI. He wanted the country's friends and its enemies to understand how Pakistan sees its security environment, its threats, and how these two important organizations work to protect the Pakistani people and their culture. He understands that there is danger from adversaries, foreign and domestic, who manipulate and misuse information and information technology to create societal divisiveness, ethnic strife, and national instability. In this, he distinguishes himself from those who continue to build armies to fight the last war. His book is a worthy effort and should be read by Pakistan's friends and foes.

There is a sense of betrayal by the United States in his writing, and the botched US effort in Afghanistan figures prominently in his thinking. He argues that Pakistan was the most effective and loyal US partner in the effort to defeat the Soviet Union's 1979 invasion and occupation of Afghanistan. Once the Soviets left, however, the US withdrew hastily without consulting its partners and before having done anything to address the conditions that led inevitably to extremism and violence in that war-torn country. Also inevitably, extremism and violence crossed the border into his country, causing a myriad of social and security challenges. Brigadier Khan believes that Pakistan did not fare well from its partnership with the United States and fears the disastrous US withdrawal from Afghanistan will let loose even greater and perhaps more destabilizing forces upon his country. His greatest fear is that the current US policy toward South Asia will enable India to dominate the region at Pakistan's expense.

While I do not agree with Brigadier Khan's assessment of the American effort in South Asia, clearly, his views regarding the United States align with those of many Pakistan officials and offer insight into how Pakistan will respond to future initiatives in the region. They also explain why his country is moving increasingly to embrace China.

This book, however, is much more than a listing of policy grievances against the United States. It is the story of an honourable Pakistani patriot who gave more than forty years of his life to keep his country and its people safe. Brigadier Khan began in a two-room mud hut in the Kashmir Mountains, a place he named the 'red-clay castle'. He went to a school with no desks, no chairs, and no classroom. During his first three years as a student, he learnt his lessons while sitting outdoors on the ground, on a torn mat called a 'taat'. His parents instilled in him moral values and a love of education, refused to let him think there were things he could not do, and taught him the value of work. He learnt that with work came rewards, and he came to believe that he could "touch the sky" if he worked hard enough. He fought his way out of a hard living through education and climbed the army's ranks through professionalism and hard work to become one of Pakistan's most trusted and powerful security officials during some very dangerous times.

As an army officer alternating between troop and intelligence assignments, Brigadier Khan set three guiding principles for himself: 'Always honour my oath, always take care of my men, and always stay mission-focused.' How he came to adopt these values offers much food for thought and much to be admired. You will find it not spoken, but clearly present in his words and his actions. His love of Pakistan with all its imperfections; his determination to take care of his children by educating them as his parents educated him; his work ethic—'if you can't outplay your opponent, outwork him'; his persistence in the face of adversity—'Tough times never last, but tough people do'. These are the values that drove his military professionalism, guided him through the crucible of three Afghan wars, and earned him the trust and confidence of his nation's highest officials. They are a tribute not only to him but to the system that produced him.

After his retirement from the army, as a man of honour, he found himself in a very awkward position, faced with some false allegations of dishonourable behaviour and abandoned by some of his friends. It is unfortunate, but such situations are not uncommon. All armies shield their senior officers from mundane administrative tasks to make them more efficient, and to give them more time to focus on military matters that are important to the country. There is no comparable system in the civilian world and once that protective cocoon of support is withdrawn, it is easy for a person, unfamiliar with how the civilian world works, to become embroiled in situations that can expose him to much difficulty. When that happens, the threat of dishonour in the hands of unscrupulous actors creates unwarranted leverage over honourable men. In Brigadier Khan's case, he remained true to his guiding principles. He focused on fixing the problem regardless of merit and emerged with his honour intact. Consequently, the effort to taint him with dishonour only magnified the ethical and professional values that made him such an admired and trusted army officer.

In war, moral authority can counterbalance organization and weapons as is evident in Ukraine today. Brigadier Khan set out to convince you that his army and the ISI are professional and capable organizations, and of great value to Pakistan. He uses tales of his years in military training, his time as a regular army officer serving with troops, and his work as an intelligence operative overseeing counterintelligence operations to illustrate their professionalism and capabilities. The stories make for interesting reading, but I would argue that the best evidence of what he says is true is Brigadier Khan himself because an institution's importance and value to a nation are reflected in the kind of senior leaders it creates and puts in place to handle the nation's problems. The Pakistan Army made Brigadier Khan who he is. If it makes more officers like him, then it is indeed as important to Pakistan's future as he believes it to be.

PREFACE

My lifelong association with the Pakistan Army and Inter-Services Intelligence (ISI) spreads over four decades, and its impact on my life continues to shadow my way in the years ahead. Besides a long-time soldiering in an elite self-propelled (SP) artillery regiment during peace and war, I served with ISI, Pakistan's premier intelligence agency for more than two decades. I started with ISI as a major and gradually rose through command and staff appointments to the rank of brigadier, where I handled critical security issues at national and international levels. My time in ISI coincided with historic developments in my country and in the region, with far-reaching effects on Pakistan's national security paradigm. Among those developments were the Russian Invasion of Afghanistan (1979 to 1989), the Afghan Civil War (1990 to 2001) and the aftermath of 9/11 which completely altered international security norms, particularly in South East Asia. I also had to deal with Pakistan's continuing issues with India and some of our internal sensitivities seriously affecting our national security.

Pakistan's strategically important location in the region, its strong nuclear capable armed forces, and its built-in strengths as an irrepressible nation have earned us adversaries who consider us a formidable obstacle to their strategic plans for the region. Unfortunately, some of our internal fault lines offer them opportunities to meddle in our internal affairs and weaken our strength as a regional power.

Pakistan's army, being the centre of gravity of our national strength and cohesion has become the priority target of our enemies. Misperceptions, intentionally created through well-thought-out conspiracies aim to weaken the Pakistani people's trust in our armed forces and to create a wedge between the army and the people. It is a much more severe challenge to our national security than most of us realize.

The current political turmoil in the country with extremely damaging consequences on civil-military relations, is also continuation of the similar efforts that have been going on in the country during past four decades and even before that. This trend needs to be analysed to its entirety and countered as a national priority.

I did not fully understand the gravity of the situation until my post-retirement experiences with the private security sector in Dubai, where I had many opportunities to interact with leading security professionals from around the world. I was shocked to discover how badly we are misunderstood abroad because of flawed perceptions built by our enemies, both internal and external. With that understanding came recognition of the need to portray a realistic picture of Pakistan's army to the world to counter this poisonous propaganda.

Knowing about our army and how it works is important not only for the Pakistani people but also for the international community so that we and other nations can establish international relationships and cooperation in the region based on ground truth. Many international security professionals from the world's major powers lack authentic knowledge about Pakistan and its armed forces. They are confused about who we are and what we do and that makes them vulnerable to information that is entirely fabricated by our enemies and used to hurt Pakistan's national interests.

I thought the officers who witnessed and participated in Pakistan's recent struggles need to come forth and record their views and experiences to help the international community perceive us as we are. It is in this spirit that I have written this book, to tell the truth about Pakistan's army and correct faulty perceptions about us, in an organized and proactive way. I hope my experiences in Pakistan's security and counterintelligence operations, during a period of unprecedented regional turmoil, will help people understand what Pakistan has endured during the past forty years and what it must deal with in the years to come.

There is a responsibility and a duty to help future leaders of Pakistan's army, the next generation of national leaders, the intelligentsia, Pakistan's youth, and readers at large, to know about Pakistan's army, and how it contributes to safeguarding the country's physical and intellectual frontiers against an array of complex threats. That includes an assessment of the international and regional security trends that Pakistan be forced to navigate and the emerging threat scenarios that it will confront.

My involvement in security issues at regional and international levels began in the late 1970s during an era that witnessed two superpowers playing a tit-for-tat chess game in our region. I had been in the thick of operations to support the Taliban against the Russian invasion and occupation of Afghanistan and was deeply involved in handling the civil war that followed Russia's withdrawal of its forces from Afghanistan. Dealing with the aftershocks of the 9/11 bombing in New York was a different ball game, but that too became part of my job.

PREFACE

The long years of intelligence work have been very rewarding professionally. Fighting for my country as an invisible warrior for nearly twenty-three years; quietly penetrating the strongholds of its enemies; operating too often in a storm of bullets; stealing our enemy's secrets while protecting my country's own information and plans; these are the memories I cherish most.

My work in Dubai in the private security sector has given me another perspective on the region and Pakistan's role in it. All of it contributes to the book's observations and conclusions.

Every one of us plays different roles at different times in our lives. That is certainly true of me and to put my points of view in perspective, I thought it appropriate to write this book as a memoir of my life, using my experiences from my childhood until today to describe and illustrate the individuals, institutions, and organizations that produced my hard-won understanding of the dynamics that drive army and the life of a Pakistani soldier.

The first part of the book is my effort to retrace the arc of my learning, the role of my parents and siblings, and the institutions that built my educational and moral values. The second part is aimed at helping people to understand the Pakistan Army and its culture; its make-up, mentoring process, and how it fulfils its obligations to ensure the security of the country. Along the way, I have tried to explore critical elements of its emerging strengths, the principles that govern it, and the primary reasons behind its unquestionable success. For the young, I hope this part of the book serves as an incentive for them to look more carefully at an army career. For those who are older, the narrative presents a more accurate picture of Pakistan's army than what is portrayed in descriptions written by our internal and external adversaries.

The third part of the book is basically the crux of the narrative and presents an insight into Pakistan's national security hypothesis from the viewpoint of an insider who has been part of its first line of defence for nearly four decades. The conclusions are primarily based on my personal experiences while being part of many crucial operations conducted against our adversaries, foreign as well as domestic. With an exceptional mix of personal experiences and effective access to information and intelligence about international political and strategic manoeuvrings in the region, I have tried to analytically identify and underline the direction and intensity of the crossfire that our security forces have to continuously confront while they perform their responsibilities. Based on my understanding of some of the fault lines within our internal realm, that are deceitfully exploited by our adversaries to their advantage, I have also recommended certain counter measures at the national level, to fill the gaps.

In the same contest, the ongoing political, social, economic, and governance catastrophe in the country, has also been briefly discussed from my personal perspective. I think it would be naive on our part to look at the prevailing scenario just as an internal political issue that would end in due course. There is a lot more to see into it and contemplate the consequences that might follow.

Being a counterintelligence operative, having first-hand knowledge about many of the conspiracies hatched against Pakistan by its adversaries, both internal and external, I view the current turmoil in the country, from a different angle than most analysts do. In this context, I thought it appropriate to share my perception of the prevailing crisis from a non-political angle and limit my comments to share my serious apprehensions about the outcome of this turmoil from a security angle only.

The last part of the book is a story about my own battle to continue the voyage after my retirement. It highlights the difficulties that some army personnel have when they retire and transition from **khakis** to *civvies*. Unfortunately, many of us find adjusting to civilian life difficult. My transition initially was a tough one. It did, however, teach me critical lessons about moving on to my new life with dignity and honour.

My post-retirement venture in the private security industry has introduced me to well-known strategists and security professionals from around the globe. It has been an eye-opening experience and a source of great support for me to successfully continue my security-related work. The trends in the worsening global security environments that shape the security challenges for the private security sector, have been suitably highlighted, in this part of the book.

The book as a whole is a tribute to the hard-won successes of the Pakistani army and ISI in guarding the country's security during these challenging times. Their sacrifices need to be recognized at home and abroad.

PART 1
THE ARC OF MY LEARNING CURVE

CHAPTER 1

THE OPENING SHOT

The Spotlight

'You have a call, Naseem!' said my wife Khansa, knocking on the door of my room where I had just gone for some rest after a long day in the field as the detachment commander, ISI Islamabad.

It was 1982 and the Soviet invasion of Afghanistan was in full swing. While Russian forces were hammering down Afghanistan, Afghan resistance groups, fully supported by ISI, CIA, and other Western allied intelligence agencies, were desperately manoeuvring to stall their advance and push them back. Bringing together and coordinating the efforts of varying Afghan factions to build a unified resistance was a major concern. ISI had a pivotal role in this long-lasting campaign which, in one way or another, continues today, except that the players and the manipulators have changed according to their strategic interests in the region.

My wife informed me that the director general (DG) of ISI who at that time was the late General Akhtar Abdul Rehman, was on the phone. After we exchanged a few pleasantries, he told me, '*Put on a decent shalwar kameez; keep a small pistol in your pocket, fully loaded; and drive the best car in the detachment. You are to pick up a very important person from a pre-selected location near GHQ in Rawalpindi and bring him to my residence for an important meeting.*'

A strong word of caution followed these specific orders. He informed me that although a lot of invisible security would be in place in the area, I alone would be responsible for ensuring the highest level of security and secrecy during the operation. That was enough to make me realize the importance of the operation. After giving me some more details to coordinate, General Akhtar wished me good luck and hung up the phone.

A little nervous but determined, I immediately got ready and left home to undertake the assigned task. Sensing the gravity of the situation and the security risks involved, I informed my wife that I was off for an important job and would be back by midnight. I told her not to worry if I got home late and that in the event of any problems, she should take care of herself and our child, the only one we had at the time.

Precisely at the given time, 8:00 pm, I reached the rendezvous. It was dark, and a haunting silence prevailed. A few streetlights glowed, but there was hardly any sign of life. From behind a small line of delicately trimmed bushes a middle-aged person appeared, dressed as I had been told he would be. He was wearing a white shalwar kameez and a dark blue sherwani (jacket) with a golden chain stylishly hanging between the top two front pockets. At first sight, there was no confusion about the gentleman's identity. He was none other than the President of Pakistan, the late General Zia-ul-Haq.

The task at hand was much more important than I had anticipated. Controlling my nerves as much as possible, I looked to see if I could spot any extra security measures that might help me in case of trouble. Though I sensed a very tight cordon of invisible security in the area, I did not know how much, what, or where it was. I was sure there would be enough and there would not be any loopholes in the president's security system. All I had to do was to carry out my task professionally and as instructed by my boss.

I drove the president of Pakistan to DG ISI's residence with extreme secrecy and the utmost caution. I knew I was being used as a trustworthy team member to provide extra secrecy and personal security for the president.

I welcomed General Zia into the car. He sat gently on the front seat next to me. He responded to my greeting in a very polite and fatherly way, something for which he was generally known, and immediately put me at ease. After exchanging a few pleasantries, I drove him to nearby Harley Street where our DG ISI used to reside during those days. The fact that I was performing on my own a job that would normally require thirty to forty security vehicles and a vast number of security guards with guns and ammunition to protect the route weighed heavily on my mind. It was incomprehensible to me, but I had been working in ISI long enough to be somewhat battle-hardened when it came to taking on unique situations. I was nervous but confident that I could do the job. I did not let the president see any nervousness in me.

Within fifteen minutes, we were at DG ISI's residence. He was waiting to receive the president. In a very swift movement, General Zia was escorted inside the house. I stayed outside awaiting further instructions. Meanwhile, General Akhtar, the head of ISI came back and personally escorted me into his residence. He guided me to the hall where the president was sitting. I was greatly surprised. The president was meeting with the top Afghan leadership fighting Russian forces in Afghanistan. The next moment was an even greater surprise for me. General Akhtar asked me to join the meeting and offered me a chair next to his. Suddenly, I was sitting next to the DG ISI, and just a chair away from the president. It was all happening very fast, and I was in a different world.

For me, it was something unimaginable and difficult to digest. I never dreamt of being part of such a high-level forum, even as a spectator. At the meeting, the war was discussed in detail and strategies to handle the Russian onslaught in Afghanistan and push them out of this country were agreed upon. Pakistan had a major stake in this campaign and being in such a meeting gave me the feeling of practically 'touching the sky'.

Flashback

Was I touching the sky? The sentence sounded familiar, and so were the feelings. My mind flashed back to an incident in my childhood when I was four or five years old.

'I can almost touch the sky Bhai,' excitedly shouted my younger sister Tahira as we jumped on an old wooden bed, known as '*charpai*' in Urdu. The bed was lying in front of our newly constructed small mud house on top of a hill 'Danna' in the village of Pothi Balla, Azad Kashmir. We had recently moved from our ancestral home at Kotari in the village of Pothi Makwalan, located at the mountain's base. Living at about 9,000 feet above sea level was a new experience that brought broader horizons and perhaps new hopes. The open space at such height and the closeness of the sky was an inspiring change for the family. We, the young ones, were excited and soon were busy exploring new places. Playing outside our new home was like playing in space. We thought that we could touch the sky by jumping in the air just a little bit higher. We all did our best to touch the sky. My younger sister Tahira was convinced that she would be the first to put her hand on the sky. I remember her shouting at us, urging us to jump higher to touch the sky.

As I sat in the high-level meeting with the President of Pakistan and the top hierarchy from varying Afghan factions, I wondered if my presence at that forum had anything to do with our innocent childhood play when our ambitions were to touch the sky. I still think about that question, now and then.

Incidentally, I belong to the **Sudhan tribe**, also known as **Sudhozais**. The tribe is historically linked with Afghanistan. Sudhans trace their roots to the Pashtuns and moved to the Poonch District of the Kashmir region several centuries ago. Their common ancestor is Jassi Khan, who was an Afghan chief. He earned the name of 'Sudhan', a word from Sanskrit meaning 'justice, fair and honest'. Jassi Khan arrived in Kashmir with a sizeable group of followers about five hundred years ago. The new arrivals had to fight for their existence, but with Jassi Khan's leadership, they quickly emerged as a solid and powerful tribe.

Sudhans have a history of fighting against the domination of Sikhs and Dogras and of never reconciling to their rule. Their uprising in 1947 turned into a general revolt against the Maharaja of the princely state of Jammu and Kashmir. The Pakistan Army fully supported the Sudhans and some other tribes in their fight to liberate Kashmir. With the active support of Pashtun tribal lashkars, from Khyber and Waziristan tribal agencies, they eventually liberated a small region, now called 'Azad Kashmir'.

Their immediate successes on the battlefield resulted in a hurriedly arranged ceasefire under UN sponsorship. Kashmir's future was to be determined by a free and fair referendum that gave the people of Kashmir the right to determine their future.

For those who may not be familiar with the background of the Kashmir dispute, I would like to briefly explain its root causes, and how Kashmiris came to reside in Indian Held Kashmir (IHK) for the last seven or eight decades. Unfortunately, despite the so-called civilized world order that guaranteed Kashmiris the right to self-determination, the impasse that began in 1947 continues unabated, killing thousands of innocent women and children in IHK.

The story begins with the British East India Company coming to India as traders on Aug 24, 1608. The company gradually gained control of the whole Indian subcontinent and annexed it to the British Colonial Empire. In 1857, general distrust and dissatisfaction with the company's leadership resulted in the 'Sepoy Mutiny', a widespread mutiny of army troops. The British government responded in 1858. It abolished the East India Company and imposed direct British rule by appointing a British Raj to manage the subcontinent. The change did not matter much, but it did introduce a more personal note into governance and removed unimaginative commercialism that had existed for many years. It also reorganized government machinery and the army and provided for consultation with local Indian notables, giving them significant participation in the new governance system. These reforms improved the situation to some extent.

However, the 'Sepoy Mutiny' had changed the people of India. There would be no going back to the way it was. A strong middle class had emerged with a hardened sense of Indian nationalism. At the same time, the Government of India's increasingly centralized internal autocracy and its enormous imperial bureaucracy, generally known as 'Pukka Sahib' (British Super Bureaucrats), mostly remained aloof from the population in private clubs and guarded military cantonments. This disconnection created a vast gap between the rulers and the public and contributed to fast-growing Indian nationalism.

The last quarter of the British Raj was a period of Hindu-Muslim conflict and intensified agitation. There were demands for India's independence with separate states for the Muslims and the Hindus. More than a century of British technological and ideological unification of the South Asian subcontinent thus ended after the Second World War with communal civil war, mass migration, and partition.

In 1946, the British made a last-ditch effort to transfer power to a three-tiered Federation of India under a single Indian-led administration but failed to manage it. Resultantly, the British Parliament passed the Indian Independence Act in July 1947 and ordered the territories of India and Pakistan to be demarcated by 14-15 Aug 1947. The *Princely States*, with Muslim or Hindu majority populations, of which there were quite a few, were to be integrated into neighbouring provinces.

Kashmir, being a princely state, has a little different but interesting story. On 16 March 1846, the British government sold the state to Maharaja Gulab Singh and his descendants under the Amritsar Pact for seventy-five lac rupees. The pact contained some very interesting clauses that explicitly describe the British intent to keep control of their colonies through a cleverly orchestrated arrangement of penalties and incentives. Under the pact, the Maharaja was required to obtain the British Raj's consent for all interactions with neighbouring states and to provide full support to the British Army as and where required. Additionally, as a token of obedience and loyalty to the British government, he was also brought under obligation to present gifts to it on an annual basis, including one horse, twelve goats of good breed, and three pairs of top-quality Kashmiri shawls. The written pact signed between the British government and Maharaja of Kashmir is an interesting read and helps to explain Britain's politics, deceptive manoeuvring, exploitation, and governance during colonial times.

Selling the state of Jammu Kashmir, with a ninety-five per cent Muslim population, to Dogra Raja Gulab Singh for seventy-five lac rupees was a traitorous and disgraceful act, one of many such acts by the British in the subcontinent, for which they will always remain accountable to the people of the state of Jammu and Kashmir.

I am proud of the substantial contributions some of my ancestors made to the cause of the Kashmiris during the British Raj and later during the war of liberation of Azad Kashmir in 1948. They played an important role and remained relevant in the state's affairs till the end.

When the British government was consulting with local notables and increasing their involvement in local administration, my paternal grandfather,

Sardar Muhammad Bulour Khan was a prominent figure in the District of Poonch in Kashmir. He was appointed as a member of "Judge and Jury" in four towns in the district. "Judge and Jury" was an ad hoc British arrangement to supplement the local courts with some notable Indians. While holding this position, he was a great help in delivering justice to the locals under the prevailing legal system. He was also the head official of his town to manage its administrative and revenue issues. His younger brother Sardar Muhammad Ameer Khan was the Town Clerk, a position of responsibility and respect, in charge of maintaining records of landholdings. Subsequently, during the rebellion in Kashmir in 1948, my paternal grandfather and my maternal grandfather, Sardar Sajawal Khan, and other family members actively participated in military operations to liberate their towns which are now part of Azad Kashmir. Interestingly, my mother, Sahib Jan, was head of the women's wing of the village and led them in organizing the defence against attacks by Hindus and Sikhs.

These are some of the memories that passed through my mind while I sat at the conference table with General Zia and the other high-level dignitaries, discussing regional and international strategies for a campaign in Afghanistan. The discussion seemed to connect my past with the present. It reminded me of my life story commencing from that remote village life with the belief that '*we could touch the sky if we tried harder*', my family background, and our tribal linkages to the Afghans. I wondered if it had any relevance to the journey that brought me to this meeting. I believe that the events and progress in my career during the subsequent years of my life were probably a continuation of the same process.

The Storyline

William Shakespeare said, "All the world's a stage, and all the men and women merely players; they have their exits and entrances, and one man in his time plays many parts".

Looking back at my journey, I think how accurately Shakespeare's words describe my own life. With that thought in mind, I have set forth my experiences in the field of Pakistan's national security. Each phase of my life brought a new role for me to play, and a new stage upon which to perform. To make it easier to follow, I have tried to show how the different phases of my life prepared me for the next role I was given to play.

Being an army man, I thought the best way to share my story is as if it was a military operation, involving choices, preparation of capabilities to achieve the mission, a bridgehead from which to launch myself, and finally multi-echelon manoeuvring to reach the objective. I have tried to explain valuable lessons that I have learnt along the way through the hard realities of life. My goal has been to help the people of Pakistan and people abroad understand the dynamics that drive the Pakistan Army and its affiliated security agencies. This chapter entitled 'The Opening Shot' is an attempt to link my life's most important events with the prior experiences that prepared me to be part of it.

The foremost responsibility of an army commander is to clearly conceive the mission that needs to be accomplished. In my case, the mission of this book is to share my hard-won understanding of the security challenges that Pakistan faces today and make people aware of the role played by our armed forces and their affiliated intelligence agencies in safeguarding our national security and cohesion. That, I have done by narrating first-hand scenarios with facts and figures to illustrate my point of view.

Pakistan is located on a subcontinent with a history of animosity among its neighbours. India's unending attempts to undermine Pakistan's national security and disrupt our internal cohesion are serious threats that have existed for years and continue to this day. Identifying these dangers and neutralizing them before they do irreparable damage to our country is the essence of planning and conducting successful counterintelligence operations.

Pakistan and India's long-standing troubles are well known, but there are other regional and global powers that seek to gain an advantage from Pakistan's geo-strategic location. The subcontinent has become a playground for more powerful nations to advance regional and global conspiracies.

Unfortunately, Pakistan also has internal fault lines that make its external threats more dangerous. The challenge is to understand the external threats and the internal vulnerabilities, and how they interact with each other to undermine the country's safety and well-being. The hardest task in this effort is to distinguish between friends who are true friends and adversaries who are pretending to be friends. The most dangerous enemy is the one that betrays your trust.

There are also challenges presented by changes in the prevailing international security landscape. Major powers are able to manipulate the actions of weaker states through a new kind of warfare that relies on information. It seeks to destabilize an enemy country by exploiting vulnerabilities created by social, political, cultural, and religious differences within society. Every Pakistani should know that, unfortunately, Pakistan, with its nuclear capability and formidable armed forces, also finds itself embroiled in this new form of conflict.

The information in this book is based on my four decades of experience as a military officer and one of Pakistan's invisible warriors. Though confidentiality prevents me from sharing some parts of my story, there is enough here for

Pakistan's people to get a true sense of what the country has gone through during the past forty years.

During that time, I was personally involved in the capture and arrest of many foreign intelligence operatives who were caught red-handed inside Pakistan. Details of third-country intelligence operations inside Pakistan, especially, concerning Afghanistan, will surprise many in the West who hold limited knowledge about the proxy war in South Asia. Which country facilitated India's use of Afghanistan as a launching pad for terrorist attacks against the Pakistani people and why it was done, remains a big question. There is also an inquest about many Indian agents of influence operating clandestinely in Western countries against Pakistan's interests.

I have also included stories of some of my most frustrating operations, the ones that uncovered spy networks against Pakistan run by countries that were supposed to be our friends and allies. Unfortunately, this happened more often than one might expect.

I have offered my recommendations to address imbalances in our domestic governance systems in vogue in the belief that they will help us to better manage the threats we face. Finally, I have included a message for the international community to build strategies and relationships in the region based on ground truth rather than on false perceptions built by our adversaries within and abroad.

CHAPTER 2

AT 'RED-CLAY CASTLE'

The Red-Clay Castle, as I like to refer to it, was a two-room newly constructed mud hut on top of a mountain in our ancestral village where my family lived after we left a multi-family house. Red clay is a reddish type of mud that is stronger than the typical brown clay and is usually used to construct mud houses in the villages to keep them strong and safe from severe weather hazards. It especially helps to keep the homes warm during heavy snow in the winter. Luckily, red clay was plentiful on our piece of land and was used to construct our 'Red-Clay Castle.' How my parents initially made this two-room mud hut and struggled over the years to gradually develop it into a comparatively more comfortable semi-concrete house is a story all by itself. Instead, however, I will concentrate on how they brought us up in Red-Clay Castle, how they raised us as a well-knit family and how they educated us beyond our imagination. It is a story of two real warriors, my parents, who fought a long, laborious, and painstaking campaign that lasted over two decades. Their hard-won victory resulted in a prosperous and honourable living for all their children, across almost all corners of the globe. I have tried to develop the story rationally, progressively, and in line with the hard facts of life, highlighting the role of good parenting, a well-knit team of responsible siblings, and my efforts to make my life worth living. The combined effect of the efforts of my family and the institutions I attended to develop my educational and moral values enabled me to make my life successful and purposeful.

The Guardian Angels

Although not highly educated, my father, Sardar Muhammad Ashraf Khan, was a very progressive man, full of courage and determination. Being very kind-hearted, he always offered a helping hand to the entire family, to his colleagues and to anyone who needed it. These qualities won him great respect among his family, the community, and local government circles. My father was a self-sacrificing person and his life's ambition was that his children would grow up to be well-groomed, well-educated people who would excel in any field of their choosing. His emphasis was always on teaching us good moral values and strong personal character. Through his continuous mentoring, he showed us how to be trustworthy, responsible, fair, and caring individuals. It was because of his hard work, motivation, and perseverance, that all my siblings are living successful and enjoyable lives.

My mother, Sahib Jaan, was equally important to our upbringing. With grace, honour, and magnanimity, she was an angel living with us, playing a pivotal role in the family throughout the long years. Describing her life is like describing human history, a path that began in the Stone Age, waded through the Iron Age, Bronze Age, and Golden Age, and finally led to the Digital Age. She worked day and night to make ends meet, and to run the house. Despite being the wife of a prominent village official, she ground the food grain at home, arranged firewood for cooking meals, cut grass for cattle, and brought water from a nearby spring. She also was very much into social work and played a leading role in helping other women in the village. She was a person who warmed every heart and affected in a positive way everyone around her. For me, without her support and inspiration, I would not have had the success in life that I was able to achieve. She was one in a million, and I feel honoured to be her son.

My parents lived a tough and barrier-breaking life and left it pain-free, regret-free, satisfied, and at ease. I think by any standard, their lives were purposeful, fruitful, and complete. My father left us too early in 1977 when I was a captain in the army. Fortunately, my mother was with me until I lost her on 24 April 2021, at the age of 101.

It is painful to find her missing on launching of this book. She was a source of continuous support and motivation for me when I started to write it. She told me her life story while I sat at her bedside. How she participated in the 1948 war in Kashmir that liberated Azad Kashmir from Dogra rule. She led the women of the village, fought, side by side with the men, and endured the bloodshed. They fought with wooden sticks, iron rods, shovels, and even red chilli powder to throw in the eyes of their attackers. Her story was heroic, fascinating, and motivating. I make it a point to share her life with my young ones. They listen with passion and pride, and they are as motivated by her as I was.

My parents' hard work, motivation, and perseverance made them role models for my siblings and me, and we all have made it a point to follow in their footsteps in raising our children. Losing them both has been a great loss, but we can still feel their guiding hands on our shoulders as we move forward. Someone has rightly said, *'Sometimes, even the people with meagre resources leave their children the richest inheritance.'* My parents are among those people.

My Comrades

We were seven siblings of varying ages who accompanied our parents to the 'Red-Clay Castle'. My two elder brothers who were quite grown up at that time had joined the government education department as schoolteachers and helped my father run the family, chipping in with money whenever they could to make our lives a little more comfortable. My two elder sisters were going to school while the rest of us remained at home.

My father was always keen to educate each of us as best as possible, but his financial position prevented him from doing as much as he desired. He believed that because of his financial constraints, his goal of educating all of us would come true only if we became a closely-knit family and supported each other. To that end, he ensured that sharing and caring were at the core of our upbringing and that we developed matching character traits. He taught us to help each other with our studies and to share responsibility when it came to running the household.

I remember cleaning the house, bringing water from a nearby spring, doing laundry work on a fortnightly basis at a pond about three kilometres away from our home, and showering. I would take showers under fresh cold spring water briskly coming out of mountain rocks. It was fun. As a family, we shared financial obligations and supported each other in our studies. The additional coaching by my elder brothers was a great help with our school assignments and enabled us to learn under less-than-ideal schooling arrangements.

After we settled in the Red-Clay Castle, my father managed to send our eldest brother, to the United Kingdom and encouraged the other to move to Karachi for his higher education. Subsequently, he also went to the UK to join our eldest brother. While living in the UK, they were able to financially support our father in educating the younger ones.

My father motivated my eldest sister to join the education department as a teacher after passing her matriculation examination. She continued with her educational pursuits privately, for many years thereafter, and went on to achieve a master's degree and became an accomplished teacher. She rose to a senior position in the education department before she retired from teaching. She is the family's brain and has been instrumental in keeping our family together as a well-knit team and continues to provide mature guidance to all of us in running our family affairs. In addition to her schooling, my middle sister remained a great helping hand to our mother to run the household during all those difficult years we spent living in the village.

My father dreamt of my youngest sister Tahira becoming a doctor. He arranged for her to receive additional tutoring. To provide her with the educational foundation she needed for admission to a medical college, he rented a small house in Rawalpindi and sent her to a well-recognized girls' college to prepare for her examination to study medicine.

During those days, the education of girls was not a priority among the common people, especially in the villages. My father faced severe criticism from his relatives and friends, who were generally not in favour of girls' education and who were particularly against sending girls to boarding schools. One of my uncles remarked disapprovingly, 'Look at my brother, wanting to make his daughter another Fatima Jinnah,' referring to the highly educated sister of the founder of Pakistan, Muhammad Ali Jinnah. Fatima Jinnah was a dentist by profession, active in the struggle to create Pakistan, the first woman to contest a presidential election in Pakistan and carries a great name in our national history. To my father's and her great credit, Tahira, our baby sister, went on to study at Fatima Jinnah Medical College in Lahore, became a doctor, served in Pakistan, United Kingdom and United Arab Emirates, and presently has dedicated her life to bringing medical services to disadvantaged rural areas through a country-wide charity organization in Pakistan.

As soon as our youngest brother became eligible for proper schooling, he was sent to Lawrence College, a highly well-reputed boarding school/college located in Murree, Pakistan. He subsequently joined Pakistan's Air Force becoming a fighter pilot and rose to the rank of Group Captain.

I enjoyed a special place with my parents, who provided me with astonishing educational opportunities that enabled me to achieve things I never thought I could achieve when I was living in the village.

My siblings were my team-mates, and my father and mother were our guardian angels. They gave us the learning and the confidence to compete at all levels and ensured that we did not suffer from any complexes. It was all because of them, their nurturing at our Red-Clay Castle and the team spirit they built within the family that helped each of us to reach so far. Thank you, my comrades; nothing could have been possible had we not all played our parts as active team members.

One of my elder brothers in the UK, Muhammad Anwar Khan is no more with us. He passed away in the UK after a prolonged illness on 10 September 2020. He was among the first to suggest that I write this book. He thought that my story might inspire other people who grow up in un-privileged and challenging environments. He believed that my army career, particularly my experiences at the national and regional levels during the past three to four decades, would be of great interest to many at home and abroad, particularly to those who wanted to know more about Pakistan Army warriors.

I wish to take this opportunity to pay homage to Anwar Bhai and pray for his departed soul to rest in peace. He was a great mentor during my school days at the village and greatly influenced my life during the later years. He died fighting very bravely for almost four decades against severe muscular atrophy. His life story is a personal triumph in the face of adversity. His doctors gave up hope long ago. Yet, he fought till the end and lived a very purposeful life. Instead of bowing to the circumstances, he stood up to the challenges and fought back, ignoring the doctors, and choosing to live his life to its best. Despite his gradually increasing physical disabilities, he was always there to provide us with guidelines about important decisions in life. He influenced our behaviours, helped us to shape our goals, offered us a sense of direction and guided us on everything linked to our family. He was very active in social work within his community. He was a true example of a people person and was always available to provide the necessary support and guidance to anybody looking for help. His unparalleled contribution and hard work made a visible difference to those around him and earned him tremendous respect, honour, and a reputation for excellence and integrity in Kent, England.

He remained particularly attached to all family members back in Pakistan and was always there to support us through thick and thin. To conclude my tribute to this great gentleman, here are a few words which I found during my readings that perfectly express my heartfelt feelings for him:

> *Hats off to you, my brother!*
> *Your actions were always kind,*
> *a generous hand and an active mind!*
> *Anxious to please and loath to offend,*
> *a loving brother and a faithful friend!*

Our father must have been very proud of what his son Anwar Khan accomplished in his life before joining him to live the life hereafter. God bless their souls, Amen.

The 'Taat' School

The word 'taat' in Urdu means a mat, primarily used in schools by students in rural areas to sit on the ground to attend classes where proper sitting arrangements are unavailable. My initial memories of formal schooling involve my father taking me to and from a nearby school about four kilometres away from our house. Holding my school bag in one hand, helping me with the other to negotiate the rugged mountainous terrain, he walked me to school and brought me back home every day. It is a memory I cherish most. It was the beginning of a lengthy pursuit that my father started to groom me for a life I have enjoyed ever since.

The first school I attended, Middle School Rawalakot in Azad Kashmir, was housed in an old building with only three classrooms to accommodate students in classes one through eight. The three senior classes: classes six, seven, and eight were held in the available rooms inside the building. The junior classes from one to five were held under the open sky, exposed to all kinds of weather, in the school's backyard. The class I attended outside was run under a thin tree providing minimal shadow from the sunshine, with a torn *taat* and some stones suitably arranged to make a sitting arrangement for the students. However, the school's competent and mature teaching staff, supplemented by the effective mentoring I received at home, became the basis for my success later in life. As I progressed to the senior classes, my teachers, parents, and siblings encouraged me to participate in the school's extracurricular activities. My participation for two years in the school's scouts squadron was probably one of the reasons for me choosing the army as a career.

The gallant personality of my maternal grandfather, Sardar Sajawal Khan, who always behaved and acted as a warrior, also significantly influenced me to live the life of a soldier. He was a warrior who significantly contributed to the war of liberation of Azad Jammu and Kashmir (AJK), during 1948. I remember vividly a fascinating collection of arms and weapons at his house that he used in that war and afterwards for local hunting games. He was fearless and bold. On one occasion, he staved off a lion attack single-handedly. The lion had entered the village to attack people and their cattle. When the local people responded, the lion went into a cave. Later, it jumped out to attack people who were standing near the cave's entrance. My grandfather jumped on the lion to save people from being injured. The lion struck my grandfather in the forehead with its claws and tore the skin from his head, but his action prevented the lion from attacking the people, and they were able to overpower it as it was attempting to escape. The incident earned my grandfather a reputation for being brave, bold, and forthcoming in the face of adversity.

The Breeze at the Dawn

Since my father was working in the District Education Office, he had a fair idea about the leading educational institutions in the country and their admission processes. After completing my class seven examination, he surprised the family by asking me to get ready to sit for the competitive examination for admission to class eight in two of the best educational institutions in the country! One school was Cadet College Hasan Abdal (CCH) which is a semi-government autonomous body, being managed by a Board of Governance (BoG) having a minimum of three official members who are civil officers from the provincial government. The chairman of the BoG is the governor of Punjab, and the vice-chairman is the head of the Pakistan Ordinance Factory, Wah, who is always an army officer.

The other school was PAF Public School Lower Topa, Murree, which is run by the Pakistan Air Force. I had not thought about attending either school because neither I nor anyone else in my family, except my father, thought it was a viable option. A big question was, did I possess the educational background to compete at that level? The idea seemed unrealistic considering the village school that I had attended. Yet, despite the odds, my father insisted that I try because he thought I could compete at that level. He told me to have faith in my abilities and he was confident that I would do well on the tests. With such strong encouragement, I decided to accept the challenge and apply for admission to both institutions. It was quite scary for me to compete in these examinations because they are held in English, and English is always very difficult for students from Urdu medium schools. I know it was for me.

To everyone's surprise, including me, I passed the written tests held at Rawalpindi. This unexpected success encouraged me to work harder, and I started preparing for the interview, the last requirement for admission to these colleges. These interviews were held two to three weeks after the written tests. My father requested my uncle, a schoolteacher, to help me prepare for the interviews.

It was winter, and the weather was freezing in our part of Kashmir, with snow covering the mountains and road slides suspending traffic for months at a time. While I was waiting for the call from CCH for the interview, the road between Rawalpindi and Rawalakot was blocked by heavy snowfall and avalanches. When the road was finally cleared for traffic about two weeks later, my father received written notice for me to appear for an interview in Rawalpindi on the following day. It was already late in the afternoon when he received the letter. The weather was freezing and windy that day. Nobody in the area owned private cars in those days, and the bus journey from our village to Rawalpindi took nearly eight to ten hours over winding mountainous semi-concrete roads. Every day, one or two buses travelled between Rawalakot and Rawalpindi. They started early in the morning so that they would arrive at their destinations before the last light, enabling the passengers to reach their homes by nightfall. Finding other transportation during odd hours or travelling at night was a big challenge.

Under ordinary circumstances, the average person would have given up going as being impossible, but not my father. He was determined to get me to Rawalpindi in time for the interview. He convinced one of his friends, an inspector in a local government office, to give us a ride. The inspector told his driver to take us in the inspector's jeep as far as the bridge at Kohala, about thirty kilometres short of Murree. Kohala is located on the river Jhelum, where the administrative authority of the AJK government ends, and Pakistan's administrative authority begins. We had to stop there because the inspector was not allowed to use the jeep outside of AJK territory.

My father thought that we would find alternative transportation in Kohala to take us the rest of the way to Rawalpindi, but by the time we reached there, it was already midnight, and there were no routine passenger vehicles going to Rawalpindi.

After waiting for hours, the inspector's driver came up with a brilliant but risky idea that would help us and at the same time help him. His native village 'Bassian' was about five kilometres beyond Kohala on Murree Road. It was a popular stop for all types of transport between Kohala, Murree, and Rawalpindi. He thought that we might find some transportation there for Rawalpindi, and he could spend the night in the village with his family. He thought his boss would not object to his spending one night with his family and was ready to take the risk and help us out. My father was concerned about misuse of the jeep, but the driver insisted that he would settle it with his boss and there would be no issue on that end.

We had no other option but to take the chance and we arrived in Bassian at about 3:00 am. The driver dropped us off and left. We sat in a local restaurant, ate a midnight dinner, and waited for nearly an hour for our luck to change. We finally saw a truck carrying some goods from Muzaffarabad to Rawalpindi. My father asked the driver for a lift, and he was kind enough to give us a ride for three hundred rupees. That was quite a bit of money in 1963, but there was no alternative, and we accepted his demand as a blessing.

As we approached Murree Hills, known for frigid winters and heavy snowfall, the temperature was getting colder with each kilometre. By the time we reached Murree, there was five to seven feet of snow on both sides of the road. My father tried to shield me from the cold winds by wrapping his arms and legs around me while we sat in the truck's front cabin. It was half open on both sides and, as we rode through the snow, he bore the brunt of the strong cold winds blowing through the Murree Hills. His cheeks were almost frozen, but he kept a smile on his face and remained optimistic. He thought his efforts were about to bear fruit.

We reached Rawalpindi early in the morning, two or three hours before the interview. We went to a small hotel on Railway Road, fortuitously named 'Hotel Paradise', and rented a room for one night. It was like paradise after the hectic journey. We rested for an hour and then got ready to go for the interview.

I had a reasonably good pair of trousers and a shirt to wear for the interview, but I did not have a jacket and it was very cold outside. On the way to where the interview was to be held, my father bought me a second-hand coat from 'Landa Bazaar,' a type of market for second-hand clothes that is found all over Pakistan. Now with me suitably dressed, we arrived at the place of the interview fifteen minutes before it was scheduled to begin. The first phase of our desperate effort was successfully completed.

The interview candidates were taken to a big room inside the building, while their parents and guardians were told to make themselves comfortable and wait in a grassy area outside the building. We were briefed about how the interviews would be conducted and each candidate was made to enter the interview room through one door in front and leave through another door in the back to prevent us from sharing information about the questions. It also spared the boys who were waiting to be interviewed the psychological pressure of seeing the boys who were not selected.

When I entered the room for the interview, the head of the interviewing panel asked, 'Son, will you be comfortable being interviewed in English?' I suspected my educational background as an Urdu medium student triggered them to ask me this question. The temptation was to ask that the interview be done in Urdu, but I declined to make such a request and instead answered confidently, 'Sir, please interview me in the same language as you are interviewing others.' This was not an effort on my part to impress the panel. I wanted to be treated equally with no impact, one way or the other, because of my underprivileged educational background.

The second question the panel president asked me was, 'Where did you get this coat from? It suits you so well. I think your brother from London must have sent you this.' I was sure they must have learnt about my brothers in the UK from my application form. I answered, 'No, sir, my father bought this for me early this morning from Landa Bazaar.'

The people on the interview panel looked surprised by my answer and thanked me for my forthrightness and honesty. There were a few more questions that I answered very confidently. When the interview was over the president of the panel smiled and informed me that I was being recommended for admission to the college. That sentence changed my life. I felt the battle was almost won.

Most of the candidates before me failed the interview and were not recommended for admission. My father, who was waiting outside, learnt of their failures and had lost hope about my selection. When I came to meet him, his first words were meant to encourage me and cheer me up. 'Son, don't worry if you have failed. Even those from big schools who came in big cars have also failed.'

'What are you saying, Abba Ji? I passed!' I said. He was surprised, delighted, and overwhelmed with gratitude. With tears in his eyes, he hugged me tight and congratulated me on my success. His dream had come true. Within minutes, we were celebrating at the 'Muslim Grand Hotel and Restaurant', a good and affordable restaurant nearby. We ate our fill of chicken karahi (curry) and hot tandoori roti (bread), my father's favourite dish.

Our effort to complete the interview makes me think of Rumi's poem *The Breeze at Dawn*, which advocates getting out of the comfort zone to achieve one's ambitions and avail oneself of the best in life. It was an example of what great fathers do to keep their children upbeat during adversity, give them the courage to face challenges and join them in celebrating their successes. From the time we left home for the interview until my acceptance into the college, his care, motivation, guidance, and love made things easy for me to handle. Honesty, straightforwardness, perseverance, and self-confidence won us the day.

In addition to the CCH, run by the army, I was also accepted to PAF Public School Lower Topa, Murree, run by the air force. I had the choice to attend either. My success was a source of great pride and joy for all who knew us. It was also a great lesson for many people in our village who had a similar background about the importance of ambitious planning and determined follow-up in the struggle for a better future.

After consulting with his senior colleagues in the education department about the matter, my father decided it would be best for me to attend the CCH, undoubtedly one of the best educational institutions in the country.

The two days I spent with my father trying to reach Rawalpindi for my college interview was a life-altering journey that influenced me when the time came for me to help my children with their education. Our fight to overcome the odds kept me utterly committed to seeing that my children received the best possible education, and it remains with me even today.

CHAPTER 3

THE GAME CHANGER

In a Different World

The day I began at the CCH, was 4 April 1964. My father took me to college. He wanted to make sure that I did not have any problems with the admission formalities and that I got settled into my dormitory without any difficulties. As a precaution, he thought it appropriate for us to reach Hasan Abdal a day early so that I could get familiarized with the environment before formally joining the college. Accordingly, we reached the college gate around the afternoon of 3 April.

The moment we got off the bus and I first saw the college campus; it was something I could never have imagined. We could see a huge red brick building, as big as Buckingham Palace, pictures of which my brother in London had sent to us. It was just as impressive. I was thrilled.

At the gate, we were welcomed by two security guards who rightly thought that I was one of the new entrants who would join the college the next day. While my father was exchanging some pleasantries with them, they told him that they were also from Rawalakot. They were excited and proud to know that someone from their village was going to be a student at this great institution. Since there were no official arrangements for us to stay overnight at the college, the security guards invited us to be their guests for the night at their one-bedroom apartment near the end of the campus. It was a kind gesture, and we gladly accepted it.

My first night on the campus as their guest in a small apartment is a lovely memory I cherish even today; their kind hospitality, the sumptuous dinner and the two beds they prepared for us in the grassy playing ground field in front of their apartment. I stayed awake for many hours that night, unable to sleep, staring at the beautiful sight of the dark indigo sky with thousands of shining stars and a cool breeze blowing across the vast green parade grounds. It was a new place, and a new experience, to set my expectations for the days to come.

THE GAME CHANGER

The next morning, our hosts brought us to the college administration offices to complete the admission process. I got a closer look at the college campus with its matchless dormitories, the best possible classroom facilities, and its huge playing fields. It was fascinating.

CCH admits about 110 students each year. It was opened in 1954 as a cadet college under the direction of Gen Ayub Khan, then commander in chief of the Pakistan Army. The college prepares students to become future global leaders in their chosen field of influence.

What a change from my *'taat'* school! From a three-classroom building to a complex spread over hundreds of acres, I was in a different world. I had no words to thank Almighty Allah and my father who made it possible for me to be an 'Abdalian.' It was a game changer in my life.

With a comparatively weaker educational background, my initial days in college were tough. My biggest issue was English. Most of the subjects were taught in English and I struggled to keep up with my studies and be at par with the other students who had a better educational foundation. Being in boarding school and away from my family for extended periods of time was depressing for me, and I became homesick. I had hoped to settle in quickly, but feelings of loneliness and frustration were overpowering at times.

Overwhelmed by the despair, one day I wrote to my father, "Abba Ji, please take me back home. This is a *jail khana* (prison). We have no liberties here, and I feel trapped…"

I requested my father take me back to the village and put me in the *taat* school. My letter caused him great shock and pain, and within no time there came a strong reply. His words were harsh, but I could feel the love and affection in what he wrote.

"Go and find a job as a waiter in some restaurant in Rawalpindi, but don't come back home," was his blunt reply. That said, he gave me very thoughtful and encouraging advice, "bear with the change for a better future, and you will settle down in a couple of months." I decided that I had no choice but to hang on and fight my frustration.

Mr A.W.E. Winlaw, the principal of the college, was a retired Lieutenant Colonel from the British Army. One day, while he was making his late afternoon rounds of the school complex, he found me sitting alone under a tree, looking gloomy. He came and talked to me. "Hey, son," he said gently, "cheer up! This college is your second home, and I am here to care for you just like your father. If you ever feel lonely, don't hesitate to come, and talk to me." I did not understand some of his British accent, but what I did hear significantly boosted my morale, and inspired me to take on the challenges ahead.

My *taat* school background haunted me for quite some time, and I struggled with my studies during the first year. At the end of the first term, I ranked nineteenth in a class of twenty-three, mainly because I was having trouble with English.

The situation improved slightly during the second term. I got better at taking notes, and my English improved. I worked hard and improved my position to thirteenth. By the end of the final term, I was comfortably ranked seventh in the class.

My hard-won progress during the first year also earned me a scholarship of twenty-five rupees per month. I did not care much about the amount, but the fact that I had been awarded a scholarship was a great morale booster. It was also a huge relief for my father, who had to pay my college fees out of the family's limited financial resources.

With a scholarship in hand, I was set to undertake the demanding five years of studies to complete my intermediate standards certification. When I reached class ten, I was selected to be a prefect in the dormitory. I was given the appointment of a section commander. It raised my profile and helped me to grow within college. My physical fitness gave me a significant advantage. I was a member of several sports teams and was recognized as one of the leading sportsmen in my class.

The Formative Process

These five years moulded me from a kid to a well-organized young man, capable of shouldering important responsibilities. Living through a meticulously planned 24/7 routine was the most rewarding aspect of my college life and helped to prepare me for my duties later in my career.

Mr Bokhari Sahib, our housemaster, used to wake us early in the morning of each day for our prayers, '*Uthiyay, Uthiyay, Uthiyay, namaz ka time ho gaya hai,*' he said, telling us to 'wake up, wake up, wake up, it's prayer time.' At his commanding wake-up call, we would jump out of our beds before he reached and pulled us out.

Making our beds in the prescribed manner and going through well-organized physical training exercises or a drill period began our mornings. Then, we would change into uniforms and go to breakfast in the mess, followed by academic classes until midday.

After lunch and an hour of mandatory rest, we participated in sports programmes, studied in our dormitories, and went to dinner in a mess, formally dressed, in one of two main dining halls. One dining hall was for senior students from classes eleven and twelve and the other was for junior students from classes eight to ten. Each hall had rows of dining tables that would seat ten students per table. One student from class ten was the designated 'table head' and he always sat in the same chair at the head of the table. He was responsible for ensuring discipline during the meals. The other students at the table rotated their seats at each meal. The student who sat at the opposite end of the table from the table head was the server, fetching trays of food to the table. The table head would place his fork and knife parallel in the middle of his plate to signal that the meal was over. Meals began by proclaiming en masse '*Bismillah*' and ending with '*Alhamdulillah*'.

After dinner, there would be another study period of an hour before the prefects blew whistles for lights-out. Strict adherence to the schedule was the hallmark of our routine.

We were required to attend extracurricular activities, covering various aspects of social life on a weekly basis. I chose to become a member of the college squadron team that engaged in activities akin to scouting. The squadron was run by the college adjutant, who was always a serving captain or major in the Pakistan Army. It engaged routinely in light military training. My participation in this club was of great help for my later training at PMA.

The college had a huge variety of sports facilities and I, being physically very fit, made use of most of them. I was captain of the college football team and was also a member of the college hockey and athletics teams. I was encouraged by my instructors to take part in the boxing competition and managed to win my bout in the Inter-Wing Boxing Competition.

As luck would have it, my opponent for the boxing competition was the opposing team's captain. He was an excellent boxer, and I had no chance of winning against him. I thought the best I could do would be to save myself from too much of a beating. My boxing coach and I had to build a strategy that would avoid his strengths and exploit his weaknesses. He knew how to box, and he was much taller than me. That gave him the advantage of being able to reach out and punch me while keeping himself out of my ability to hit him back. The only weapons I had to face him were my physical fitness and my stamina.

As they say, if you cannot outplay your opponent, outwork him. My strategy was to fight a defensive fight and work to protect myself from his punches. During the first two rounds, I hit him once and then withdrew quickly to avoid his counterpunches. I wanted to survive the first two rounds and tire him out for the third round. Then I would exploit my physical toughness to beat him. The plan worked. My opponent fell into the trap, and when we reached the third round, he was out of breath. I gave him hell in the third round and was about to knock him out when the round ended, and I won the bout. For my effort, I was awarded the college colour in boxing, something I could not have imagined before the bout. My participation in boxing also helped me during my training at the PMA.

At the year-end sports gala, I was honoured with college colours in football, athletics, and boxing in recognition of a good performance in each of these sports. The colours gave my college blazer a mark of distinction.

The extracurricular activities gave us opportunities to develop circles of close friends and associates that later would develop into lifetime relationships.

Narrow Escape

During the last year in college, we became complacent because we were in our final year, and some of us inadvertently became involved in serious mistakes. I, along with a few friends, got into one that almost cost me my career. I crossed the line.

I attended an anti-government protest rally at the college against Gen Ayub Khan's administration. My friends and I knew that such political activities were not allowed but with our final exams around the corner, we nevertheless went ahead and joined the rally. We had no political agenda, and our actions were purely a spur-of-the-moment reaction to country-wide student unrest. Still, our behaviour was immature and likely the first of its kind in the college's history. There were bound to be consequences.

Those of us who were engaged in planning and leading the rally were expelled and asked to leave the college on the same day. Unfortunately, I was also amongst those expelled from the college. It was a great shock, something that I never anticipated would happen because of my involvement. I thought my life had ended before it had even begun. Fearing the backlash at home, I went to the home of my best friend, Khawaja Khurshid, in Rawalpindi to figure out what to do. Khurshid had also been expelled. He passed away a few years ago after fighting a tough battle against cancer, a good person with a good heart. His parents were incredibly loving and always treated me like a son when I stayed at their home.

His father told us that we should return to the college the next day and ask for forgiveness from the college principal. We followed his advice but when we reached the college gate, we were refused entry. After repeated requests and waiting for hours, we were told that the principal would not meet with us and that we might try again the next day.

The following day we went back to the college, and after waiting for a couple of hours, we were able to meet briefly with the vice principal. He gave us a very tough lecture, had us prepare a written apology, and made us sign a promise of good conduct in future before we could meet with the principal. We did what was asked and were then taken to the principal's office.

Mr J.D.H. Chapman, the college principal, was furious. With very strict and carefully chosen words, he made us understand the damage we had caused, not only to ourselves but to the college's reputation. Finally, to our great relief, he gave us permission to return to the college conditioned on our agreement not to repeat such irresponsible behaviour in future. A major disaster that could have had life-altering consequences for me was averted.

I learnt some essential lessons from this misadventure, the main one being not to make decisions based on emotion but rather with a level head recognizing and being ready to accept all the consequences that might flow from them.

Unfortunately, while Khurshid and I were trying to address what we had done, a letter from the college reached my father in the village telling him of my expulsion. He was not aware of our efforts to be readmitted and sent Anwar Bhai to assess the situation and see what could be done under the circumstances. Anwar Bhai was greatly relieved to learn that I was back in college and the problem had been resolved. He conveyed to me our father's anguish about my behaviour and gave me valuable advice about how to modify my behaviour and continue to prepare for my intermediate examination. He was kind and supportive because he realized how badly shaken, we were about what we had done. Khurshid and I were back in the college routine after a week's break, a little subdued but determined not to repeat such blunders in future.

Thank You, CCH

My remaining time in college was smooth sailing. I passed my intermediate examination with an 'A' grade, Alhamdulillah. The stage was set for me to test for selection into the Pakistan Army.

Looking back, I realize what a fundamental role CCH played in shaping my personality and career. It wouldn't have been possible for me to get this far without the guidance I received from CCH. I am particularly grateful to all my incredible teachers. They helped me to overcome my deficiencies and made me confident and competent enough to compete at par with my peers. Most of them are no more in this world, may their souls rest in peace, Amen!

PART 2

IN THE KHAKIS

CHAPTER 4

THE BRIDGEHEAD OPERATION

Assault Across

The minimum requirement in Pakistan to become an army officer is an intermediate school certification, in other words, a high school diploma. Students taking the entrance examination during the same year they graduate can apply and go through most of the selection processes. Their final selection by the Inter-Services Selection Board (ISSB), however, must wait until they complete their intermediate certification. This accommodation enables regular college students to apply for entrance into the army without losing a year because of examinations and other scheduling conflicts between civilian educational institutions and the Pakistan Military Academy. The procedure permits candidates to complete the initial written examination, interview, and medical tests before taking their intermediate examination and then appear before the ISSB immediately after passing it.

An Unexpected Jolt

Being an Abdalian, physically fit, and expecting an A grade in the intermediate examination, I thought I would qualify easily for selection into the army. The earliest course I could apply for was the forty-fifth PMA Long Course, and I decided to apply for admission into that course while I was still preparing for the Intermediate School Certification examination. I qualified the written examination and passed the interview test. However, while going through the medical tests, I was shocked when the commandant of the military hospital in Rawalpindi told me that I was being deferred for selection for three weeks due to a systolic heart murmur. He provided me with medicine to take for three weeks. Then I was to reappear for a second medical test.

Being an athlete and a regular sportsman in college, I could not believe that I had a heart ailment that required me to take medicine. I returned home very disappointed and hoping against hope that it would be over in a month.

After taking the medicine for three weeks, I returned to the hospital for retesting. To my absolute disgust, I was told I was still not fit for duty. The forty-fifth PMA Long Course was scheduled to start soon, and I was advised to continue the medication and apply for a later course.

I was stunned. I thought that my dream of becoming an army officer was over. The question of "what next" was agonizing because I had never thought about any other career.

My father, a great fighter, worked to keep my morale up. He encouraged me to apply for admission to several engineering universities as an alternative to the army, but I was so focused on the army that nothing else seemed to matter, and I refused my father's advice. Unbeknownst to me, he sent an application for admission on my behalf to Engineering University Lahore.

Justice Delivered

About two weeks later, my father came home with a brown envelope addressed to me. I opened it, and I was surprised and delighted to find that it was a letter from the Military Hospital Rawalpindi asking me to report immediately for a re-examination of my heart condition. The start of the forty-fifth PMA Long Course had been delayed for a few weeks, and there was still time to give me another chance to qualify for admission. All of us at home were over the moon, and my late mother led the prayer, requesting God Almighty to give me the success I so passionately wanted.

I went for my re-test on the scheduled date, and when I reached the commandant's office to receive my results, I learnt, once again, that I was still considered not qualified. My hopes were shattered, and I was extremely frustrated.

A thousand people can say *no* to you, but all it takes is one to say *yes*. I requested the commandant to reconsider the decision based on my physical fitness. I showed him all the sports awards and certificates I had won during my time at CCH, particularly the certificates for winning marathon races. Pointing at the colour badges on my blue college blazer, I argued, "Sir, please look at these colour badges that I have won for my extraordinary performance in different sports and still my health is being questioned?"

The commandant looked at my awards and considered what I had to say. He was himself surprised by what the doctors had decided because he thought there was no reason for me to suffer from this kind of disease. He summoned a few other doctors who had more experience with systolic heart murmurs. After discussing the case thoroughly with them, he ordered the re-examination of my case by a board of heart specialists. I was immediately taken to the hospital's cardiology department for retesting. After various physical exercises and medical tests, the panel determined that I was fit for army service. The commandant cleared me medically for acceptance into the forty-fifth PMA Long Course.

It was excellent news for me, and I thanked Almighty Allah for all His blessings. This incident convinced me that in the army cases are decided based on merit, and not on who one knows. If one has a question, all one needs to do is present the issue logically, and justice will be delivered fairly based on merit.

When I reached home, I was surprised because before I could break the news of my selection, my father welcomed me joyfully, "Congratulations on your selection; your mother told me a few hours back that you had been selected."

"How could she know it? I haven't told her about the decision yet." I responded.

I was astonished by what my father told me, "Your mother was offering her prayers, and she heard a voice say—*your son got selected for the army.*" That may surprise some people, but such things do happen. It all depends on your conviction and trust in God. My mother was a very religious person, and she was known for her strong spiritual beliefs. She knew that her earnest desire and prayers had been accepted by God.

References Don't Matter

On clearance by the medical board, I was immediately called to appear before the ISSB for final selection. During three days of board proceedings, I was given written tests to evaluate my intelligence and general knowledge and performed several group tasks to test my abilities to command a team and to work as a part of a team under the command of someone else. I participated in a detailed interview in the presence of psychiatrists who had made recommendations based on their observations about certain specific personality traits the army wants its officers to possess.

There were five of us from CCH who were tested, and four of us, including me, were selected for admission. The four of us selected were from middle and lower-middle-class backgrounds, and the one who failed to qualify was the son of a serving major general in the Pakistan Army. It was another example of the army making decisions based on merit, irrespective of a person's references or family background.

I was now a Gentleman Cadet of the PMA, Kakul. I received the final notice of selection and further instructions regarding my admission a couple of days later. I had overcome the obstacles and established a bridgehead in the 'Khakis'.

During my last few days at home before joining PMA, I received a call from the Engineering University, Lahore, offering me a seat in the Bachelor of Science Engineering class starting in about two months. The application that my father had sent without my knowledge while I was fighting the battle against my medical examination had been accepted. It was a repeat of when I was in class 8 and applied for admission to two of the best colleges in the country and had been selected by both. That had given me the latitude to make a choice. Here too, God was providing me with the opportunity to choose the army as a career or become a civilian engineer. My choice was the Pakistan Army. Allah be praised for all His blessings. He always granted me success and kept options open for me to choose my own path.

The Bridgehead Battle

The VIP Reception

I joined PMA as a first-term Gentleman Cadet on 3 November 1969. As before, my father accompanied me on the bus from Rawalakot to Rawalpindi. The bus broke down en route, and we had to walk nearly fifteen kilometres before we could get another bus to Rawalpindi. I carried my rolled-up bedding on my shoulders, and my father held my bag during our journey on foot. It reminded me of when my father walked me to school, across the difficult streams and mountainous terrain of Azad Kashmir, carrying my school bag in one hand and holding on to me with the other. When we reached Rawalpindi, I said goodbye to my father and caught another bus that took me to PMA Kakul.

When I arrived at the academy's gate, the PMA instructional staff took me along with other new Gentlemen Cadets to a parade ground nearby. The senior cadets from the third and fourth terms, appointed as corporals and sergeants briefed us, assigned us to platoons and companies, and then took us to our barracks. I was assigned to Sala-ud-din Company (S-26), which was housed in black wooden barracks with a tin roof. After dropping off our luggage in our rooms, we were made to fall in line in front of our barracks for a briefing by our corporal and the sergeant. After short menacing remarks, our military life began with a dose of "ragging," a process of transforming civilians into soldiers. It is a mixture of harsh language and physical punishments, designed to eliminate personal egos and acclimate one into obeying commands immediately and without question. It is a difficult time for new cadets, but care is taken not to insult a new cadet's character or damage his self-respect.

Despite the November cold, we were made to dress in our shorts and a vest until late that night. After an hour or two of sleep, we arose early the next morning to continue the ragging. It was the beginning of our first-term training as Gentleman Cadets, and after a while, we got used to it. We became part of the military culture. My two years in PMA were a memorable period of my life. Apart from various military and academic subjects, the academy taught us discipline and moral values. That was important because character goes a long way in our lives and, in most cases, is transferred to our children.

Learning the Hard Way

Some of our instructors were junior commissioned officers (JCOs) and non-commissioned officers (NCOs). They played a vital role in our lives as cadets. Physical training is equal to academic and military subjects in the academy's curriculum, and they used it to build character, teamwork, and comradeship amongst the cadets.

The Bleeding Elbows

In one instance, a cadet from our platoon mimicked the voice of our NCO instructor Havildar (Sergeant) Suba Khan during physical training. The instructor was annoyed but could not identify who had done it. He asked the offending cadet to step forward and accept responsibility for his action and he called upon the platoon to identify the guilty party, but no one gave him up. As punishment, the instructor made the platoon crawl for hours on our elbows in the snow along the side of the road. When we were done, there were lines of blood in the snow from injured elbows for hundreds of metres. Still, nobody disclosed the name of the offending cadet.

The NCO instructor suspected that someone from my group of cadets was involved in the incident and ordered that four of us, including me, report to the Academy Adjutant, Major Nadar Pervez, Sitara-e-Jurat (Bar), for inquiry and disciplinary action as appropriate. "Sitara-e-Jurat (Bar)" is Pakistan's third-highest military award. 'Bar' means the same award given to the recipient twice or more. Major Nader Pervez had received it twice. He was also an Abdalian, and he knew me well as his former college mate. When it came to discipline and his duty, however, none of that mattered. He did not hesitate to order a punishment of twenty-eight days 'restrictions' for all four of us. That meant we had to attend all scheduled punishments, were banned from social activities, and could not leave the PMA campus during that period. We also lost our end-of-term break of about four weeks because the break coincided with the time of our punishment. The only good thing to come out of it for us was that the loyalty and comradeship we had shown to save one of our own were appreciated at all levels.

THE BRIDGEHEAD OPERATION

Haye Lassi, Haye Paratha

We also learnt character, teamwork, and comradeship on another occasion, during a week-long field exercise. A few cadets bought some cooked food at night from a nearby village, which was forbidden. The exercise, named 'Initiative,' was primarily about endurance training although there were a few minor tactical exercises also included in its schedule. The cadets were made to march about sixty kilometres in full battle dress, carrying weapons, and dry rations that we were supposed to cook for our meals.

The purchase of food items from a local village somehow got leaked, and the entire cadet corps, about 110 of us, was made to stand in parade formation for hours with Full-Service Marching Orders (FSMO). FSMO includes personal weapons as well as individual equipment, including bedding, clothing, and other items of personal use. The culprits who had bought the food were asked to step forward and own up to their mistakes voluntarily.

Most of the cadets knew who purchased the food, namely diluted yoghurt called 'lassi' in Urdu, and fried bread called 'Paratha' in Urdu, but everyone decided not to name them. We were made to do push-ups and sit-ups and shout, '*Haye lassi, Haye paratha*' for hours. Everyone was soaked in sweat. Still, no one identified the culprits. Yoghurt and fried bread were very popular among the cadets, and we all had to pay a hefty price for the few who got to enjoy them. When the ragging ended and we resumed the exercise, the instructors quietly appreciated the esprit de corps that prevented us from disclosing the names of the culprits.

Battle Inoculation

To familiarize cadets with combat and make them battle-hardened, an exercise named 'Battle Inoculation' is conducted during the middle of the PMA course. The cadets move through various obstacles under live fire conditions to assault an objective. Small arms, light and medium machine guns, mortars, and even artillery guns firing, make the exercise realistic. Many precautions are put in place to keep the cadets safe, but of course, the risk can never be eliminated completely.

During a 'Battle Inoculation' exercise, a cadet lost his life when he failed to follow safety instructions. Suddenly, whistles were blowing everywhere, and the firing stopped. The body of the cadet was recovered, put into an ambulance, and dispatched to the academy. All the cadets, instructors, and other staff members, stood in parade formation and offered funeral prayers. Everything in the exercise area settled down and in about an hour or so, the live fire exercise resumed. For the cadets, it was a lesson in how to overcome one's emotions and carry on with the mission despite terrible losses. A similar incident had occurred earlier on as well, and necessary precautions had been taken. But there are always risks in the profession of arms that have to be accepted as part of the game.

Conquering the Five 'Ss'

The five S's are stamina, speed, strength, skill, and spirit; the greatest of these is the spirit. Being a sportsman and having a cadet college background gave me a grip on all of them, which was to my great advantage during my training. I continued my sports activities in PMA and became a Sports Sergeant in the final term of the course. Boxing is an essential sport at the academy because it requires boldness and courage. My hardest-fought boxing bout was fought against Gentleman Cadet Asad Kayani. We both were known for our physical fitness and stamina, and we were evenly matched. I beat him, but it was a close match and Kayani received an award of 'Best Loser' for his brave fight back. The referee was none other than Major Shabbir Sharif (Shaheed), Nishan-e-Haider (NH). His holding my arm up to declare me the winner is one of the most cherished memories of my PMA stay. Major Shabbir Sharif NH, Sitara-e-Jurat (SJ) was a military officer in the Pakistan Army who was posthumously awarded the NH, the highest award in the Pakistan Army, during the Indo-Pakistan War of 1971. He is the only person ever who received both NH and SJ for his bravery.

The D-Day

Our graduation parade was scheduled for the end of October 1971, but we graduated a month early, on 28 September 1971, due to the war with India. In addition to being commissioned as an officer, cadets who completed their academic examinations successfully were granted a bachelor's degree from the University of Peshawar. I was also among those who received that degree. The month holiday cadets normally receive at the end of their coursework was shortened to a week, and we were ordered to report to our units at their battle locations.

Several of my classmates were foreign cadets from friendly countries. I remember two Iraqi cadets who completed the training with us and later rose to the rank of Lieutenant General in the Iraqi Army. Both cadets were very sound professionals and were highly regarded as officers. They represented the highest standards of the Iraqi army of that time. We also had several cadets from East Pakistan (now Bangladesh) who were later repatriated to their country. Many were professionally good, and some later rose to the rank of major general and lieutenant general in the Bangladesh Army. One of them became chief of the general staff in the Bangladeshi army. Some of the cadets from Bangladesh were saddened by the events in East Pakistan and would have preferred to remain in the Pakistani army if they had a choice.

After enduring PMA training for two years, my classmates were like a family. It is a unique relationship, hard to explain in words and generally expressed between friends through the wink of an eye. I think quoting someone much wiser than me may help to explain what course mates mean to each other.

> *"Young hooligans thrown together by fate,*
> *Bound together thereafter for life*
> *with the magic word 'Coursemate'!*
> *One gets preference over family & wife,*
> *In a course mate's house, you demand a bite,*
> *Whether it is day or night!*
> *You can borrow his shoes or favourite dress,*
> *And then dump it back in a total mess.*
> *Coursemate is your friend, philosopher, and guide,*
> *Who must stand by you and not take you for a ride!*
> *When in trouble, just give him a ring,*
> *Problems solved before the bee can sting.*
> *May not have met for many years,*
> *But that should not give you any fear.*
> *Just a reference of passing out date,*
> *Brings back remembrances and opens all gates!*
> *Knows your darkest secrets never to be told,*
> *Even if he is offered a bag of gold.*
> *Will look you in the eyes & give a wink,*
> *Come sunset he will join you for a drink.*
> *Course mate's bonhomie cannot be matched,*
> *Conspiracy to break them cannot be hatched,*
> *They are bound together by blood and sweat.'*
> *The closest to a person you can ever get....!!"*
>
> By 'A Coursemate'

A reunion for the forty-fifth PMA Long Course was arranged in 2010 by General Ashfaq Pervez Kayani, ex-chief of army staff (COAS), Pakistan Army who also happens to be from the forty-fifth Long Course. Several Bangladeshi officers from our course attended as 'The Bangladesh Chapter' of the forty-fifth PMA Long Course. This contingent comprised both serving and retired Bangladeshi officers who wholeheartedly participated in the reunion. It was an occasion for reviving old associations, sharing sweet memories of our days in PMA and an exemplary illustration of army culture and heritage. Some of the souvenirs they presented to us as a gesture of goodwill occupy the best place in my house, along with my other army mementos.

CHAPTER 5

THE BREAKOUT MANOEUVRES AND THE MENTORS

My 'Breakout Battle' in the 'Khakis' has been multi-directional. My army career progressed through three distinct manoeuvres: as a regimental soldier, an intelligence officer, and as a diplomat. While two main manoeuvres were regimental soldiering and intelligence work, a subsidiary effort has been an opportunity to represent my country as a diplomat abroad for nearly three and a half years. Though I call this effort 'subsidiary', it is purely because of the limited time frame that I was in the diplomatic role and by no means lessens its importance in any case. The role of armies internationally has made military diplomacy an important part of international relationships, probably as important as diplomatic channels. Besides providing me with an opportunity to learn the art of diplomacy and get to know the nuts and bolts of regional and international strategic and political manoeuvring, service as a diplomat abroad was of immense value to me while discharging my duties as a senior military officer during the later years of my career.

Looking back on almost four decades of my time with Pakistan's army, I can safely say that what the army has given me is much more than I have been able to give back. I had great opportunities to serve in the field, command valiant soldiers, undertake intelligence work, and travel extensively at home and abroad. The only thing I have sought is to leave an unblemished legacy behind me. For soldiers, it is not about who we are but what we can do for the people and the institutions we serve.

I owe a great deal to my mentors who encouraged me to push through all the long years of being a professional soldier. I am particularly grateful to ex-Chairman Joint Chiefs of Staff Committee (CJCSC), General Akhtar Abdul Rehman and ex-president, ex-COAS, General Pervez Musharraf. Their patronage and peerless mentoring during various stages of my career remained a guiding light for me until the very end of my career.

One of my commanding officers in the 16 SP Artillery Regiment—'*The Dashing Sixteen*' Lieutenant Colonel Rashid Ahmed, SJ, mentored me through the early part of my career. He fought gallantly in the 1965 war against India and participated in the famous 'Chawinda' battle in the Sialkot sector. It was a desperate battle, in which many of our soldiers wrapped explosives around their waists, laid down in front of Indian tanks, and blew up themselves and the tanks. Lieutenant Colonel Rashid, then part of the 1 SP Regiment, employed his artillery gun as a direct shooting weapon and destroyed many Indian tanks, forcing the enemy to withdraw, leaving behind massive wreckage that burnt for days, filling the air with acrid smoke. He was awarded SJ for his bravery during this battle.

The Dasher's Way

A Royal Welcome

After training at PMA, the graduating cadets are posted to various army units as second lieutenants. Their assignments are based on key considerations, such as the individual's aptitude in a particular field, and his position on the merit list which ensures fair distribution of cadet talent throughout the army. An individual cadet's choice and claim for a specific unit also plays a role in his postings. For example, if a cadet's blood relations served in a particular unit, the cadet can claim that unit and request to be sent there. All other things being equal, his request will likely be granted.

I was posted to 16 SP Regiment Artillery 'The Dashing Sixteen' on merit. I was honoured to become part of this great unit which was well known throughout the Pakistani army. Sixteen SP was raised in 1956 and equipped initially with vintage Sherman tanks from the Korean War. The unit distinguished itself in the 1965 Indo-Pak War during furious tank battles between India and Pakistan in the Kham Kern and Sialkot sectors. Many of its officers and men were honoured with gallantry awards.

President of Pakistan, General Pervez Musharaff was also one of the award winners who fought the war as a lieutenant in one of the 16 SP Batteries as a gun position officer and was awarded Sitara-e-Basalat for his bravery and courage.

I, along with another coursemate, Abid Ali Khan reported for duty to 'The Dashing Sixteen' at Lahore about a week after our graduation. We were warmly welcomed at the railway station by one of its officers, Captain Rahim, and soon were on our way to the unit mess in Lahore cantonment.

Abid and I had a long association that spanned more than two decades until his death. He was a valued colleague, an excellent man with a good head and a good heart. When I was at CCH, he was a student at Military College Jhelum. We played sports against each other during our college days, especially during inter-college sports tournaments. He was an outstanding hockey player who attended national training camps. He was one of my closest friends throughout my career.

When Abid and I arrived at the 16 SP mess in Lahore cantonment, we were introduced to our batman, a helper the army provided to officers to maintain their uniforms and to perform minor administrative tasks. Our batman took our luggage to our assigned room and guided us to the sitting room, where other unit officers were waiting to welcome us.

This time the reception was not as cordial as it was at the railway station, and once again, we were reminded of our cadet life. One officer who introduced himself as the regimental adjutant gave me a stern lecture about my attire that he said was below the standards an army officer should possess. After delivering his critique, he introduced us to an older officer who was the unit's second in command. He gave us a second dose of 16 SP's special welcome although not as strong as the adjutant's.

He told us to deposit a few hundred rupees with our batman, so that we and our room would be maintained at a living standard expected of army officers. We had hardly any money but had to give whatever we had. With a few more admonitions about what was expected of us as 'Dashing Sixteen' officers, we were sent back to our room to refresh ourselves and return for dinner.

When we entered our room for the first time, we felt that we were finally officers in the Pakistan Army. Beds, an armchair, a study table, and a few decorative pieces of furniture were all neatly laid out. The batman, who had taken our money, was not there. We took a shower and dressed ourselves carefully in the best clothes we had, hoping to satisfy our mighty adjutant and meet the dress standard for dinner.

On reaching the dining room, we could not believe our eyes. The smiling officer who stood at our table in formal dress to greet us was none other than our pretended batman! He introduced himself good-naturedly as Captain Fida, the regiment's real adjutant. Three other officers joined him, laughing and enjoying the ruse they had staged to welcome us. One of the officers, the one who lectured us as the second in command, was the regiment's senior captain. Another senior officer present on the occasion was my acting battery commander, Captain Hasan Shah.

While they were all joking and enjoying how they had fooled us, I was thinking about the money we had given to Captain Fida, thinking that he was our batman. I did not have to wait long to learn what happened to the money. The regiment's senior captain announced that the sumptuous dinner being served that night was being paid for by the unit's newest officers – us! We were being welcomed with our own hard-earned money.

We had no choice but to join in the celebration. With empty pockets, we ate the excellent food and waited for the day when other newly commissioned officers would pay for us to have a lavish meal. Although it cost us almost all our money, the meal turned out to be great fun and we felt very welcomed by the unit. It was part of the unit's traditions and the army's culture and it helped to make us a team.

Briefing Notes

The next day, we drove in a mini truck a few miles outside the cantonment to the unit lines. Our reception there was very different to the one we had received the previous evening. The regimental adjutant briefed us and told us to review the unit's Standing Operating Procedures (SOPs) before we met the 16 SP's commanding officer, Lieutenant Colonel Mumtaz Ahmad Khan Niazi. This time nothing was said about my appearance. Now it was serious business.

Our interview with the commanding officer turned out to be very inspiring. He was very fatherly and gave us valuable tips about life in the army. Much of what he said guided me throughout my career. His basic theme was that we, as officers, should maintain self-discipline, high moral values, and team spirit, and conduct ourselves professionally. He told us to learn about the unit and army life from the second in command, from other unit officers, and importantly from the unit's sergeant major. In Pakistan's army, the sergeant major is a rank between sergeants and lieutenants, akin to warrant officers. The position is held by only the best and most senior enlisted men.

I met with Sergeant Major Ibrahim Sahib after my meeting with our unit commander. He welcomed me on behalf of all other ranks of the unit. Despite his age and a bit of a waistline bulge, he stood fast in front of me, saluted smartly, and was very gracious. I responded in the way I had learnt in PMA and offered him a chair next to mine. The waiter brought us tea and snacks. We exchanged pleasantries briefly, then the sergeant major began his thoughtfully prepared briefing. He was very polite and respectful, sprinkling his comments with 'sir' and 'sahib.' The briefing lasted nearly two hours. It was full of wisdom and guidance, each word bolstered by decades of army experience. He painted, as I came to understand, a true and accurate picture of the tradition and culture of the army's enlisted ranks. It was fascinating to hear this wise man speak.

He described in detail the life of an enlisted soldier and the expectations of their officers. He talked a great deal about the general conduct of young officers, their professionalism, and important aspects of their personal lives, their social, moral, and financial behaviour. He offered personal guidance that was particularly noteworthy. With a knowing smile, he told me, "I would keep track of your mess and canteen bills and be sure that you stay within your financial means. Do not smoke, drink, or follow a lavish lifestyle."

His last words of caution were delivered with a laugh. He told me that if he learnt that I had a girlfriend who was not aligned with our culture and religion, he would write a letter to my father. Sergeant Major Ibrahim retired as an officer and an honorary lieutenant. He was one of my best mentors during the early stages of my career, and I remember him quite often. May Allah rest his soul in peace, Amen.

My meeting with Sergeant Major Ibrahim was followed by a series of briefings by senior and junior regimental staff officers and a visit to the gun park. I spent the afternoon in the office and participating in the sports programme, during which I met most of the other members of my gun battery. That evening, I was shown the cookhouse and dining hall for other ranks and ate dinner with them. During these brief introductory visits, my role as a young officer to ensure high standards within the unit was emphasized.

Life in the Bunkers

With the clouds of a war with India hovering above us in 1971, the 16 SP moved into the front line. In the weeks that followed, we spent our time preparing for combat. It enabled me to see the unit implement its standard operating procedures on a war footing. My days were filled with getting to know the men and capabilities of various operational teams within the battery.

Soon we were deployed in our pre-designated battlefield positions. Being a new second lieutenant, I shared a bunker with the other ranks next to our tanks. I was there for two weeks before moving to share an underground bunker with my Battery Captain Muhammad Farooq Malik. Living with troops in the field was a unique opportunity to know them better and to develop the team spirit that is essential for army officers to be successful.

We started each day with physical exercise, followed by 'On the Gun' training until noon. After lunch, we participated in sports and attended entertainment events in the evening. The evening's activities were important to maintaining good morale after a hard day of physical activity. I developed a close association with my under-command during the prolonged period we spent waiting in anticipation of the 1971 war. It remained with me during war and peace all along subsequent years.

In addition to preparing for a possible war with India, I and two other young officers, Lieutenant Abid Ali Khan, and Lieutenant Aejaz Gilani had to attend a basic artillery course at the School of Artillery at Nowshera. Lieutenant Gilani was a classmate from CCH and is a long-time friend. He graduated after me and had requested an assignment to the 16 SP Regiment because of me. We remain very close friends.

Our second in command, Major Akhtar, who himself had been an instructor at the School of Artillery, arranged for us to take a general preparatory class before we reported for the formal training. He was a Bengali officer with a reputation for professionalism and being a devoted Pakistani. He condemned Indian subversion in East Pakistan and often expressed concern about anti-Pakistan political and subversive activities in that part of the country. He was one of many Bengali army officers who refused to be repatriated to Bangladesh after its separation from Pakistan.

The preparatory training lasted nearly two months. During this time, Major Akhtar personally mentored us. His guidance was of great help to us during our time at the School of Artillery. All three of us received good results. I graduated from the course with an 'A' grade.

After my basic course, I was posted as a gun position officer in my battery and managed the training of an excellent team of technical assistants and gunners who went on to win many competitions at the unit, brigade, and higher formation levels.

Though our unit was not directly involved in the main theatre of war, we were moving constantly from one sector to another, as part of the Corps Reserve Independent Armoured Brigade Group. We were a frequent target of the Indian Air Force that tried unsuccessfully to locate and strike us. We were on continuous alert and ready to move with our armour formations into Indian territory for a counter-offensive. We received food in haversacks each morning and kept them in our vehicles in case the attack order came. Dry fruit and other non-perishable items were stuffed in our packs in case we ran out of cooked food. Channa, a form of lentil that can be eaten for many days once roasted, was the most common food we carried for such situations.

Finally, our formation headquarters received orders to launch a counter-offensive. Everybody said goodbyes to each other and mounted their combat vehicles and tanks to move forward towards our objectives, hoping to meet again after the battle. Spirits were at the peak, each tank roaring with slogans of 'Allah-O-Akbar' and 'Pakistan Zindabad'.

The fight was not to be. At the last moment, the unit headquarters received a radio message that the attack had been cancelled and that the war was over as far as the 16 SP was concerned. Everyone was shocked and there were tears in the eyes of many that the war for us would end without confronting Pakistan's enemy.

The ceasefire and the painful loss of East Pakistan sent a shock wave through the army from top to bottom. How we had failed as field soldiers was the question on everyone's mind. We had not seen a single Indian soldier during the entire war who was prepared to engage us. It was demoralizing and unimaginable, and many of us could not digest it for years afterwards.

We remained in the operational area for nearly two years after the war ended. We trained rigorously and worked hard to restore our morale and confidence. There were frequent training events at all levels, followed by honest critiques and debriefing sessions to improve our professional standards. We increased close interactions between various command levels, and they helped to rebuild an esprit de corps within the ranks. We revamped our operation teams and restored their trust in the unit's capabilities. We rebuilt Dashing Sixteen's morale.

Fumbling for the Better

As a young officer, new to the unit and war, I was learning much about the army. Every day there was something new, something more to know. Staying with the enlisted troops on a 24/7 basis was an excellent opportunity to know them better, to win their confidence, and to understand their experiences. I learnt valuable lessons about maintaining a balanced relationship between the command and its subordinates during this period. There were ample opportunities to provide leadership under demanding circumstances. Making decisions based on one's own judgement was one of the more important lessons I learnt.

Some of what I learnt was painful. I was participating in three days of training at Brigade Headquarters in the Changa Manga Forest, about two to three hours from Lahore. My unit was deployed on the forward defence lines (FDLs) near Kanganpur, about an hour's driving distance towards the Indo-Pak border from Changa Manga. I was given a jeep and one of the battery's best drivers, Naik Fiaz, to carry me back and forth to the training.

One day while we were returning from the Changa Manga Forest, I asked Naik Fiaz to let me drive for a while. I had some driving skills from driving around inside the camp, but I did not have a driving licence. Naik Fiaz gave me the wheel.

THE BREAKOUT MANOEUVRES AND THE MENTORS

Unfortunately, I had gone just a few kilometres, maybe four or five, when I failed to negotiate a sharp turn, and the jeep overturned, falling into a nearby stream. I was thrown from the vehicle, but Naik Fiaz stayed inside until it came to a stop, upside down. I rushed to the jeep to see if he was safe. Luckily, he was unhurt and was cautiously trying to crawl out of the side door.

I helped him out of the jeep that I saw had been significantly damaged. Within minutes, several people gathered at the accident site and helped us to roll the jeep back onto the road. I was happy to see that Naik Fiaz was safe and moving about without difficulty. He was in his usual self, with high spirits, and expressing his gratitude to Almighty Allah that we both were safe. While he was trying to put the jeep in a condition to drive it back to the camp, I was thinking about the consequences for me. I was driving the jeep without a licence.

We both thought that disciplinary action would be taken against us. Naik Fiaz believed that he would be held responsible for allowing me to drive without a licence. He did not want me to get into any trouble and thought that he should accept responsibility for causing the accident. I rejected the suggestion and told him that I would take responsibility for what I had done and try to save him from any disciplinary action. Fiaz insisted, however, that by agreeing to his suggestion, we both might escape serious consequences. I relied on his experience in the unit and agreed to his suggestion. It was a terrible mistake that later turned out to be a life lesson for me.

Fiaz managed to drive the jeep back to the unit and turn it over to the LAD, the electrical, mechanical, and engineering section, attached to our unit. A report was submitted saying that Fiaz was behind the wheel when the accident happened. Later in the evening, I was called by the regiment's adjutant to meet with the regimental commander Lieutenant Colonel Rashid, SJ who had by then taken command of the unit. He was a very experienced and thorough officer who always sought all the facts before making any decision. We met and it did not take him but a few minutes before I confessed to what had happened.

A lengthy counselling session followed, including a verbal reprimand to make me understand that my conduct in this matter was unbecoming of an officer. He made me realize how such irresponsible behaviour by an officer is very damaging when junior rank personnel are involved. I should have taken responsibility for the consequences even if Naik Fiaz had done something wrong under my supervision. I was terribly ashamed of my behaviour and confessed my guilt. I knew what he was saying was true, and I had agreed to Naik Fiaz's suggestion immaturely.

Lieutenant Colonel Rashid decided that while my actions were wrong, they were not done with malicious intent. He let me off with a warning letter and a strong verbal reprimand. He mentioned the incident in my annual fitness evaluation but noted that my behaviour had changed ever since and improved subsequently. His words were critical of me but written in a manner that did not damage my career. For me, it was the lesson of a lifetime, one that I will never forget.

It changed my behaviour. I became a different man, willing to accept responsibility for my behaviour, good or bad, without hesitation. I became more willing to express my opinions on matters involving moral values and principles.

Lieutenant Colonel Rashid later appointed me to the position of regimental adjutant based on merit. It is an important job. The adjutant assists the commander with unit administration and the officers appointed to do that job enjoy the commander's trust and confidence. How I came to have the position is an example of how the Pakistani army works to develop its workforce, taking appropriate corrective measures when necessary while mentoring its people who have made mistakes.

Walking in Rhythm

Our prolonged stay in the field after the 1971 war was used thoughtfully to rebuild the troops' broken morale, develop our operational teams, and carefully reconnoitred our operational areas to update our contingency plans. There were active Forward Defence Lines (FDLs) on each side of the border, and we were able to monitor closely our enemies in the area and identify vulnerabilities that we could exploit in future encounters. The troops on both sides had comparatively relaxed routines of operational activities. We always found Indian Army soldiers subdued and hesitant to face us at the border posts. Where the border posts were close, within hearing distance apart, the sentries on both sides could interact with each other. Our sentries were proactive and willing to engage with them, but their soldiers were always impassive, just waiting and counting the time until their duty hours were over.

On occasion, our unit *cookhouse* on the border was almost opposite the Indian *cookhouse,* and it made for an interesting situation at mealtimes. Our unit had music to entertain the troops. Our motivational songs for the soldiers were so popular that the Indian troops often requested that we play them louder during mealtimes. Malika-e-Taranum Noor Jahan, a well-known Pakistani singer, was their favourite. They did not seem to mind that the songs were full of praise for Pakistani soldiers.

We wondered if the passivity of Indian troops was because of their training or because of the nature of the Indian soldier. I know that the Indian Army has some brave and skilled fighting regiments, but I did not encounter them during that time along the border.

Back to Barracks

On returning to the barracks, our first challenge was to defend our Armoured Brigade Hockey championship trophy. We had a winning history in this sport, but that year our team was weaker because some of our key players had retired. Our commanding officer was a great hockey player, but he was getting older and had developed a heart problem. Still, he was very concerned that our team be well prepared to defend its title, and he took on that task as a personal challenge. Despite his busy schedule, he spent a lot of time on the hockey field. Even when he was in his office, he was planning strategies and brainstorming various combinations of players to overcome the team's weaknesses. As his adjutant, I was always there to help him. He used a whiteboard to identify and plan all the possible playing options and to discuss the tactical manoeuvres that we needed to employ. He decided to field a team of seven young officers, including me, and himself as defenders. The other team members were young soldiers, full of energy and regimental spirit. We trained ourselves as a well-knit team for about a month, day, and night, before our game against the First Frontier Force Regiment (1FF). It was a very experienced team and many of its players had been members of the all-army hockey team.

Colonel Rashid designated me and Captain Sikandar Ghumman, to defend against their two most dangerous players by staying next to them continuously, irrespective of where the ball went. We both did our jobs well and with the other players contributing equally, were able to prevent our opponents from scoring.

Then Captain Farooq Malik, from our team, stole the ball from an attacking player near our goal post, dribbled through the opponent's defence down the entire length of the field, and scored the lone goal to win the match and allow us to retain the championship trophy. A young, energetic squad of officers and Colonel Rashid's leadership won us the day, surprising everyone in the corps. Captain Sikander who later rose to the rank of Colonel, recently died due to kidney failure and heart ailment. He was a wonderful comrade and very reliable friend. May Allah bless his soul.

Learning the Intelligence Craft

Within a few months after our unit returned to the barracks, I was selected to attend the basic intelligence course at the School of Military Intelligence. It is a course for upcoming young officers with a good service record and the potential to be posted as operations/intelligence staff officers at a brigade or divisional headquarters. Some officers are also selected for posting to various intelligence services or units.

I was promoted to the rank of major upon completion of the course and assumed command of my former battery. Being the commander of an outfit, I had joined as a second lieutenant a few years before, was fascinating. Everyone from the sergeants to the cleaning staff celebrated my appointment and gave me their complete support.

I improved the subunit's administration as well as its operations and had a successful command. We won several inter-batteries operational and sports competitions and were declared the best subunit in the annual inspection. I received an outstanding fitness evaluation and together with my above-average performance in my educational and professional courses, including the intelligence course, I was nominated for consideration as an instructor at the PMA. Serving as a PMA instructor is considered a highly prestigious assignment. The selection process takes place at the PMA and lasts six weeks. We were evaluated for our suitability as an instructor and as a member of the PMA faculty.

At the end of the evaluation, I was recommended to become an instructor. I was asked, however, to attend a three-month course at the School of Infantry and Tactics before joining PMA. I was trained as an artillery officer and the training for PMA cadets is focused on infantry skills. A spot was found for me in an already scheduled course at the Infantry School at Quetta, but before I could make travel arrangements to attend the course, I received an immediate posting order for ISI.

The posting was a surprise that altered my career trajectory towards long-term employment as an intelligence officer. I was not very happy about it because I did not want to lose my prestigious appointment as an instructor at PMA and I did not want to abandon the hardcore military career path that I was following. Nevertheless, I had no option but to obey the orders. Although we cannot predict it at the time, things coming from heaven always have something good in store for us. That turned out to be true for me as I realized later in my career. Though not a very welcome posting which I thought was most untimely, it put me on a voyage that consumed more than half of my four decades in the Pakistan Army.

The best thing that happened in my multi-pronged professional pursuits has been that all endeavours had been mutually supportive, for successful progression in my career 'In the khakis'. Timely shifting the path from regimental soldiering to intelligence field and vice versa, kept me relevant to both sides. Resultantly, everything went perfectly for me to get the maximum out of my military career. Serving as a diplomat abroad, was an invaluable advantage for me to successfully shoulder my professional obligations in senior ranks while I served in ISI and remains equally handy today as I serve in the private security industry in Dubai.

Battling in the Silent War Zone – Part 1

Upon joining ISI in 1979, I was assigned on a temporary basis as the commander of ISI detachment, Sargodha. I was kept in that job for nearly 11 months. Sargodha was a peaceful place with few significant security issues. The Pakistani Air Force base was the only defence organization that required continuous monitoring from a counterintelligence point of view. There were also a few other small army organizations to look after, but they were easily managed. In general, life at Sargodha was quiet, and I enjoyed my stay there, playing squash in the company of some new friends in the Pakistan Air Force. I also kept busy with organized hunting trips to exciting places.

The most significant development during my short stay in Sargodha was my engagement with Khansa Shaheen, an educator, and a friend of my elder sister. It was a lucky encounter for me that changed my life.

I was posted as officer commanding the ISI detachment Islamabad in 1980. It was a prized appointment for an ISI major. Things changed dramatically when I arrived in Islamabad. I was introduced suddenly to a long list of duties and responsibilities. It felt like when I transferred from the '*taat*' school in my village to the CCH. In addition, Khansa and I were married a couple of months after my arrival, and we set out as a newlywed couple to explore what is undoubtedly one of the best cities in the world.

As the officer commanding the ISI detachment Islamabad, my first task was to coordinate security for a Foreign Ministers Conference of Islamic Countries. The meeting was important because it was being held to follow up on decisions taken at a previous conference of Heads of the Islamic Countries held in Lahore. This high-profile event had far-reaching consequences on the geopolitics of the region. All eyes were on its proposed actions and on how the important decision taken during this meeting would affect global politics. Security of the delegates and the information was of prime importance. That was probably the reason my posting to Sargodha was so short.

My time as Officer Commanding ISI Detachment Islamabad completely changed my career profile from a purely professional soldier to a hardcore intelligence operative. On the professional soldiering side, the plan was for me to move to the PMA and become an instructor. That would have put me on a career path of high-profile professional soldiering. On the intelligence operative side, I was holding the best possible appointment I could get as a major. This is called destiny, and we all have no choice but to submit to it unconditionally. For the most part, it worked out much better than I anticipated. My experiences during the later years of my career made me believe that God has a plan for every one of us, and following it is the best thing we can do. Our job is to work hard and put the rest in God Almighty's hands.

Islamabad, Pakistan's capital city hosts all foreign diplomatic missions, and it is a hub of overt and covert intelligence activities. My posting there coincided with Russia's invasion of Afghanistan, an event that created extreme turmoil in the region and threatened the interests of all the regional stakeholders. The war caused a manifold increase in intelligence activities in the region and particularly, in Pakistan.

The foreign diplomatic corps in Islamabad became very active. The number of hostile intelligence operatives operating undercover suddenly increased. Concurrently, we increased our counterintelligence efforts to keep track of them. We had succeeded in gaining access to their strongholds where they used to hide their secret documents and plans to target our national security interests. In many cases, we were able to procure these documents through our moles which were effectively used by us for counterintelligence purposes on different occasions.

Because we were working on joint operations in Afghanistan with allied intelligence agencies, it became difficult to distinguish between allied efforts against the common enemy and allied intelligence efforts against Pakistan. Our counterintelligence activities led us to disagreeable conclusions about what our allies were doing. Unfortunately, in a few cases, our investigations led us to some trusted people who were not working in Pakistan's best interest.

During my time in Islamabad, the security of senior government officials was among our primary responsibilities. However, Indian agents operating under diplomatic and non-diplomatic cover and undercover agents from a few other non-friendly countries remained high-priority counterintelligence targets. We were able to identify many active intelligence networks being run out of the Indian Embassy. There were some major breakthroughs. We arrested and prosecuted several members of these networks. Some of the members we were able to turn and use as high-value double agents. In a number of cases, high-profile diplomats, including Indian diplomats, fell prey to our counterintelligence efforts and were caught red-handed while participating in undesirable activities. We also turned some of them into double agents and they remained very useful sources of intelligence for us for a number of years thereafter. We also neutralized several non-Indian undercover agents who were involved in third-country operations.

In 1980 and 1981, we busted a spy network of twelve Pakistani scientists and engineers who were planning to sabotage Pakistan's nuclear programme at various locations. The network was working on behalf of a foreign intelligence agency and had planned to develop significant technical faults in our nuclear weapons production system that would have taken years for our scientists to uncover, repair, and fix. On an important lead, the ISI Detachment Karachi developed the operation and subsequently, ISI operatives from Karachi and Islamabad jointly conducted the operation to take down the network. I was commanding the ISI detachment in Islamabad at the time and was personally involved in the arrests of the culprits in my area of responsibility. The investigation revealed that five agent handlers, three males and two females, who were running the network, were in Pakistan at that time to personally monitor the operation.

It is painful to mention but we also had to deal with many internal enemies. We identified and neutralized several journalists, politicians, and many other prominent figures among various segments of society, who were working on behalf of our adversaries. Dubious politics under complete elite capture, has been the most damaging aspect of our internal realm. Corruption and ethnic/sectarian divide make the system more fragile. Politicians with foreign linkages have been a serious security risk over the years. Unfortunately, there has been no dearth of high-profile political figures in the country playing double games to gain their personal ambitions. Interestingly, many high-profile politicians who used to pretend to be true democrats at the public forums would always hover around me to arrange their meetings with top military brass for political favours and were always willing to play the role of a loyal subservient for personal gains. Unfortunately, the trend continues even today, with dangerous consequences for our national security and cohesion.

We smashed a group of four terrorists from the 'Al-Zulfiqar' group who were planning to assassinate President Zia-ul-Haq and attack sensitive government installations in the capital. Many people, especially the younger generation, may not be familiar with this terrorist organization. It was organized by Murtaza Bhutto, son of Zulfiqar Ali Bhutto, after General Zia-ul-Haq overthrew the Bhutto government. The group called itself 'Al-Zulfiqar' and received the backing of certain foreign countries. It was a short-lived terrorist outfit that we effectively neutralized during its infancy. Hijacking a Pakistan International Airline flight to Kabul was one of its major terrorist acts.

I learnt about the presence of some members of this organization in Rawalpindi/Islamabad, as the Officer Commanding ISI Field Detachment Islamabad from my second in command, Major Makhdoom Hussain. He gave me a lead on a gang of terrorists belonging to this organization who were operating in the area. It consisted of five men who had been trained abroad and sent to Pakistan via Kabul. Their targets were President General Zia-ul-Haq and sensitive installations in the capital. One of the main targets was the main Islamabad electricity grid station in sector H-9 which they intended to blow up.

The terrorists hid at various locations in Rawalpindi and Islamabad and changed their locations frequently to avoid detection by law enforcement agencies. We were able to identify a person who was providing them with support, and through one of our very reliable contacts, bought the man's loyalty and his agreement to become a double agent in exchange for a heavy payment of money.

Based on the double agent's information, we were able to locate all their hiding places in Islamabad and Rawalpindi. During a swift night operation, we captured all of them. The last arrest came at about 4:00 am. We picked him up at the Jinnah Supermarket in Islamabad. A sizeable number of firearms and explosives were recovered from each one of these terrorists. The magistrate and police officers who accompanied us during these raids did an excellent job. A potential threat to the president and other vital installations in the capital was averted.

Besides VIP protection and other counterintelligence duties, ISI detachment Islamabad also played a significant role in acquisition of operational intelligence for the organization. In the process, we significantly contributed to ISI's effort in Afghanistan. We were in a non-stop mode in those days. Each day, we became increasingly involved in dealing with operations linked to the war. Not a day went by when we were not deliberating on our ongoing operational pursuits and exploring new possibilities to support the campaign against the invading Russian forces. The nature of warfare demanded effective and continuous intelligence support, and we contributed our bit. When I look back on our operations, there is a sense of achievement, and I am proud of what we accomplished.

A glimpse of the importance of our work in support of allied forces in Afghanistan during those days is suggested in chapter 1, 'Opening Shot', the story I chose to start this book. As the officer commanding ISI detachment Islamabad, I was given the responsibility of driving the president of the country covertly and alone from Army General Headquarters to the residence of my boss, the DG ISI, General Akhtar Abdul Rehman in Rawalpindi. The DG ISI organized a high-level meeting between Afghanistan's top leaders and the president. Its purpose was to eliminate differences among various Afghan groups and unify them into a single joint strategy to fight the Russians.

Among others, I remember distinctly the face of Gulbuddin Hekmatyar, a notable Afghan politician, former mujahideen leader and head of the Hezb-e-Islami Gulbuddin political party. He was sitting just opposite me at the meeting table. Many other prominent Afghan leaders were actively participating in the discussions. The president of Pakistan meeting directly with these Afghan leaders to guide and motivate them, with the DG of ISI sitting next to him, speaks volumes about how the war was conducted.

The task given to me to drive the president from headquarters to the DG's house underscored the importance of secrecy in moving the president to this meeting. It also showed the president's faith in our ISI team members. General Zia was the architect of Russia's defeat in Afghanistan and ISI was his primary weapon to bring about that victory. As the officer commanding the ISI detachment in Islamabad, I am proud of ISI's role in this sensitive operation, in which the president of Pakistan was the key player.

ISI remained at the forefront in every aspect of the campaign in Afghanistan, whether planning the strategies, fighting on the front lines, or providing the highest level of intelligence for effective operational planning. The Soviet Bloc countries worked in unison to help the Russians conquer Afghanistan and other countries in the region. At one point, the Russians had a plan to seize territory inside Pakistan to the Attock River, reducing the country's size by almost three-quarters.

During the early months of 1983, I picked up a lead from one of my reliable sources about some suspicious movements of Afghan diplomats at their embassy in Islamabad, late at night in the nearby Margalla Hills. We were watching the movements of all Soviet Bloc diplomats around the clock, particularly the Russians and the Afghanis. The descriptions of the suspicious diplomats enabled me to determine that they were the Afghan military attaché and his undercover colleague. Margalla Hills in those days was not as developed as it is today, and a late-night visit by diplomats to such a deserted place was an abnormal activity that needed to be taken seriously.

This intriguing piece of information made me curious, and I decided to visit the area the same night with Captain Kirmani, the officer in charge of the Afghan desk. We found nothing of interest in the bushy darkness of the Margalla Hills and decided to drive up to Pir Sohawa, a picnic spot at the top of Margalla Hills about fifteen kilometres from Islamabad city. Today, Monal, a most attractive restaurant, and a favourite spot for visitors to dine out, is located there, but in those days, there was a small one-room guest house maintained by the Capital Development Authority.

We learnt from the watchman that the two Afghan diplomats were planning to use the rest house for a secret meeting, which they planned to hold in two days. They told the watchman that they were expecting between fifteen and twenty people. Sensing the importance and sensitivity of what they were planning, we decided to bug the meeting with an audio and video recording system. We recruited the watchman into our plan and paid him double the amount he had received from the diplomats. Using the dark hours to their best, we immediately set out to make the requisite arrangements, as best as we could.

The trap was in place before the first light of the meeting day. I established an operational command post in some thick bushes, a few yards away from the rest house, with a dominating view of the meeting place. The meeting's participants began arriving around 9:00 am. In half an hour, the house was packed. The cars bringing the guests had diplomatic number plates. Among the participants were ambassadors from almost all the Soviet Bloc countries, including the Russian ambassador. Other participants were the military attaches and undercover diplomats associated with the intelligence agencies from these countries.

The meeting lasted nearly five hours, and luckily, we had planned the electronic coverage to last that long. During those days, the technology was not as advanced, and we relied on big tape recorders with large spools of tape. My team and I stayed in position for all these long hours, alert and holding our breaths because we knew the attendees were using anti-bugging precautions. After everyone had left, we were happy to find that our bugging effort was a success. The first thing we learnt was that the Soviet ambassador and the KGB (Russian Committee for State Security) station chief were the meeting's hosts, and among the attendees were the ambassadors from the leading Soviet Bloc countries and their intelligence representatives.

The purpose of the meeting was to coordinate KGB operations in the region for that quarter of the year, particularly as they affected Russia's invasion of Afghanistan. The KGB's upcoming operations were discussed in detail, covering the nature of these operations, where they were to be conducted, the organizing teams, and their schedule.

The recordings were passed to the DG ISI, General Akhtar Abdul Rahman for his review. Our efforts were greatly appreciated. The information we developed was shared with President General Zia-ul-Haq, all relevant sections within ISI, the Pakistan Army, and relevant allied foreign intelligence agencies. They all were excited to receive it and conveyed their wholehearted appreciation for our professional excellence and for sharing this vital intelligence with them. The intelligence gathered during the operation became the base for many operations conducted by the allied intelligence agencies, subsequently.

A small lead picked up from a well-placed source and vigorously followed helped us to know the KGB's operational plan for the entire region. It was a matter of great pride for my team and me. I recently learnt that Captain Kirmani, who assisted me during this operation, passed away about a year ago. That is unfortunate news, and I wish to take this opportunity to pray for his departed soul to rest in peace. He was an excellent comrade, trustworthy intelligence operative, and valuable friend.

To ensure a continuous, authentic, and timely flow of intelligence on Russian forces invading Afghanistan and the activities of the puppet Afghan government, installed by them, we needed to penetrate the relevant Afghan government organizations in Pakistan and gather the latest information about their strategies, operational plans, and future intentions. I cannot resist briefly mentioning another intelligence operation we planned and successfully conducted in 1983. Our target was a sensitive enemy organization in possession of important intelligence information. Without going into details about the organization itself, within weeks, we had one of their senior executives in our pocket enabling us to collect valuable intelligence that we required about the Soviet-Afghan War. My second in command, Major Makhdoom, who led the operation, did an excellent job, and we were able to gather enormously important and credible information about the war. In some cases, complete files were procured through our plant which carried highly confidential information about their plans.

Stories about ISI operations in support of the Afghan war can go on forever. Simply said, Pakistan played a critical role in the Soviet-Afghan War, and there is no doubt that General Zia's supervision and ISI's wholehearted commitment to the campaign brought about Russia's defeat. The Afghanistan operations desk at ISI headquarters managed the campaign and ISI's field detachment in Islamabad along with field detachments based in some other parts of the country, especially those located in the north-western part of the country served in a supporting role. Together, they made the difference that ended in victory.

While dealing with Afghanistan, we did not neglect our other adversaries who were always looking for gaps to exploit in our counterintelligence efforts. My people were overworked, but even during these testing times, we destroyed their espionage networks in our area of responsibility and apprehended many of their important agents.

ISI's hectic schedule in Islamabad kept me so busy that I did not realize it when I passed the normal amount of time that an army officer with my merit standing is supposed to spend on such assignments. The army has a schedule of various courses that officers must attend to advance their careers. I lost sight of that and put my career development in the army at risk. My army career was at a point when I should be attending mandatory professional training courses, and I had missed most of the opportunities to do so. The most important course I was about to miss was the Staff Officer's Course at Command and Staff College, Quetta. Every officer has four opportunities to take the entrance examination for selection to attend this course. My extended stay in ISI had caused me to miss three of them. When I realized it, I had only one chance left.

Having been away from professional soldiering for years, being selected based on an examination that focused purely on military-related subjects, was obviously going to be a very difficult task. I was facing the prospect of leaving it as a bad job, reconciling myself to the rank I was holding and enjoying my intelligence assignments in the capital as long as I stayed in the service. A 'Surprise Guest' at my house made me realize that it is never too late to accomplish something that we have the capability to achieve and motivated me to pay attention to that part of my life with a realistic and positive approach.

One day, late in the evening, my batman knocked on my bedroom door to inform me that a guest had come and was waiting for me in the sitting room. I immediately went to meet him. My guest introduced himself as Lieutenant Colonel Pervez Musharraf, Commander of the 16 SP Regiment, my parent unit. I knew the name immediately. He was not in the unit when I was there. He was probably serving as an instructor at Command and Staff College in Quetta at the time, but he was one of the regiment's most famous and respected officers. Everyone admired him and prayed for his return to the unit. I knew that he had been posted back as commanding officer, but I had not had the chance to meet him. I did not know it then, but I was hosting the future COAS and the president of my country.

Lieutenant Colonel Musharraf had already asked my batman for a good cup of tea and some fried *pakoras*. He greeted me very warmly, we sat comfortably, and began to discuss how the unit was doing and my career progression. I felt that I had known him for a long time. I found a real mentor and a very kind senior officer whom I could trust and take guidance from.

We had a wide-ranging conversation and discussed everything from the profession of arms to family life. He asked me if there was any reason why I was prolonging my stay in ISI. When I said there was no reason, he very candidly reminded me that to remain relevant in the army I needed to come back to the unit and take the entrance examination for the staff course. He thought I could qualify if I worked hard and told me that it was my last opportunity to qualify for the course. I told him that having stayed out of the army for nearly six years, it would be difficult for me to qualify, even if I worked hard.

He was persistent that I return to the unit immediately and apply to take the examination. He would coach me and make sure that I was well-prepared. He was confident that I would qualify because he had been an instructor at Command and Staff College, Quetta and had experience in coaching students to qualify for the course. His words were so motivating and thoughtful that I had no choice but to agree. Given his professional reputation, and his willingness to coach me, I thought that it would be worth a try. I gave him my consent and he promised to arrange for my posting back to the 16 SP as soon as possible. He left my home with a promise to visit me the next day. True to his word, he was there the following day with my posting order in hand, asking me to return to 'Dashing Sixteen' ASAP.

Within a couple of weeks, a truck from 16 SP, which had come on some official duty to Rawalpindi, stopped at my house and carried my luggage back to the unit at Kharian Cantt. I was back in the army garrison after a gap of nearly six years.

Thus began my deep-rooted association and friendship with General Pervez Musharraf. It lasted almost four decades. In him, I had found a lifetime mentor and friend. Incidentally, while I was in the process of writing the script of this book in Dubai, he too had settled there. I did discuss with him the outline plan for the book, and he was quite keen to write a foreword for it once I had done with its writing. But unfortunately, he did not live that long to see the book published and write the foreword for it. I owe a lot to him for his continuous guidance and support throughout my army career and even after I retired. May Allah bless his soul.

Back to the 'Dasher's Den'

I will never forget the welcome I received upon my family's arrival at the mess in the Kharian Cantonment. All available unit officers were there to greet us. My family, which had very little exposure to army life, was pleasantly surprised to feel the warmth we were shown upon our return to the unit. My children were very young at that time. One of the young officers, Lieutenant Raza, who later became Brigadier Raza, ordered a bottle of milk and personally fed my daughter Maryia who was barely 2 years old.

My daily routine after settling into the unit included a mandatory coaching class for my staff college entrance examination at Lieutenant Colonel Musharraf's residence. It continued for nearly two months. Almost daily, his wife, Sahiba *bhabi*, served me a cup of hot tea or coffee. This is what made General Musharraf and his wife so special to me.

With his expert coaching in military subjects, especially military tactics, not only did I manage to pass the exam but was also chosen to be among those selected to attend a foreign staff officers course in any of the countries allied with the Pakistan Army.

General Musharraf's willingness to respond boldly and promptly to all kinds of issues had been the hallmark of his approach to command and leadership. On one occasion, I contacted him regarding some minor issues in our unit when he was a brigadier and had been posted as an instructor at the army war college in Rawalpindi. He promptly told me to be at his house in half an hour. When I got there, I was astonished to see him dressed in jeans and a sports shirt, ready to personally accompany me in my old vintage jeep to Kharian Cantonment where the unit was stationed.

When we reached Kharian, the sergeant major told us the unit had gone for training at the Tilla ranges near Jhelum, about two hours away by road. It was already getting dark, but then Brigadier Musharraf insisted that we drive to the training area. We arrived there around 10:00 p.m., met with all the officers in the mess tent, and discussed their concerns in detail. We were able to resolve all the problem areas in about an hour, and after dinner, we drove back to Rawalpindi to be on duty the following day. It was not the only occasion that General Musharraf gave generously of his time to help 16 SP. He considered 'The Dashing Sixteen' his second home and was always there to support each of us in any way he could.

An Exposure to Martial Law Duties

Before I went to Command and Staff College, Quetta in 1986, I was sent to the deputy marshal law headquarters in Rawalpindi. For several months, I was the officer in charge of the complaint cell. I also served as the security adviser to Major General Muhammad Afzaal, the General Officer Commanding (GOC) 6th Armed Division and the deputy marshal law administrator (DMLA) at Rawalpindi. General Muhammad Afzaal later rose to the rank of lieutenant general and was among those who died in the unfortunate air crash along with General Zia-ul-Haq, the president of Pakistan and a number of other senior military and civilian officials including the then US ambassador, Arnold Lewis Raphel.

It was a different kind of job I thought unnatural for a soldier. Many critics of the role of the army in governance in the country, may not agree but to the best of my knowledge and experience, most army officers do not like martial law duties. I too found the job to be unpleasant, but in fairness, there was some good along with the bad, and the experience came in handy in the later part of my life.

The job helped me to understand how the civilian government works, and how best to interact with civilian bureaucrats. It also made me aware of the deplorable state of the social structure in which most people in rural Pakistan live, and how much it needed the government's attention. It was painful to see. As the officer in charge of the complaint cell, I confronted cases that opened my eyes to the dismal state of our social structure, especially in the villages. There was deep-rooted corruption everywhere, in all walks of life, in politics, administration, or just routine social activities. A corrupt feudalist mafia exploited poor people in the villages. I did my best to address what I could at my level, and I tried to bring the problem to the attention of my seniors who mattered in the administration, but it was all very depressing.

In one case, a lady came to my office with one of her young daughters. She complained that her landlord was exploiting her and that her daughters were continuously being harassed and molested. Tears streamed down her face as she told me her story and how she felt helpless in seeking justice from the current system. She begged me to help her escape the continuous torture that she and her family were suffering at the hands of influential people in her village. I did what I could to help her, but I was disgusted.

In another instance, some con men had swindled a poor family of all their belongings. When I confronted the culprits, they tried to pressure me not to get involved. They followed me one day after work while I was driving back to Kharian for the weekend. They were driving very close to the back of my car, and it irritated me to the extent that I decided to respond. I stopped at a roadside restaurant near Dina, Jhelum area and waited for them to approach me if they dared. My military instincts had taken over, and I was ready to do battle if necessary. Finding me furious, they decided not to confront me. Instead, after sheepishly exchanging a few pleasantries and praising my leadership as the officer in charge of the complaint cell, they left. They were another example of the rudeness and rebelliousness that has overtaken our society and caused people to think that they can get away with rowdyism and foul play. I was surprised to see them come to my office the next day to let me know that they had paid back the money they had taken from the poor family.

On another occasion, I had to attend the execution of a man convicted of murder by a civilian court. I went to the jail, intending to meet the man and be present when he was hanged. It was a very unpleasant duty, but I had no choice. When I reached the death chamber, I found the man praying for mercy a few minutes before his death. When he saw me, in uniform, he turned to me and raised his hands as if I could save him in this last stage of his battle against death. He begged me for justice and swore to God that he had been wrongly sentenced by the court. He told me that his brother had committed the murder, but he had been arrested and sentenced to death. Had something gone wrong and now an innocent person was condemned to die? Why was it done? Who was to blame? I had no answers. I also had no authority to save his life.

The law said he had to be hanged, and he was, but I felt helpless and disappointed by our justice system. There was nothing I could do but make my comments on the register at the hanging site and submit a written report to the DMLA the next day. I feel the justice system in our country has some inherited shortcomings. While it does not protect innocents in most cases, the rich and influential people who are accused of large-scale crime and corruption remain above the law. The poor remained victims of tyranny and oppression and it was happening while the country was under martial law, but the civilian judicial system was in part playing its role. Many of the judges were known by their political affiliations rather than their competence.

During this period, parliamentary elections were held throughout the country, and as the adviser to DMLA on security and intelligence matters, I was tasked with vetting all the candidates. I personally visited every village in the Rawalpindi division, met with hundreds of people and local civilian government officials, and conducted a fair survey to assess the quality of the candidates who were likely to be chosen in these elections. Wherever I went, I found the elite in full control of the political processes. Feudalists and industrialists determined everything. The electorate was at the mercy of powerful elites. I assessed that the forthcoming elections were unlikely to contribute anything positive to the country's governance system. Instead, the powerful mafia would continue to mock the rule of law and give the government a bad name.

All the candidates were landlords and industrialists who had been contesting each other in elections for decades based on inheritance and family patterns. Poor voters were made routinely to vote for their landlords or the owners of the factory where they worked. Nobody dared to go against this system; lest they be punished, in one way or the other.

I submitted my survey results, indicating the likely winners in the Rawalpindi division, along with my comments and reservations about the election's outcome. My report said that most government institutions had been politicized, corrupted, and lacked efficiency. People had no liberty to contest the elections or cast their votes independently and on merit. Subsequent events proved my assessment to be correct.

It is an unfortunate fact that Pakistan has a history of similar episodes. The same pattern is repeated; elected officials remain vulnerable to corruption, nepotism, and exploitation, creating the conditions that lead to army takeovers. In most cases, the intelligentsia, and the opposition parties appeal to the army to either change the government or assume government leadership. All roads lead to the General Headquarters and the army chief of staff gets sucked into the power struggle. The army is considered to be a stabilizing force and is requested to intervene or guide the government. That leads to the blurring of boundaries between military and civilian control.

The rigmarole between democratically elected officials who become dictators and military takeovers has become an unending game. Military takeovers distract civilian officials from fulfilling their vital government roles, and critical government institutions cease to function. When martial law ends, these official institutions remain ineffective. Their growth is stunted. How to end the cycle is a question worthy of consideration by every patriotic Pakistani.

While martial law is not an option for us, at the same time, Pakistan's prevailing democratic norms do not provide sustainable solutions to our problems. There are significant challenges for democracy in illiterate, feudal, and parochial societies. People who come to power are not elected based on merit. They rise in the political hierarchy because of their family connections and financial resources. Their priorities are often self-centred, and their national interests become secondary to their personal interests and their political agendas.

We must remember that if democracy is to be functional and sustainable, it must be tailored to meet the local conditions and the people's needs. Unless we realize this, we will remain wandering in the woods, directionless and purposeless. Pakistan is a country of great significance, not only for the Muslims of the subcontinent but for the region and the world.

My survey report with all the facts and figures was submitted to my bosses and was much appreciated. The government had their plans, the elections were held as scheduled, and the same people were returned to the corridors of power. I did my job satisfactorily, and I was at peace with what I had written. I believe that honest reporting, even at the lower levels, whether it aligns with the plan or not, is always a valuable contribution to an administration.

Becoming Wiser than an Owl

A few months later, I was on my way to the Command and Staff College, Quetta for my staff officer's course. Completing the course is important for every army officer who wishes to further his military career. The Staff College at Quetta is one of the best army staff colleges in the world. It is on par with the British Army Command and Staff College at Camberley and the US Army Command and Staff College at Leavenworth. The image of an owl was part of the college's old insignia. It signified the intelligence and planning ability for which that bird is famous and the institution's goal of embedding those qualities in its students. Somehow, the insignia was changed in 1979.

The Command and Staff College at Quetta is Pakistan's premier institution of military education. It prepares students to become the army's future leaders by giving them the knowledge and skills they need to handle the most senior military assignments. The curriculum focuses on two main areas, professional competence, and ethical behaviour. Its graduates are assigned to command and senior staff positions in army divisions. British Field Marshal Bernard Law Montgomery served as a member of its faculty.

I completed the college's staff officers' course and received my graduation certificate, along with a Bachelor of Science degree, with honours, from the University of Baluchistan.

While most graduates were posted to senior staff positions at various division headquarters, because of my extended time with ISI, I was sent to the field to gain the experience I needed for promotion to lieutenant colonel.

On the Line of Control

I was posted to the 46 Mountain Artillery Regiment, as a deployed battery commander on the Line of Control (LOC), the line that separates Pakistan from India in AJK. The battery was located about a kilometre or two from the Indian side of the line, 17,000 feet above sea level, in an area covered year around in twenty to fifty feet of snow, and it took nearly 12 hours on foot of negotiating dangerous cliffs and climbing mounting trails to reach it. The first time I entered the battery's position, it was almost dark, and a reception party had to come to help me cross a dangerous cliff to reach the camp. It was a unique and challenging assignment but one that gave me an excellent opportunity to learn the art of mountain warfare under near combat conditions.

It was also challenging for my family. As a major, I had no option but to dispatch them back to my village before joining the unit. Things were more difficult for my kids, who had to attend a village school with far fewer educational opportunities than they had at the Kharian Cantonment. Still, the educational environment in the village was better than it had been when I went to school there.

My time on the LOC was an excellent learning experience and a memorable period of my army career. The mountains welcomed me with a life-threatening incident. On my first full day at the LOC, I decided to hike along the ridge line about four kilometres to visit one of our observation posts which was located 200 hundred yards from an Indian observation post. A senior technical assistant and another sergeant from my gun battery accompanied me during the trip. We followed a narrow, slippery track through the snow, along the edges of steep cliffs that fell sharply into valleys below.

We had hardly walked for a few hundred yards when my foot slipped and I fell down a steep cliff in a thousand-foot drop, free-falling, and headed toward the bottom of the mountain. I thought this is it; I am going to die. I saw a bush in my path in the snow, about 200 hundred feet below, and somehow, I managed to grab it. How I did it, I will never know. It just happened. It broke

THE BREAKOUT MANOEUVRES AND THE MENTORS

my fall, and I was able to stabilize myself by digging my feet into the snow. It took me a few minutes to settle my nerves, regain my senses, and understand what had happened.

I did not know how long the bush would hold me. I had no doubt, however, that if it let go or I lost my grip on it, I was done. There was another tree branch sticking out of the snow a few metres away that was a little bigger and had a slight bend at its base with enough space for me to sit and wait for rescue. Getting to it would be risky, but I thought it was my best chance of getting off the cliff alive. I took the chance and clawed my way toward the branch and managed to reach it safely.

I sat on the branch and for a few moments, there was nothing but pin-drop silence. Then, I began to hear the other members of my group calling my name. I waved a handkerchief, shouted back to them, and was able to capture their attention. They worked their way to a place above me, threw down a rope, and pulled me back up to the ridgeline.

My knee was injured but it did not appear to be serious, so we continued to the observation post. The officer in charge there greeted us warmly and briefed us on the area and the enemy locations. Indian soldiers and their officers stood on the other side of the line, about 100 feet away from us. They went immediately inside their bunkers to avoid being observed by me or my team. It reminded me of the 1971 Indo-Pak Border War. There was a remarkable similarity in their behaviour, pessimistic in their approach and shy about making eye contact with us. In contrast, the high morale of our soldiers was heartening, and I was proud to be part of a great fighting force known internationally for its courage, determination, and fighting skills. After a long and tiring day trip, we returned to the battery headquarters camp late in the evening.

Living under challenging conditions had turned all ranks of the battery into a tightly-knit family. In addition to operational duties, social activities were an important part of our routine. During off hours, we played games in our bunkers until late at night, especially on weekends. It was fun. One of the cleaning crew and I would play cards against the senior JCO and another NCO in my bunker. We would play for hours while eating boiled eggs. We were well received by the civilian Kashmiri population. They gave us food and handmade gifts, and we used to reciprocate with return gifts, and with our appreciation and gratitude.

About a year after my arrival in Kashmir, the regiment held a formal dinner at its headquarters near a small village at the base of the mountain range. My commanding officer used the occasion to announce that the army general headquarters at Rawalpindi had approved my promotion to lieutenant colonel. All the officers congratulated me, and we had a fantastic dinner to celebrate the news. I passed this good news on to my family. They were all excited and prayed that I would soon be posted back to my unit at the Kharian Cantonment where they could join me. I also prayed and hoped the time would come quickly when I received my promotion and was ordered back to my parent unit—The Dashing Sixteen.

About a week later I received a phone call from army headquarters informing me that it would take some time for me to be adjusted as lieutenant colonel commanding officer of a unit. In the meantime, they wanted to assign me to an operational staff position at a division-level headquarters. They planned this move because my posting to Kashmir considered a hard assignment but a necessary one for my career development, had caused me to miss the operational staff appointment that normally follows completion of Command and Staff College. They explained that my performance during the staff course qualified me for an operational staff position at the division level and that it would be more than a year before I was promoted to lieutenant colonel. They told me that it would be a tremendous professional boost for me to complete an operational staff assignment while awaiting my promotion. The only drawback was the staff position immediately available was a little lower in professional status than what I deserved based on the merit list maintained by the military secretary's branch. They thought this problem was outweighed by the career benefit to me of serving as a major in this higher-level staff position. I gladly accepted the posting, and in a couple of weeks, I was at divisional artillery headquarters at Murree as the brigade major. It is an example of how the Pakistani army takes care of its people and grooms them for higher responsibilities.

'Hannibal' of Murree Hills

Hannibal of 'Carthage' was one of the top ten military strategists in the history of warfare. During the Second Punic War in 219 BC, he attacked and conquered Saguntum, an independent city allied with Rome. Then he marched his massive army across the Pyrenees and the Alps into central Italy in one of the most famous campaigns in history. My job as brigade major of the division artillery headquarters at Murree made me understand what Hannibal must have felt when he took his army across the Alps.

The division headquarters at Murree commands all artillery field units and formations deployed for hundreds of kilometres along the LOC in the mountains of Kashmir. As brigade major, my job was to be the principal staff officer to the commander and to be responsible for preparing all operational plans and issuing all execution orders to the units under his control. Keeping the plans updated to meet the changing operational requirements along the LOC is a continuous task. I became so immersed in mountain warfare that I felt like what Hannibal must have felt like two thousand years ago.

My time as brigade major was a period of great learning. Besides being responsible for the division's operational footprint along the LOC, I was also part of the divisional headquarters' team that prepared operational plans for various contingencies including the Indian Army aggression in 1986/87.

The Indian Army moved troops up to the LOC and was planning to conduct attacks in our area of responsibility. Finding us fully prepared to defend ourselves, they cancelled the attacks and abandoned their plans. It was a great strategic and tactical victory that demonstrated our ability to plan for defensive operations in mountainous areas. I gained much professionally from watching my commander, Brig Arshad Mahmood SJ, during this time. His bold and calculated approach to problem-solving was an example of military leadership that I have tried to follow. I learnt a great deal as Brigade Major and had been there almost two years when I received my promotion and was ordered to report to 'The Dashing Sixteen' as its commanding officer.

Leading the 'Dashers'

Being in command is the dream of every army officer. My personal goal was to be promoted to lieutenant colonel and given command of my parent regiment, the 'Dashing Sixteen'. Eventually, I achieved my goal, but it took some effort.

I wrote a letter to the military secretary's branch requesting that it assign me to command my parent unit. My request was denied because the service term of its current commander had some time to go before its completion. I then requested that my promotion be delayed until the current commander's tenure of duty ended. That request was also denied based on service requirements.

I was being told to shut up, cool down, and do as I was told. I decided to take one last chance and approached General Akhtar Abdul Rehman, the then chief of the joint staff committee, who had been my boss when I was at ISI. Initially, he tried to convince me to accept the military secretary's branch's decision. When I argued against that, he offered to get me posted as the commander of his parent unit. I suggested that I wanted to command the 16 SP so that I might have the same relationship with my parent unit as he had with his parent unit. He was exceedingly kind and convinced by my passion to command my parent unit. He personally asked the military secretary's branch in GHQ to consider my request, even if it took them some time to do so, and they did.

Finally, I was assigned to command 'Dashing Sixteen'. The affiliation that every soldier develops with his parent unit is very important in Pakistan's army. It is where colleagues and comrades serve and die together in peace and in war. The help of my senior mentors, strong army traditions, and persistence enabled me to achieve my goal. It was the most incredible honour I could ever wish for.

In Dasher's Mode

I was warmly welcomed when I arrived back in my unit. However, this time I was not welcomed by an undercover batman, nor were there any lectures about my uniform. It was a formal welcome to begin the best period of my army service. I had a graceful nameplate prepared with the inscription '**The Dasher's Den**' and hung it at the gate of my official residence.

Expectations for my time in command were very high and there was much work to do. I had my own ambitious plan for what I wanted to do as the commander, 16 SP. My biggest asset to achieving my goals was the support I received from the ranks and from serving and retired unit officers. I outlined my work plan, prioritizing what I believed to be the unit's needs.

Achieving a set goal requires honest and down-to-earth leadership to motivate others to do their best. One must lead from the front and display good personal qualities to convince people to follow them in pursuit of common goals. Army commanders must be firm, compassionate, and considerate toward the men. They must look after their welfare and help them with their personal problems. Timely feedback from the unit and purposeful discussions with senior colleagues help to focus the unit's efforts. All important operational and administrative tasks must be prioritized and pursued vigorously. If that is done, the unit will give the commander its respect and be willing to follow him. I had an added advantage. I was from the unit, had grown up with them, and most of them knew me well. I worked hard to make sure that people knew they could always count on me, and I believe I could lead them to achieve anything.

One of my PMA classmates, Major Muhammad Ilyas, was my second in command. He had also been in my class at the CCH. It can be awkward when an officer has to serve under one of his classmates, but that was not the case when Maj Ilyas served as my second in command. He was my most significant support. I knew without question that I could trust him, and he was always forthcoming for any task or assistance that I required from him.

The regiment's operational readiness was our top priority. We needed to upgrade our weapons and our technical systems. We converted from old 105 mm howitzers to newer M109 SP 155 mm guns. I spent most of my time fielding the new equipment and training the men to use it. We were commended for our success during the regiment's annual gunnery exercises at the Tilla firing range.

Esprit de corps at its Best

Not everyone in the unit and those who were either retired or posted out to other units knew about what we were trying to accomplish. Yet, expectations of good performance were at their peak. I, too, was excited and optimistic, but I knew the tasks ahead would be demanding.

I set out to create closely-knit teams and assign specific tasks to them. I started organizing get-togethers on one pretext or another and used them to get everyone on board with our planned initiatives. The regiment's innate spirit made it relatively easy to organize around our goals. Within a couple of weeks, we were working in unison with each other in unit formation, on the playgrounds and during operations. Soon thereafter we had a vast team of Dashers, totally involved in the unit's affairs.

Our effort brought attention and support to The Dashing Sixteen from all levels of the army. The support of senior officers was exceptional. General Pervez Musharraf, for example, carried huge responsibilities on his shoulders during those days, but he was always just a telephone away to provide support or advice whenever I asked for it. Being the commander of an armoured artillery unit was exciting and challenging.

Self-propelled guns when manoeuvring are generally led by the unit's second in command. The commander travels in his command vehicle and coordinates the regiment's movement. In my case, I wanted one day to lead my self-propelled guns as they manoeuvred in the field and ride in the leading tank as the operational commander. I got that chance in an army exercise named 'Zarb-e-Momin.' It was a large army-level exercise, conducted with full arms and equipment and involving the movement of troop columns between multiple zones of military operations based on various future war scenarios. Exercises at this level were difficult but helped us greatly when it came to building well-knit teams and matching esprit de corps.

I led the unit, personally during the exercise, riding aboard the lead tank, and manoeuvring the unit from one operational sector to another. We were using a mix of old Sherman tanks and new M-109 howitzers which made the rapid movement of our gun columns very difficult. Halfway through a night move of about sixty to seventy kilometres, one of our Sherman tanks broke down. When I received word of the broken tank, I immediately ordered the march to halt. I jumped off my tank, signalled for the commander's jeep, and drove back to the disabled tank. The tank's commander was Sergeant Mohammad Hussain, an outstanding wrestler, and a leading member of our regimental sports teams. My goal was to rectify the fault and continue the march as soon as possible because we were facing an operational deadline to be at our new location by first light of the following day. We worked for an hour or so, could not fix the tank, and were left with no choice but to leave it behind and recover it the next day. I instructed the tank commander accordingly and ordered the rest of the men to prepare to resume the movement.

When I moved toward my jeep to go back to the front of the column, Sergeant Mohammad Hussain came and stood in front of me causing me to stop. He was infuriated by my decision to leave his tank behind. I was astonished that he was standing face to face with me, trying physically to keep me from leaving his tank behind. He was very emotional, and near tears. He said being left behind was a great dishonour, and he begged me to delay the move a little longer so that the mechanics could fix the tank. I decided to grant his request and stayed a short while longer. Luckily, during that time the tank was fixed and made ready to go. Sergeant Mohammad Hussain and his crew were over the moon. Shouting regimental slogans, they joined the convoy full of enthusiasm. In the end, we reached our new location in time.

My treatment of Sergeant Mohammad Hussain was influenced by the outcome of my own confrontation with a senior officer in the past. When I was a captain, I had a similar run-in with Lieutenant Colonel Inayat, my commanding officer and a hardcore professional but a very kind-hearted officer.

Our unit was conducting a field exercise, and we were having lunch in the officers' mess, located under a tent in a half-finished bunker. I got into an unnecessary argument with Lieutenant Colonel Inayat during a general discussion of non-military matters. The argument grew heated on my part, and I was insulting and unreasonable to the commander in front of all the unit officers. Everyone was surprised by my behaviour and urged me to stop the discussion before the situation escalated. But I ignored them, I had gone nuts. I was overtaken by my emotions, and I went beyond the limit of what army discipline and decency required. I continued to argue rudely until an annoyed Lieutenant Colonel Inayat left the table before finishing his meal.

Everyone at the table was perplexed, and we left the mess to await what the commander would do. His response was sure to be very severe. Some officers finished their lunch, but realizing what I had done, I was suddenly not hungry. I too left the mess without eating.

THE BREAKOUT MANOEUVRES AND THE MENTORS

The situation became more tense when the Commanding Officer did not even turn up to the mess for dinner. None of the officers was able to take the dinner properly and we all dispersed without having proper food. I went straight to my tent and tried to sleep but my rude behaviour with the commanding officer kept pricking at my conscience and kept me awake. I feared there would be strong disciplinary action against me the next day. It was almost midnight when the rear curtain of my tent opened, and our favourite mess waiter, Fazal Hussain, entered my tent with food from the mess. He wanted to be sure that I had something to eat before I went to sleep. That was the kind of man he was. Fazal died a few years back. A great buddy. May Allah bless his soul.

The next day, I was mentally prepared to be brought before the commander and subjected to appropriate disciplinary action. I waited in his adjutant's office for him to have me reported, but nothing happened. His door remained closed, increasing my apprehension tenfold. I thought he was probably coordinating with the brigade commander about what to do with me. I waited there the whole day with no sight of the commander. He did not even leave his office for lunch that day. It was late afternoon when Lieutenant Colonel Inayat called for me to enter his office.

I steeled myself for strong action and reported as ordered. It was tough looking into his eyes. I was surprised when he graciously asked me to sit down in front of the table he was using as a desk. For the next hour or so, he spoke nothing but kind words of advice, many of which are still engraved in my mind. He told me that he appreciated my stance on the topic we discussed the previous day and offered that I needed to be more decent and argue more sensibly when presenting my viewpoint. He told me that I had the potential to go far in my army career, and that was why he did not intend to spoil my career because of the argument. He would end the matter with a counselling session only. What a great man! I learnt a great deal from Lieutenant Colonel Inayat, and I have tried to follow his example since then. Gradually, I learnt how to handle such discussions more tactfully while remaining true to my beliefs and principles. I found most of my seniors willing to consider my recommendations and suggestions, and even constructive criticism, if these were based on facts and expressed in good spirits.

Excelling in Sports

Athletics play an essential role in developing a successful army. Units take great pride in fielding good sports teams, that win championships at various levels of army competition. Traditionally 16 SP was a champion in hockey, and I wished to add another sport to its reputation by winning a division-level championship. Since we had a number of excellent basketball players in the unit, I chose to emphasize this sport, along with hockey. I travelled to the Artillery Centre at Attock to meet with the commandant and search for basketball talent. I requested him to post new recruits who might be potential basketball players to my unit. He sent me to the concerned training regiment to look for new soldiers who were tall and had the potential to become good players. The effort worked and I got a good number of recruits posted to my unit. We trained them day and night to play basketball and built them into a professional squad that won championships at the army level.

Installation of Colonel of the Regiment

Installing an honorary colonel of the regiment is another army tradition. The unit will select one of its senior officers, serving or retired, who has contributed to the unit and show its appreciation by making him an honorary colonel. As colonel of the regiment, he maintains close contact with the unit's commanding officer and with the other ranks. He supports the unit with his knowledge, experience, guidance, and connections. When I took command, the 16 SP had never had a colonel of the regiment. I decided to change that.

After consultation with all the ranks and with our senior officers, including General Musharraf, I installed one of my ex-commanding officers, Brig (Retd) Riaz Ahmad Qureshi, as our first colonel of the 'Dashing Sixteen'. The regiment lost him about a year ago. He left behind some cherished memories as a very active member of the Dashers family. May Allah bless his soul.

Having a colonel of the regiment has proven to be very fruitful. It promotes cohesion between serving and retired officers and improves unit administration. Many of our old comrades who attended the installation ceremony had lost contact with the unit but once again became active members of the team. It particularly helps retired junior-ranking personnel and their families.

Later, I was lucky to be part of the team that worked with the then unit commander, Lieutenant Colonel Shafi Akeel Mufti, to arrange for the installation of the second colonel of the regiment. We chose General Pervez Musharraf as the new colonel of the regiment and combined his installation as colonel of the regiment and the 16 SP's Golden Jubilee. The celebration was attended by a large number of ex-16 SP officers and other ranks, as well as many senior officers from the garrison and from various branches of GHQ in Rawalpindi. With General Musharraf's installation, the unit was renamed **'Dashing Sixteen, The President's Own'**.

The event was an illustration of our regimental history, culture and traditions developed over the years since its raising and induction as one of the leading artillery units of the Pakistan army. A huge banner hung over regimental lines with the names and pictures of our martyrs during the 1965 war with India.

General Pervez Musharraf, who happened to be the chief guest and was being installed as the new colonel of the regiment, had joined The Dashing Sixteen as second lieutenant just before the 1965 war began and fought that war as a 16 SP gun position officer. Some of the martyrs whose pictures and names were dominating the big banner had died while they were fighting as part of his command.

They gave their lives on 22 September 1965, during the famous Battle of Chawinda in the Sialkot Sector. The battlefield became known as 'the graveyard for Indian tanks.' During the fighting at night, an enemy artillery shell hit one of our SP guns operating under then Lieutenant Pervez Mushrraf and set the rear compartment on fire, lighting up the sky. There was great danger of the gun's stored artillery shells catching fire and bursting and causing a chain reaction that would destroy the entire position. Then Lieutenant Pervez Musharraf dashed to the damaged gun and entered the burning vehicle. Another brave soldier Sepoy Abdul Rehman followed him. Inside the tank, they found three crew members lying in a pool of blood. Lieutenant Pervez Musharraf began throwing shells of ammunition out of the vehicle before they could explode. Sepoy Abdul Rehman began to help him. The two men took off their shirts and used them to protect their hands from the hot shells. Inspired by Lieutenant Musharraf's bold action other men also rushed to the gun and joined them in removing the ammunition. Finding one of the injured crew members still alive, Lieutenant Pervez Musharraf tried to bandage his wounds, but the man died before it was done. Lieutenant Pervez was given the Gallantry Award for his bravery and courage in battle. Gunner Abdul Rehman was awarded Tamgha-e-Jurat for extraordinary heroism.

When I was promoted to the rank of brigadier, I became the colonel of the regiment after General Musharraf's tenure ended. He attended the installation ceremony, and he did me the honour of putting the badges of honorary rank on my shoulders.

The End Result

My command tenure with the 16 SP of almost three and a half years was rewarding. The unit improved across the board, and I achieved most of the goals I set to achieve when I assumed command. It was a period of great learning. I experienced the challenges of leadership first-hand and learnt that it is an art, not a science. It is about interacting appropriately with people, junior and senior, and it can be learnt. Reacting boldly to situations, accepting challenges head on, a cool temperament under pressure is what wins us the race. For an army commander, understanding the prevailing environment in all its complexity, and having one's finger on the pulse of his men are essential.

One should always push for optimum results, but one must be willing to accept partial successes as long as the unit is moving in the right direction.

There were many young officers who helped me during my command tenure; Captain Kureshy, Captain Raza, Captain Altaf, Captain Fida, Lieutenant Rana, Lieutenant Mufti, Lieutenant Zafar, and many others who stood with me like a rock when it came to the well-being of The Dashing Sixteen. The devoted Dasher Lieutenant William John always impressed me with his straightforwardness, hard work, patriotism, and commitment. The die-hard retired 16 SP officers were always just a phone call away if I needed them. I remain indebted to Major (Retd) Shamim Khan, who was one of the most prominent members of our group, and Brigadier Riaz Ahmad Qureshi who was my primary support, and always available.

The unit was blessed with my successor, another 16 SP officer. Lieutenant Colonel Mughni, an equally motivated 'Dasher', was ready to take over, and we all felt confident that the unit would keep moving forward under his able command. I cherish my lifelong association with 'The Dashing Sixteen'.

"Dasher's Den is ... where life finds you!!"

At Army General Headquarters

A few months before my tenure as commander 16 SP was to end, we held the installation ceremony of the first Colonel of the Regiment and many principal staff officers from the army's general headquarters at Rawalpindi were invited to attend. Among the guests, was Lieutenant General Khalid Latif Moghul, Military Secretary of the Pakistan Army. After the official function, he asked me for a one-to-one meeting with him in my office. During this meeting, he congratulated me on arranging the celebrations and for a successful period of command. He asked me about my choice for my next assignment. I was moved by his kind gesture and thanked him for allowing me to express my choice. However, I thought it would be better to leave the planning of my next assignment to the Military Secretary's office system. I avoided saying openly what I would like to do and said that I would be satisfied with any posting or appointment that matched my efficiency index, as shown on the grading system for officers that is maintained in the military secretary's branch.

A few months later, I received a telephone call that Lieutenant General Khalid Latif wished to meet with me in his office the next day. After getting permission from my brigade headquarters, I went to his office. Once again, he praised my performance during my command and told me that based on merit, I deserved to be posted to the military operations directorate as a grade-1 staff officer. It was the best posting any officer could hope for. He went on to express his regret, however, that there was no current vacancy in that directorate. He offered me the second best posting based on my profile, as a grade-1 staff officer in the military training directorate. He said that he wanted my consent before issuing the posting order.

I was grateful to him for being so considerate to call me from Kharian to ask for my consent for the assignment. He thought it appropriate to consult me before issuing orders because he knew it was not fair to me based on merit. I consented to the assignment and within a week, I was posted to the military training directorate, at army general headquarters as a principal staff officer. I was made responsible for all army training institutions. Prominent among these were the Command and Staff College Quetta and PMA.

The selection of candidates for the staff officer's course at Quetta is done through a competitive entrance examination. It was one of the most sensitive tasks I had to perform, and it required a lot of hard work. Unquestionable integrity was its hallmark. A strong check and balance system was in place to ensure that candidates were selected based only on merit. The selection process had never been compromised and by the grace of God, my two years in the Military Training Directorate were to the entire satisfaction of my seniors. I thoroughly enjoyed my stay in Rawalpindi.

After my time in the Military Training Directorate and a successful command tenure in the unit, I was looking forward to my next operational assignment. I was surprised when my boss Lieutenant General Assad Ahmad Durrani, inspector general of training and evaluation, called me on the intercom and told me that, once again, I was being posted to the ISI directorate Islamabad. Frankly, I was not expecting it. I had assumed after working so hard during my operational assignments, completing a successful command tenure, and performing good staff work at general headquarters, that my career path would be in the hardcore professional army. Upon inquiry, Lieutenant General Assad Ahmad told me that my name was among a small number of officers ISI had asked for specifically. Once again, I was among the intelligence community.

Battling in the Silent War Zone – Part 2

My second posting to ISI began in 1992 when, as a lieutenant colonel, I was assigned as the officer commanding ISI detachment Rawalpindi with additional oversight responsibility for the ISI detachment at Islamabad. By then, I had served in army operational assignments at grade 2 and grade 1 levels, and I had completed my command tenure at 16 SP, thereby fulfilling the requirements for subsequent promotions to the senior ranks. Though I was expecting another high-profile operational postings within the army before I was promoted, this posting to ISI, was equally well rewarding during my subsequent progression in the army.

During their prolonged stay in Pakistan in connection with their operations in Afghanistan, foreign allied intelligence agencies had ample opportunities to penetrate different segments of our society. Most of these agencies had established their embassies and non-embassy-based networks to enhance their agendas in Pakistan. Their access to some of our sensitive national security institutions was a serious concern. It was because of the gravity of the situation that those of us with hardcore intelligence experience were once again posted back to intelligence agencies to increase their counterintelligence capabilities and make them more prudent. I was now holding one of the most important positions to identify and neutralize Pakistan's enemies hidden within our ranks and files, a more challenging task at hand.

My primary responsibility as the officer commanding ISI Rawalpindi was to look after the security of the three Services Headquarters and the Joint Services Staff Headquarters. I served this assignment for two years and it was quite rewarding. Through continuous and systematic monitoring, we identified and arrested several resident agents operating in some of our defence organizations. The timely elimination of these espionage nets averted severe consequences.

After completing two years as Officer Commanding, ISI Detachment Rawalpindi, I was promoted to Colonel and posted as Sector Commander ISI at ISI Sector Headquarter, Lahore. There, I was responsible for the great majority of ISI field detachments in Punjab province and some parts of Kashmir. This posting provided me with an opportunity to dwell on the counterintelligence efforts that I had initiated while I was commanding ISI detachment at Rawalpindi, and we were able to smash some well-established espionage networks operating in some of our very sensitive institutions.

My time as an ISI commander at Rawalpindi and subsequently, as Sector Commander, Punjab, handling regional security issues, was actually a continuing progression within the organization and was immensely rewarding. I learnt a great deal about the vulnerabilities within our security realm and various other internal issues having adverse bearing on our national security. There were also ample opportunities for me to interact with civil bureaucrats and with political personalities. This opening greatly helped me to know and understand how the civilian setups work.

During my second week as ISI Sector Commander, I had an official call on the Chief Executive in the Government of Punjab. We had a good chat, and after assuring him of my support on all security issues, I returned to my office. At 11:00 p.m. that night the Chief Executive called to invite me personally to a private breakfast at his residence the following morning. I was a Colonel and receiving such an invitation from the province's chief executive was very unusual. I had no choice but to accept the invitation. The next day, I went to his residence, and he spent most of the time trying his best to win me over to his political point of view and seek my support. I managed to avoid having the discussion go beyond official matters under my purview and left after a sumptuous breakfast.

It is not unusual for some politicians and journalists to blame ISI and/or the army for unwarranted meddling in civilian governmental affairs. In my experience, it was just the opposite. My breakfast at the Chief Minister's residence and his efforts to haul me into politics in the province, were just an example of how things actually move in Pakistan. Civilian government officials and politicians tried time and again to drag me into their affairs and personal agendas. Most of the time, however, I stayed focused on matters within my areas of responsibility and was able to produce satisfying results in the field of security during my tenure in ISI.

As a counterintelligence operative, I was able to identify and neutralize many enemy agents operating in some of our sensitive institutions/installations. At the outset of my command as sector commander ISI Punjab, we identified an agent at one of our air force bases. It was a follow-up of an ongoing counterintelligence operation which I had initiated while I was commanding ISI Detachment in Rawalpindi. The agent had been tasked to obtain secret information about our aircraft and the missile systems. His handler who belonged to a foreign intelligence agency, was operating in Pakistan under a diplomatic cover. Unfortunately, this intelligence agency had been operating as one of our allies during the Russian invasion of Afghanistan. The handler had recruited this agent while he was working in the Afghan cell at one of our intelligence agencies. The agent kept working for his handler at the airbase, providing him with information about its operational activities and details about the missiles and aircraft stationed there.

Based on information from one of our local sources, we surreptitiously entered the suspected agent's office during non-duty hours and confirmed the presence of unauthorized sensitive documents and information. Later, through a well-planned operation, we apprehended the officer in his office and recovered this sensitive material. After the agent's interrogation, we decided to go after his handler.

Unfortunately, the handler was a senior diplomat and we needed to follow specific diplomatic protocols to arrest him. The first thing I did was to ensure that the agent's detention remained a secret so that his handler would not suspect that he had been compromised. I decided to trap the handler by luring him to a meeting and arrest him. I made the agent phone the handler and request a personal meeting at a place carefully chosen. It was on a small street in one of the country's larger cities.

I had fixed a spot for the meeting in front of a vacant house and planned to block both ends of the street after the handler entered the trap. A strong contingent of field operatives was placed behind the wall that surrounded the house, ready to jump out and capture the handler when he arrived for the meeting. We made the agent stand in front of the gate to the house and tied one of his legs with rope carefully so that it could not be seen by the handler, at the same time, the officer could not escape with the handler if he tried to do so. The agent was instructed to prolong his conversion with the handler as long as possible, to give us sufficient time to capture him.

I placed armed squads on both sides of the road with instructions to shoot out the tyres of the diplomat's car if he tried to drive away. A magistrate and I positioned ourselves in the courtyard to control the operation. The presence of a magistrate was essential from a legal point of view because we were dealing with a diplomat.

The handler arrived and met the agent, who did as he was told and prolonged the conversation. As expected, the handler asked the agent to get into his car, but the agent declined. At that point, I expected the raiding team to show itself and arrest the handler as we had planned, but to my utter surprise, nobody moved! After waiting a few seconds, I jumped across the boundary wall of the house, ran to the car, and grabbed the handler by his necktie. He was dumbfounded; probably, had not anticipated such a thing. The situation became chaotic. In total confusion, he started to drive away. I hung onto his necktie with one hand and grabbed the windshield wiper with the other.

The armed squads posted to prevent him from escaping were also confused and started firing at the car tyres from both sides of the street, not realizing I was there. The bullets flew on my right, my left, and through my legs. I thought the firing would surely stop as soon as the men realized that I could be hit, but they were intent on shooting the vehicle's tyres, as ordered, come what may.

Amazingly, none of the bullets hit the car's tyres. All I could see were bullets striking the concrete road, causing sparks beneath my feet and between my legs. I really do not understand, even today, how all these bullets managed to miss me. Maybe I was meant to live to write this book!

The handler dragged me for some distance until it became clear that he would not stop, and I could not make him. I let go of my grip on his necktie and the windshield wiper and rolled into a drainage ditch on the side of the road. The handler proved to be an exceptionally well-trained intelligence operative. He avoided our blockade by driving through a small stream that ran along the side of the road and got away.

Although we missed the guy, my job was done. We had made a video of the entire incident to confront him with it at the ministry of foreign affairs. In one respect it turned out well because if any of the bullets had hit him, it would have been a fiasco.

The case was reviewed at the highest levels. The diplomat was expelled from the country, the officer-agent court-martialled, and I was awarded Sitara-e-Imtiaz (Military), a medal for meritorious contribution to the security of national interests. Necessary counselling was given to team members who bungled in their task, and awards were given to those who did them well. This was just one of several spy networks that we broke up in our area of responsibility.

As a mountain boy, watching over the mountain peaks in Kashmir for acquisition of operational intelligence, was an attractive idea. More so because the type of birds I was hunting as an intelligence operative were plentiful across the border/LOC. I had identified several hot spots and found what I was looking for without difficulty. During the hunting trips I enjoyed in these mountains, I bagged some rare birds, one comes to mind.

Among my potential targets was a senior official from the Indian Army who had access to most of the information that I needed to know in IHK, specifically related to Indian Army activities in the area. I kept him under surveillance for several months, and one fine morning I learnt of his plan to travel abroad. It was an intriguing piece of information, and I decided to act upon it.

The day came, and he left on his vacation. Knowing his schedule, I planned to be at one of his stopovers to meet him. The homework paid off, and he belonged to us thereafter.

As a result, I kept ISI Headquarters updated with a complete picture of the Indian Army's activities in IHK which was of great help to timely plan counter strategies.

These were just a few glimpses of our achievements while I was part of ISI Detachment at Rawalpindi and subsequently, as sector commander Punjab. Selection of just two operations and the extent to which the information has been shared in each case, has been strictly in line with the security norms to ensure that the limits of confidentiality are not crossed at any level. I wish I could add a few more sensitive tasks that we were able to achieve but the sensitivity of the subject matter does not allow me to do that. Knowing the outcome of a few other more sensitive operations would have been a mind-blowing experience for many. All I can say is that our achievements were acknowledged as a significant contribution to the security of our motherland.

Being in charge of ISI activities in the province of Punjab taught me much about national security issues and national strategies to deal with them. My time there laid the groundwork for me to rise further in my career.

Exposure To International Diplomacy

I never expected to become a diplomat, but I did. The army assigned me to the Ministry of Foreign Affairs, and I was able to travel extensively at home and abroad. It was a great learning experience for me to meet people from different creeds and cultures. I was lucky to be selected to represent my country as a diplomat in Dubai, a place well known for being a hub of international relations. It is key to relations in the Middle East. The assignment as a diplomat was of tremendous value to me in my subsequent roles in the army/ISI and even when I am presently working as part of the private security industry in Dubai. It will be worth highlighting some of the invaluable gains that I was able to draw from this one-time opening in my career profile.

Learning the Art of Diplomacy

Learning the art of basic diplomacy is by itself an adventure and a very valuable skill set for any professional in the public or private sector. Diplomacy is essential to good relationships between individuals, groups, companies, or nations. Diplomacy's soft skills apply to any job in any industry. No matter what we do, we need at least some of the basic diplomatic skills to be successful.

As a diplomat in Dubai, my job was to represent my country and protect its national interests. Achieving these goals required me to become involved in communications, negotiations, image management, policy implementation, and the promotion of friendly relations with other countries. It was a busy time and there were many new things to learn. Effective interpersonal communication skills were necessary to create and nurture a supportive, productive, and positive network. Staying calm during periods of tension, working to understand everybody's perspective, and collaborating to find a common course of action were the important skills that I learnt during this period.

I learnt that critical thinking, a willingness to consider all factors in a situation, weigh the options and make solid choices based on facts was invaluable not only in the military but also in other professions.

Developing familiarity and skills in these areas served me well in carrying out the duties and responsibilities of various other positions throughout my military life and later after I retired.

Understanding International Strategic/Political Maneuverings

My service as a diplomat also provided me with the opportunity to closely monitor geo-strategic and geo-political developments in the region, particularly those relating to Pakistan's national security. Understanding the diplomatic, political, and economic manoeuvring of our adversaries and friends and the effects of these operations on Pakistan's national interests, goals, and agendas was a great learning experience.

Living in Dubai helped me greatly. I had the chance to meet and interact with people from diverse cultural and ethnic backgrounds from all corners of the world.

Enhancing the National Image

I also had the chance to live among Pakistan's large civilian expatriate community in the Gulf region. Getting to know them, understanding their problems, and boosting their national spirit by involving them in themes and events about Pakistan gave me a sense of great achievement. Conversely, my army background was a big attraction for them. I was warmly welcomed to their community events, large or small. I believe they cared about and respected Pakistan's armed forces and inviting me to participate in their events was their way of showing it.

Unfortunately, there were a few self-centred pseudointellectuals who mostly stayed away from community work for one reason or the other. I invited them to become part of our team and help us develop and organize national events to help boost a sense of pride in Pakistan's expatriate community. We organized many community events and invited notable people from other communities to join us and share our culture and heritage. We initiated a new tradition of celebrating 6 September every year as 'National Defence Day.' There were sporting events and an open house to which all were welcome. It became a well-attended function with a large gathering of the Pakistani community and a handsome number of ex-pats from other nationalities residing in Dubai, a day during which people of different nationalities could meet and talk freely.

I was a visa counsellor responsible for issuing Pakistani visas to foreign nationals who wished to visit the country. We worked hard to project a good image of Pakistan as a welcoming nation. On one occasion, an Indian national serving in a senior position with a respectable international company approached me in my office for a visa to visit Pakistan. His employer wanted him to visit Pakistan in connection with their business outlets. He was quite hesitant to approach our consulate to request a visa because there was a great deal of fear in the local Indian community about Pakistan's diplomatic missions in the UAE. He came to my office and asked me for a tourist visa. He was surprised when the consulate followed strictly its published procedures, processed his application promptly, and paid him due respect in the process.

Later, the consul general called me to his office and showed me a letter to the editor written by the same Indian national that appeared in the "Khaleej Times," a prominent Dubai-based English daily newspaper. The Indian national had written about his experience at the Pakistan consulate. The letter was full of appreciation for our consular services and the behaviour of our staff. He also condemned people who were using malicious propaganda to create ill will toward the Pakistani nation.

This small act earned us much respect in the international community. It underscored the impact of how our career diplomats perform their duties worldwide and the opportunities they get to boost Pakistan's image at the international level. It made me realize how important it is to have good diplomats abroad and how they can skilfully serve the national interests.

I also made myself available to many Pakistani communities living in the other northern emirates to help them solve minor issues. My staff and I made ourselves available to meet with visitors outside our offices and we would engage them proactively to offer our help. Each day, I also patrolled the consulate looking for people who needed assistance. Our visitors were always surprised to see me and my staff walking the halls and approaching them to help with their requests. I believe our effort reflected well on Pakistan.

My tenure as a diplomat was a wonderful experience, a blessing in every aspect of my life. It provided my children with the best possible education facilities, and they availed themselves of the opportunity. I also learnt a lot myself. By the time I completed my laid-out tenure in this assignment, I was due for my promotion to the rank of brigadier.

Battling in the Silent War Zone – Part 3

My third period of service in ISI began when I was posted back to ISI headquarters as a brigadier and assigned the duties of deputy director general security and counterintelligence. This assignment entailed responsibility for countering all hostile threats against Pakistan's national security at all levels. In addition to India's traditional threat, we also had many other dangerous security challenges to confront. Dealing with the aftermath of the Russian withdrawal from Afghanistan and the war on terror were among my top priorities. To complicate things, the stakeholders' changing interests in these unstable contests were making matters worse.

I served as ISI deputy DG, in uniform and as a contract civilian after my retirement, for nearly eleven years. It was the most rewarding period of my ISI service. I planned and implemented successful counterintelligence strategies and was part of the team that reorganized and modernized ISI as an institution, creating significant changes in its structure, particularly in the field of counterintelligence. As a result, the organization's performance in counterintelligence operations improved tremendously.

India has been working constantly to fuel our country's ethnic and sectarian divisions, and their efforts to destabilize us continue unabated. Besides providing moral, financial, and material support to those who would divide us, their agents have hired people to participate in terrorist attacks in different parts of the country, particularly in the Federally Administered Tribal Areas and in Baluchistan. Their involvement in Baluchistan has been very bold and conspicuous. Through very meticulously planned operations I was able to identify several networks belonging to the Research and Analysis Wing (RAW), India's foreign intelligence agency. These networks were involved in the recruitment of activists for the Baluchistan Liberation Army (BLA) and in directing terrorist activities in the province. In one such operation, I was able to identify a well-organized international network managed by RAW for training BLA terrorists in third countries and then sending them back into Baluchistan where they attacked army installations, patriotic politicians, and school children.

RAW operatives would recruit young innocent people from Baluchistan, between sixteen and twenty-five years old, and move them into Afghanistan on foot. In Kabul, RAW's Station Chief arranged for them to stay in safe houses and provided them with Afghan passports before flying them to different training camps in other countries. In one instance, I tasked my Quetta detachment commander to monitor the movement of these RAW operatives and the young Baluchis cultivated by them for training through well-trained plants in their network. Through a meticulously planned counterintelligence operation, we were able to monitor their complete movement abroad. In this case, the selected Baluchis were flown from Kabul to New Delhi for further movement to third countries for training. At the camps which RAW had established in some African countries and in the Far East, they were trained intensively for about three weeks, with an emphasis on subversion, sabotage, and terrorist activities. Then, they were launched back into Baluchistan using a slightly altered route. We kept track of the terrorists throughout their training period and grabbed them up immediately upon their return.

RAW's involvement with Baluchistan separatists has been an ongoing problem. The Indians never miss an opportunity to encourage anti-Pakistan activities in the province and create law and order issues. Their involvement with dissidents from the Bugti and Mari tribes became known widely after the uprising by Nawab Akbar Khan Bugti. Brahumdagh Bugti and Harbahyar Mari had visited India many times on Indian passports. I obtained a copy of Harbahyar Mari's Indian passport with an entry stamp of New Delhi airport through one of my well-placed agents. This copy was part of the documentary evidence that President Musharraf handed over to the US as proof of India's involvement in Baluchistan.

We also apprehended several RAW undercover diplomats in Islamabad who were maintaining links with BLA dissidents. In one instance, the RAW's station chief at the Indian embassy in Islamabad was arrested while receiving classified information from a Baluch working on behalf of the BLA. It was a classic counterintelligence operation in which the station chief was lured into the trap through a very skilfully planned penetration in his network.

I interrogated him personally and he confessed voluntarily to being involved with the funding and training of terrorists in Baluchistan and in other parts of the country. He remained my 'guest' in a safe house in Islamabad for a day and was entertained with 'fantastic cups of tea' and coffee before being expelled from the country on charges of misconduct as a diplomat. I am using the word 'fantastic cup of tea' to imitate an Indian Air Force pilot whose MIG 19 was shot down by Pakistan Air Force, while it was on a raid mission inside Pakistan territory on 27 February 2019. Wing Commander Abhinandan Varthaman who successfully bailed out of the burning aircraft, was captured by Pakistani troops on the ground and later released. In an interview, while leaving back to his country, he thanked Pakistan Army troops for the fantastic cups of tea that had been served to him while under detention. These words went viral on social media in Pakistan and abroad. During my meeting with the RAW's station chief, he also wholeheartedly praised ISI's high professional standards and competency and thanked me for the hospitality shown to him while he was with us.

Interestingly we also had the defence attaché from another major country posted in their embassy at Islamabad, in our lap while he was trying to peep into some of our sensitive nuclear installations. He also remained my guest for a day in my safe house in Islamabad before being expelled from Pakistan through the Ministry of Foreign Affairs.

I am honoured to have been part of Pakistan's premier intelligence agency, ISI, for nearly twenty-three years. I believe it is one of the longest tenures any army officer has served with this organization. My work in various capacities provided me with ample opportunities to participate personally in Pakistan's defence against many complex security threats. I was able to contribute to the security of the country at all levels and I became knowledgeable in almost all facets of intelligence know-how at the national, regional, and international levels.

To the extent I discussed my experiences during my service with ISI, I have taken care to respect the concerns of the institution about the sensitive nature of the information involved. Remaining within the constraints of confidentiality, I hope to have been able to provide a glimpse of ISI's contributions toward protecting Pakistan's national security interests. The conclusions drawn on security-related issues are mine alone, and I do not represent the views of any of the institutions that I have served while in *Khakis*.

CHAPTER 6

IN THE KHAKIS: AN INFINITE BLESSING

A Personal Treasure

My lifelong association with the Pakistan Army, extending over almost four decades, has taken my family and me on a lifelong journey filled with grace and honour. My time with the army, ISI and the Ministry of Foreign Affairs was an eye-opening experience for me in which I learnt a lot, enjoyed myself a lot, and was able to contribute a lot to my country's institutions and security. I am grateful to Almighty Allah for his blessings and to the institutions and organizations I served, for providing me with the opportunity to help protect our homeland. My association with Pakistan's intelligence organizations added tremendous value to my professional development. The Pakistan Army provided me with the foundation to grow in the profession of arms, but my involvement with ISI gave me insight into regional and international affairs, and a good understanding of how our adversaries try to manoeuvre against our national security interests.

The progression of my intelligence career facilitated the learning process in matters of security at all levels. My postings in various ISI field detachments at the rank of major and lieutenant colonel helped me to understand the basics of security and counterintelligence operations and introduced me to concepts relating to threat analysis at the national level. Posting as officer commanding ISI detachment Islamabad was an important field appointment. I had the honour to command it for nearly seven years. My primary responsibility was looking after the security of top government officials, the ministerial secretariat, and the diplomatic enclave. I managed the challenging task of neutralizing embassy and non-embassy-based hostile intelligence networks operating in Pakistan's capital region. My posting to the Islamabad detachment coincided with Russia's invasion of Afghanistan, and I was involved directly or indirectly in that theatre of war until Russia withdrew. It was a time of great learning and discovery during which I came to understand emerging international security patterns more realistically.

My subsequent postings as sector commander of ISI Punjab province and deputy DG of security and counterintelligence as a brigadier enabled me to put things into a broader perspective. In addition to handling internal and external traditional security threats, I was responsible for overseeing new security challenges that cropped up in the aftermath of the Soviet-Afghan War and the 'war on terror.' The battle seemed unending and more challenging than actual war. Unfortunately, the battle continues even today. I continue in retirement as a private security professional to use the knowledge I gained during this time.

In the context of Pakistan's national security, internal threats always foreshadow external threats. Hence, identifying and comprehending internal fault lines within our social structure was an important part of my work during these years. Our adversaries further their anti-Pakistan agenda by exploiting weak links within our society. Unfortunately, various administrations in the country aggravated some of our weak links with poorly crafted policies that focused on short-term gains. Our adversaries used these policies to manipulate Pakistan's political mafia, government machinery, and private institutions. Even religious clerics became their tools on occasion.

The democratic process in our country is unfortunately more of an illusion of democracy than a form of governance by the people and for the people. Democracy is used as a cover to manipulate the state machinery for personal gains. In many cases, this malpractice stretches beyond corruption and crosses over into the territory of treachery and betrayal. Covert foreign links and manipulation of our policies to suit foreign adversaries are, unfortunately, a reality in our country that seriously damages its politics and its democracy.

By brutally exploiting our failure to differentiate between personal gain and national interests, our adversaries neutralize our strengths, weaken our governance system, create ethnic and religious division, and damage our internal harmony. They publicly condemn and deliberately misconstrue the efforts of our armed forces and the sacrifices they make to safeguard the country's security and integrity. Unfortunately, discrediting our armed forces has become a top priority of their agenda. It is purely because, the Pakistan Army is the only unifying force in the country that ensures its integrity and cohesion against the malicious conspiracies by our adversaries, both external as well as internal.

Watching all this happening was a harrowing experience. Handling these enemies and keeping Pakistan safe has been a very demanding job, but one I believe we performed well. However, the encouraging aspect has been that the people in Pakistan have always been loving of their armed forces and expressed their solidarity with them at all odds. It is only a segment of our political hierarchy and a few others among the governing elite working on behalf of our adversaries who indulge in such anti-army campaigns for their self-interests.

While efforts to divide the country from abroad are understandable and likely to continue, the failure on the part of all concerned within Pakistan to defeat this trend is quite worrisome. Leaders among all concerned parties need to find and put in place suitable remedies as a national priority.

The story of my life in 'Khakis' would not be complete without expressing my gratitude to all my colleagues with whom I had the privilege to serve in Pakistan's army, especially to all my fallen comrades who left us during those years after laying down their lives in defence of our homeland. I have seen them, warriors sprayed with bullet wounds, and warriors frozen in the snow-covered sky-high peaks of Siachen Glacier. My youngest brother-in-law, Captain Amer Moeen, sacrificed his life at Saddle Post, on the Siachen battlefield. Like my other fallen comrades, he returned home in a wooden box, draped in our green national flag.

I knew all of them as professional soldiers who did their duty on Pakistan's behalf with grace, honour, and dignity.

The Army Values of a Pakistani Soldier

After forty years 'In the Khakis,' I was immersed in 'The Army Values,' the military code for how to live one's life and pursue one's goals with determination, integrity, and personal courage. I learnt self-discipline and the importance of one's character among the officers and the ranks. My long years in the Khakis built in me a spirit of selfless service and unquestionable loyalty to my nation. It helped me not only while I was in service but also after I retired when I had to meet the challenges of civilian life.

The army values symbolize service before self, defiance against defeat, and the idea of never giving up and never leaving a comrade behind. These are the values that create esprit de corps and move the Khakis forward.

Army officers learn to embrace the spirit upon which our country was founded and focus their lives on pursuing Pakistan's national interest. However, their patriotism can be a source of frustration and disappointment at times when they see other people in civilian setups ignoring the nation's welfare for personal gain. The willingness of some people to compromise national interests in exchange for millions of dollars in foreign accounts is infuriating. Having served in high-level positions with access to sensitive information for a long time, I can honestly say that though, for the most part, Pakistan has had patriotic and competent leaders, and their contributions to the national cause cannot be overlooked; but regrettably, on too many occasions, our country has been damaged greatly by some selfish and greedy leadership who put personal interests above their country.

While the frustrations can be great, most people in uniform believe strongly in civilian rule under constitutional provisions. No army officer worth his salt wants to be assigned to martial law duties. I was one of those who were required to perform such duties briefly during General Zia's regime. It was a very frustrating experience in my career.

Selfless service and devotion to duties are among the highest values of Pakistani soldiers. Pakistani soldiers take an oath to serve the country and guard its freedom as spelt out in its constitution. They follow their oath, bearing true faith and allegiance to the country and the institution of the Pakistan Army. In view of repeated military takeovers since our independence in 1947, many may raise fingers on my assertion about the army's loyalty and subservience to the constitution of the country. But I am sure that those who possess the factual knowledge about what forced army to intervene into politics time and again, will bear me out that in most cases, army was hauled into it, with no escape routes. Being an eye-witness to many such developments, I am privy to some undeniable facts that mostly induced army to step in. For an instance, I was Director Counterintelligence wing in ISI in 1999. A brief mention of some of the facts in case of General Musharraf's takeover, will be valuable to ponder the history of the army's takeovers more objectively and I have done that in this book in due course.

The army has an inbuilt system of accountability within its operating procedures to deal promptly with behaviour problems under Pakistan military law. In many cases, even very senior officers were prosecuted and punished in the recent past for their wrongdoings. Some of them were dismissed from service, and lost their ranks, medals, and pension, while a few others were sentenced to varying terms of imprisonment. The system does not condone abuse of power and misappropriation under any circumstances. There have been cases where officers of the ranks of Lieutenant General and Major General, being court-martialled for ignoring the official secrets act, wittingly or unwittingly.

Strict adherence to our moral values grows people's trust in the army. Personal courage in the face of danger wins us many hearts. Commitment to the cause, a willingness to face the odds, and working as a team are hallmarks of the Pakistani army soldiers.

The army works to infuse these values in its soldiers. It teaches us to stay true to our roots and be accountable for our successes and our failures. Soldiers are trained to possess the ability to cope with physical, mental, and emotional challenges. They are taught to be humble; modest when they are successful, and resilient when they fail. They are taught to accept adverse action if they mess up, but they know that what is most important is the willingness to carry on with determination and courage until the job is done right.

Intense focus, better teamwork, and advanced leadership skills are the qualities that make army officers excel while they are in service and after they retire. It is generally believed that veterans bring a sense of inventiveness, audacity, and leadership, while they serve in the private sector after their retirement, which is not often seen in employees with a civilian background.

PART 3

JOURNEY THROUGH THE CHANGING WORLD ORDER

CHAPTER 7

DIRECTION AND INTENSITY OF THE CROSSFIRE

Safety and security of a country require continuous monitoring of risks to its integrity and solidarity. It is an ongoing process that demands that responsible institutions be vigilant constantly. If a country fails to adjust its approach to meet the changing security environments, it is most likely to fall prey to conspiracies hatched by its adversaries, from both inside and outside the country.

Unfortunately, Pakistan's national security has been a primary concern since its creation. The nation exists in a complex security environment, involving internal and external military, political, social, and economic challenges. Some of them are the result of the country's past policies and practices. Others are the product of developments in the region and internationally. The problems are multi-dimensional, and they continue to haunt us today, in one form or another.

Pakistan is in an ideal geo-strategic location at the crossroads of Asia. It provides the central Asian republics, China, and Russia with an outlet to the Arabian Sea for their east-west trade connections. Its location has made Pakistan an international playground for all the region's stakeholders. They look upon it as a chess piece to play in support of their own national interest at the expense of our country.

The Russian invasion of Afghanistan during the late 1970s and 80s, the 9/11 attack on the United States and the resultant war on terror created lasting consequential effects on our nation, triggering significant developments in the region, and endangering our national security and cohesion.

Military threats to Pakistan rapidly expanded during the last two decades, from state-centric Indian conventional threats on our eastern border to transborder threats on the western front. India remains a constant factor in these regional manoeuvres and in the conspiracies that have arisen against Pakistan internationally, trying to become a beneficiary in each case. These increased threats have completely altered the dynamics of our national security paradigm.

The overall security threat to any nation generally consists of its external threats, its internal vulnerabilities, and how they interact with each other. In the context of national security, the country's internal fault lines create critical opportunities for its adversaries to exploit to further their own agendas. Unfortunately, Pakistan has to deal with a deadly combination of external threats and internal vulnerabilities.

Despite our adversaries joining forces against us, thus far Pakistan has been able to achieve positive outcomes on all fronts in the region's conflicts and that is a testament to the competence, commitment, and the ability of our gallant armed forces to safeguard Pakistan's national interests. Due to the type of warfare being employed against us, ISI has been at the forefront of safeguarding our national interests during all these conflicts.

While Indo-Pak animosity remains a constant factor in our national security paradigm, the change in Pakistan's national security situation during the past two decades was mainly driven by events in Afghanistan. It started with the 'Afghan Jihad,' a ten-year conflict, that lasted from 1979 to 1989. The conflict began with the Soviet Union's occupation of the country and was driven primarily by US aid to Afghan resistance fighters. When the Soviets left in February 1989, the Afghans began to fight among themselves leading to the 'Afghan Civil War' that lasted from 1989 to 2001. Finally, the US 'war on terror' after 9/11, resulting in the US occupation of Afghanistan, continued the conflict until the US and its allies finally withdrew from the country in August 2021. The worst for us was that the war entered Pakistan.

The Afghan conflict lasted forty-two years and greatly changed our security landscape, particularly as it relates to direct and indirect regional threats against Pakistan from India as evidenced by an increase in domestic and foreign efforts to exploit our internal fault lines. It is important that the people of Pakistan know about the country's external and internal threats and that people abroad understand Pakistan's security environment. In that way, national policies and international relations can be developed based on facts and not on false and misleading information.

Crossfire from Across the Borders

Afghan Jihad (1979-1989)

The international security environment is constantly changing as countries shift their political, economic, and strategic interests. Nations must adjust to accommodate these changes or possibly suffer harmful consequences. For Pakistan, major changes began in 1979 with the Russian Invasion of Afghanistan. Its goal was to reach Pakistan's warm water ports on the Arabian Sea, and through them gain access to the Indian Ocean. Pakistan had been put into a straitjacket. With a hostile India on its eastern border and the Soviets with their puppet Afghan government on its western border, Pakistan's security environment changed drastically. Suddenly, it had to deal with the security-related concerns, perceptions, policies, and mechanisms of countries from around the globe.

ISI played a pivotal role in coordinating the efforts of the global alliance opposed to the Soviet occupation of Afghanistan. Its work in support of the Afghan mujahideen against Soviet forces earned it unparalleled global recognition.

The regional security landscape worsened with each passing day. However, the stakeholders and their interests in the conflict kept changing in response to other global security challenges and their personal interests overlooked the interests of their partners during a decades-old conflict in Afghanistan. The fallout from this continuously changing regional landscape is the root cause of Pakistan's current security challenges.

Afghan Civil War (1989-2001) and US-Pakistan Relationship

After the Soviet withdrawal from Afghanistan, everything went into reverse gear. The US-Pakistan relationship suffered serious setbacks. Contingency planning, different priorities in Afghanistan, and mutual distrust factored into a breakdown in communications. Serious criticism was levied by each side against the other's strategies and planning. The US blamed Pakistan for harbouring Osama bin Laden and for not addressing certain groups of Taliban fighters. Pakistan had serious concerns about the US failure to control the porous Afghanistan-Pakistan border and US protection of Mullah Fazlullah and his organization who were operating inside Pakistan. Pakistan had serious reservations about providing a space to Indians in Afghanistan and allowing it a free run to encircle Pakistan through covert intelligence operations from all directions.

We had had specific and authenticated information about how a special group of Taliban fighters that had fought against Russian forces, was carved out for special treatment. Nobody would tell us why this was done. Drone strikes, the Salala incident in which twenty-eight Pakistani soldiers were killed at military checkpoints on the border, and the uncovering of a huge spy network operating against Pakistan further aggravated the anger against the West within the Pakistani society.

The devastated Afghanis were abandoned, leaving Pakistan to suffer the aftershocks. The US departure created strong feelings of betrayal within Pakistan. The US had created an unstable country on Pakistan's western border and left us to deal with it on our own. Who has been using whom became a murky issue. We all created mujahideen to fight the Russians, and the people who fought later were also mujahideen. Their lives did not change, but the world around them had changed, and nothing had been done to help them build productive lives.

Unfortunately, Pakistan was left out of the loop when the US made its decisions. It was suddenly placed on the grey list and not consulted. Simultaneously, the US imposed a military embargo against Pakistan because of its development of nuclear technology that Pakistan saw as the only way to defend itself against Indian aggression. A change in US strategic objectives accounts for this change of heart. We bought long-term pain for short-term gains.

At the end of the Soviet occupation of Afghanistan, the US pursued to maintain its dominance in our region during the twenty-first century and used multiple strategic and tactical manoeuvres to do so. It wanted to gain control over strategic global resources in the Central Asian States and dominate the region's land and sea trading routes. It also wanted to hinder Chinese emergence as a potential global and regional power, neutralize Pakistan's influence in the region and in the Islamic world, and promote India as the regional hegemon.

According to the information that we were able to gather through very reliable sources, the game plan in our national context has been denuclearization, weakening of our armed forces, and providing India with sufficient influence in Afghanistan, facilitating its operations against Pakistan in Baluchistan and the FATA. Attempts were made by our adversaries to promote internal division within Pakistan through ethnic and sectarian rhetoric, by creating anti-army feelings, and by promoting regionalism. Attempts were also made to create a split between religious clerics and the army, especially in the frontier region along the Pak-Afghan border by discrediting the army's reputation through false propaganda and disinformation. Corrupt and greedy politicians were bought to carry out their perceived agenda, an unfortunate reality that most patriotic Pakistanis regret painfully.

There were persistent efforts to sabotage our nuclear programme right from the outset and continued till the end. In May 1998, the Pakistan government and the army were under tremendous pressure from the US to refrain from carrying out planned nuclear tests. Unfortunately, both the incumbent prime minister and the opposition leader expressed their helplessness to the US authorities and asked them to approach the Army General Headquarters to stop them from making the nuclear tests. Timely information about the situation helped the Pakistan Army Headquarters to take precautionary measures and ensure that the planned nuclear test was conducted. I am personally privy to some of the facts as to how the army chief of that time, General Jahangir Karamat, stood firm and did not give up under pressure, and the tests were conducted according to the plan. At that time, our nuclear programme operated under the direct supervision of the Pakistan Army, which ensured successful completion of this vital project and has guaranteed the security of the country ever since. Even the US senior officials handling the matter at that time, later openly confirmed in their personal writings about US efforts to keep the government of Pakistan away from nuclearization and Pakistan's civilian government's inability to refrain Pakistan Army from carrying out the nuclear test.

Efforts to destabilize our nuclear programme continued even after the nuclear tests had been successfully conducted on 28 May 1998. The Dr Abdul Qadeer Khan fiasco was created by the CIA after it found some indications of his suspected involvement in nuclear proliferation in Iran, Libya, and Malaysia. It was another serious attempt to interrupt our nuclear programme. Exhaustive investigations of Dr Khan's activities were conducted in Pakistan because the allegations against him were equally dangerous for our own nuclear programme. The investigation did uncover certain shady characters and some European businesses in close contact with Dr A.Q. Khan, and a few of them were also involved with some other unwitting people in our nuclear organizations. Some Indian RAW operatives were also seen hovering around Dr Khan while he was abroad. The investigations concluded clearly that there was no official involvement of any kind at any level in Dr Khan's activities. He himself admitted to President General Pervez Musharraf that he had been lax in handling his affairs. The situation, however, provided an opportunity for people in the West to exploit and use it as an opportunity to discredit our nuclear programme and find a loophole to intervene. Dr A.Q. Khan's personal security became vital. Being the Director of Counterintelligence in ISI at that time, I also oversaw the security of Dr A.Q. Khan and was well aware of the threats endangering his personal safety. In Islamabad he was isolated and confined in his house for his safety. General Pervez Musharraf had also discussed the incident in detail in his book 'In the Line of Fire'.

In another incident, a similar attempt was made to interfere with our nuclear organizations by accusing some of our senior scientists of suspected links and support to Al-Qaeda after 9/11. These scientists were accused of providing some kind of nuclear technology to Al-Qaeda. They were arrested and put through a joint interrogation effort. I personally headed the interrogation team which had strong representation from the CIA and our other Western intelligence agencies. After an intensive interrogation that lasted two to three weeks, we all unanimously concluded that none of these scientists was involved in any such activity. All of them were declared innocent and released. I have been an intelligence operative for decades with considerable experience in similar situations, and I believe firmly that there was never any solid evidence that warranted all these investigations. It was an effort to find something where nothing existed and use it to malign our nuclear teams by accusing them of irresponsible behaviour and by suggesting an element of insecurity in our nuclear programme.

On the other hand, violating its own laws as well as International Atomic Energy Agency (IAEA) rules, the US did not hesitate to sign a significant nuclear deal with India that aimed to make it a potent force against China and provided it with massive armaments and sophisticated technology with which to subdue Pakistan.

I sincerely hope that the reported US-UK effort to proliferate nuclear technology in Australia under the AUKUS Nuclear Submarine deal as part of trilateral security partnership for the Indo-Pacific region between Australia, UK, and the US will not be a prelude to similar arrangements with India. Such arrangements can induce reckless imbalance in South Asia which Pakistan can ill afford. These types of concerns are increasing because of the US preference for Indian interests in South Asia and the disregard of Pakistan's concerns. Such a contingency could result in Pakistan taking countermeasures that will aggravate the threat to an unimaginable bog.

Additionally, overlooking the dangers of Hindu extremists controlling India's nuclear arsenal will not only aggravate the nuclear threat in South Asia, but also have consequences for the rest of the world. Overt actions signalling changes in India's nuclear doctrine have already increased the seriousness of real-time risks in the region. The Indian missile incident in March 2022 in which an Indian missile landed in Pakistan and the Indian Air Force strikes inside Pakistan in February 2019, are clear examples of Indian aggressive actions that Pakistan cannot ignore.

The US also ignored Pakistan's security interest, its main ally in Afghanistan, when it implemented its policy for a perceived new world order, by offering India as the region's net security provider. It helped India gain vital influence in Afghanistan and establish bases under diplomatic and non-diplomatic cover all along the Pak-Afghan border to operate against Pakistan. RAW agent handlers had free run in Afghanistan with the close support from the US puppet Afghan government.

The Taliban kept their resistance to the US going despite the odds, and US coalition forces began to feel the heat of the Taliban struggle just a few years into its liberation war. After years of struggle, the Taliban under Mullah Omar were able to consolidate their control over significant parts of the country. With Taliban's ascendance to power, once again, the major stakeholders' interests and priorities changed.

The external threat from across the Pak-Afghan border coupled with anti-US sentiment inside Pakistan created significant internal agitation and dissension. It was a difficult situation to handle.

9/11 and its Aftermath

Immediate Reaction by the US

I was in my DG's office (security and counterintelligence) in the ISI directorate for a briefing on certain counterintelligence operations on 9/11. The television flashed the biggest breaking news of the century, the strike on the World Trade Centre and other high-value targets in the US. It was late in the afternoon, and most other government offices were closed, except for a few unfortunate ones like us. The DG and I were both stunned. The DG ISI, who heads the organization as a whole, was abroad on an official visit. In his absence, my boss passed the word immediately to other senior officials and I immediately started calling my field detachment commanders to inform them about the news.

The next day my DG phoned me and asked me for my reaction to the news. What did I think its impact would be on our national security? It was something beyond my comprehension, but we both expected a strong reaction from the US against the Taliban. We were hosting many Afghan refugees in our country at the time, and the action against some elements within that community could not be ruled out. I suggested some protective measures be taken from a counterintelligence perspective, and with his approval passed on the necessary instructions to my field detachments. We both decided to keep our fingers crossed and to remain alert to handle unforeseen developments.

Early next morning, my boss called me again for some important updates. I was told that the DG ISI, who was on an official US visit, had been warned by Deputy Secretary of State Richard Armitage that "if Pakistan still chose to be with the militants in Afghanistan, it will be bombed back to the Stone Age". It was a very strange message, much outside the ambit of international diplomatic norms. However, the wording of the message indicated the gravity of the situation and the impact of multiple air strikes in New York and Washington. We again discussed certain additional preventive measures on our end and began implementing SOPs for such eventualities.

DIRECTION AND INTENSITY OF THE CROSSFIRE

General Pervez Musharraf, President of Pakistan, described in his book, 'In the Line of Fire,' how Pakistan was coerced immediately after the 9/11 attacks. US secretary of state, General Colin Powell had rung him directly to say: "You are either with us or against us." The US ambassador to Pakistan conveyed another strong message on behalf of his government, demanding blanket overflight and landing rights for US operations inside of Afghanistan, a complete diplomatic break with the Taliban government if it supported Al Qaeda and full intelligence sharing. The situation for Pakistan became worse when India offered its bases to the US for operations against Afghanistan. It also exploited the situation to create a joint US-Indian threat to our nuclear strategic assets. On the other side, our relationship with the Taliban government was also fragile due to its apprehensions about our role in its fight against the Northern Alliance and our relationship with the US.

Pakistan was left with no choice but to support the US against extremist elements in Afghanistan. On this matter, the US also enjoyed support from its agents of influence within different segments of our political class and within other influential sections of society. Giving US forces blanket overflight permission was impossible. However, Pakistan allowed it to use two bases in Baluchistan and Sindh for logistics and aircraft recovery.

War Entered Pakistan

We stood with the US but could not stop the war from shifting to Pakistan. Tehrik-e-Taliban Pakistan (TTP), an anti-Pakistan terrorist group, was born in Afghanistan and, with the support of a few other splinter groups, began to launch bloody attacks across the border into Pakistan. These operations were conducted often in close coordination with RAW.

TTP's activities in Pakistan increased suddenly after 9/11. We enhanced our monitoring of many of their training camps on the Pak-Afghan border, to find out what caused this sudden change. As director of security and counterintelligence in ISI, I asked my senior operative in Peshawar to infiltrate their camps with our reliable agents who would volunteer as trainees and gather information about TTP activities inside Pakistan. The operation was successful and brought back some great intelligence.

We learnt that many of the trainees in these camps were foreigners and non-Muslims with little knowledge of either the Pushto or Urdu languages. Even some of the trainers were in the same category. The blanket issued to one of our plants to sleep on during the training had a name written on it which is commonly used in the West. What did that mean? Who were the other people attending the training and who were the trainers? Was it an effort to shift the war from Afghanistan to Pakistan through a break-away group of Taliban and weaken the Taliban's resistance to allied forces inside Afghanistan, as a by-product? In follow-up operations, we apprehended many of the terrorists trained in these camps while they were on their way to assigned targets in Islamabad. Interrogation reports confirmed our assertions to a great degree. Concurrently, some known terrorists with long criminal records were provided safe sanctuaries outside of Pakistan from where they could work freely against Pakistan.

Terrorist attacks against us, one after the other, began to take place. We worked to prevent them and to follow up when they happened by trying to trace the culprits through half-blown faces, burnt ID cards, and destroyed cell phones.

Even our president, General Pervez Musharraf, was threatened personally by these terrorist attacks. Using his commando instincts and likely through special blessings from God Almighty, he survived miraculously, one attempt after another to kill him.

The first attack occurred on 14 December 2003. Religious extremists placed explosives under a bridge near the army house, his official residence in Rawalpindi. He was on his way back from the airport and terrorists attempted to activate the explosives with a cell phone. The caller failed to time the detonation accurately when his car crossed the bridge, allowing the president to avoid injury. A piece of the telephone keypad found at the site, and some other leads developed by investigators resulted in the arrest of one of the culprits, the man who triggered the explosive. His interrogation led to the identification and arrest of three others involved in the attack. All of them were junior air force employees recruited by an Afghan terrorist outfit, loyal to Mullah Omer. Sponsored by Jaish-e-Mohammad and led by Maulana Masood Azhar, they used money and religious beliefs to recruit the would-be assassins. They had rented a house in Jhanda Chichi, a place near the site of the attack to use as a base for their operations.

About a week later, there was another terrorist attack against General Musharraf at almost the same place. This time, he was returning from a conference in Islamabad, when two suicide bombers in two Suzuki pick-up trucks blew themselves up near petrol pumps about 200 yards from the same bridge. The blasts partially damaged the president's car.

During the attack, General Musharraf drew his pistol and prepared to engage his attackers. When the blasts destroyed the car's tyres, he kept it moving forward by encouraging the driver to drive on its wheel rims. They drove on the wheel rims for three to four kilometres and managed to reach his residence safely. It was nothing short of a miracle that no one was hurt.

The body of the first suicide bomber was found in a nearby police compound. The body of the second was found in an apartment complex on the side of the road. About five policemen, including an inspector, who were on protection duty on the roadside were martyred as the result of the blasts. The culprits involved in this attack were identified through DNA tests and partially burnt ID cards. The first one had been trained by a terrorist organization in the Kotli area of Azad Kashmir. He was a member of a terrorist group that had taken an oath to avenge the US attack on Afghanistan by assassinating General Musharraf. They blamed him for his support of the Americans. The would-be assassin's father had also been involved in the Afghan Jihad against the Russians.

Interestingly, there was no link between the first and second attacks. They were carried out independently of each other, according to Al-Qaeda's strategy of always targeting an objective with two separate and independent cells. Our background checks of the vehicles used in the attacks confirmed Al-Qaeda's link with the attackers.

Similar attacks were conducted against many other high-profile Pakistani personalities to create chaos and confusion in the country. Pakistan Army corps commander at Karachi, Lieutenant General Ahsan Saleem Hayat, survived a similar assassination attempt on 10 June 2004, while he was on his way to work. An improvised explosive device was placed on the road and set to be triggered by a cell phone. The driver of the general's car was killed, but his foot pressed down on the accelerator, and the car continued to move. The general's aide-de-camp had the presence of mind to take immediate control of the car. His bold action, and the cell phone's failure to trigger the explosive, saved General Ahsan from certain death.

During the same period, another general officer was attacked on Mall Road in Rawalpindi, and a lieutenant general lost his son to an attack while he was attending Jumma prayers near their residence in an army residential area on Peshawar Road Rawalpindi. Some known terrorists with long criminal records were provided safe sanctuaries outside of Pakistan from where they could operate freely inside Pakistan.

Pakistan lost thousands of lives, suffered enormous property damage, and suffered visible ethnic and sectarian strife among different segments of our society after playing a pivotal role in defeating Russia in Afghanistan. Besides the physical attacks on our army, a propaganda blitz was launched against it through the treacherous manipulation of hired politicians, journalists, lawyers, and others of similar ilk. According to a planned strategy, we were blamed as a rogue army, land grabbers, and a power-hungry mafia. We were criticized and attacked cruelly at home and abroad. Every effort was made to engineer internal dissent against our armed forces using planted moles in different segments of society. The country was choked through financial restrictions imposed by the International Monetary Fund and the Financial Action Task Force.

Besides all this, the US and its allies kept breathing down our necks with overt and covert threats of 'do more'. We were expected to follow their wishes without question, irrespective of the consequences.

Breeding the Agents of Influence in Pakistan

The prolonged stay in the region, particularly in Pakistan during the Afghanistan war, enabled the allied intelligence agencies to infiltrate Pakistan government institutions and various segments of our civil society. Taking full advantage of the opportunity to move freely at all levels of Pakistan's social structure, they created a strong network of politicians, media personalities, civil society leaders, and even members of some government departments and institutions. As a result, they were able to promote and manipulate their agenda in Pakistan and in the region.

By 2007, Pakistan's internal situation had been traumatized and the level of uncertainty was such that questions about its survival as an independent country were being circulated by national and international media outlets hostile to Pakistan. General Pervez Musharraf was removed as president through an orchestrated change in regimes. Well-known agents of influence in Pakistan were assigned sensitive positions in the chain to help maintain direct links inside Pakistan to implement their agenda. Blatant interference in Pakistan's domestic realm continues even today, through their moles in different segments of our society.

Osama bin Laden's Death Controversy

A flood of conspiracy theories erupted after Osama bin Laden's death in Pakistan on 2 May 2011, and an endless blame game has been raging since. I was not in the service at the time of bin Laden's killing in a CIA raid in Abbottabad, nor did I ever deal with matters involving him when I was in service. I have no direct knowledge of the matter but given the role ISI played during the war in Afghanistan, I want to address the allegation by multiple parties in the West that ISI provided Osama bin Laden with safe sanctuary in Pakistan.

Being an intelligence operative and having been involved in many high-profile operations in the region, I think, it would be naive to even consider that ISI would be involved in harbouring bin Laden in close proximity to the Pakistan Army's Military Academy, one of the country's most sensitive institutions. For those familiar with the terrain in Pakistan, when it comes to hoodwinking the CIA or any other intelligence agency the country's inaccessible mountainous areas provide much safer sanctuaries for such operations. Choosing Abbottabad would have been suicidal.

DIRECTION AND INTENSITY OF THE CROSSFIRE

Another interesting theory circulating in the West is that the Intelligence Bureau, Pakistan's civilian intelligence agency, was the one that helped bin Laden. This claim is probably because the then DG of the Intelligence Bureau, Brigadier (Retired) Ijaz Ahmed Shah, was a close friend of General Pervez Musharraf. I know Brigadier Ijaz Ahmed Shah and have had the privilege of serving with him. I took over command of ISI Sector Punjab from him when I was promoted to colonel. Anyone aware of the role and responsibilities of the Intelligence Bureau would never believe such an assertion. The Intelligence Bureau deals specifically with political intelligence for the incumbent government and has some other minor domestic security-related duties. Assigning it with a task to provide sanctuary for bin Laden is unthinkable.

In addition, it should be noted that before bin Laden's death, ISI and allied foreign intelligence agencies had been operating in Afghanistan for decades against common enemies. Their agents were mostly interconnected, some even playing double roles. It is difficult to perceive ISI attempting to conduct such a sensitive operation unilaterally, in isolation, under such circumstances.

Bin Laden's presence in Pakistan can best be described as an intelligence failure. It can happen anywhere and with any intelligence agency, no matter how big or how small it may be.

General Pervez Musharraf spoke about it during a London conference on the tenth Anniversary of the 9/11 attacks against the United States. When asked if he had any information prior to the Abbottabad raid about Osama bin Laden's presence in Pakistan, he strongly denied having any such information and told the audience that he was personally shocked when he learnt of it.

Pressed on how it was possible for bin Laden to be living in a sensitive area in Abbottabad, next to the PMA, without the complicity or knowledge of Pakistan's intelligence agencies, General Musharraf responded by highlighting the unsuitability of a place like Abbottabad for such an operation. The city had a population of six hundred thousand, a multi-ethnic mix of civilian and military people, making it unsafe for such an operation. To attempt it there, he argued, would be irrational.

To substantiate his assertions and negate the allegations about the planned involvement of ISI in this fiasco, General Pervez Musharraf had asked certain counter questions to the panel as to how the 9/11 attack occurred. How was it possible that eighteen foreign nationals were being trained for months to take off but not land airplanes and one of the world's most powerful intelligence agencies had no clue about it? How was it possible that four aircraft from different airlines were hijacked from four different airfields and no one knew of the plan? How was it possible that these aircraft could fly to the World Trade

Centre and the Pentagon, and the American authorities did not know where they were going? The Americans missed the case of 9/11 and the ISI missed the case of Osama bin Laden being inside Pakistan. It was an intelligence failure.

Indo-Afghan-US Nexus

Pakistan's biggest military threat has always been India. Mistrust, hatred, and animosity, coupled with India's rising stature under US sponsorship, and its emerging global influence have hardened its stance on Kashmir and other issues involving Pakistan. India's occasional overtures toward developing a working relationship with Pakistan have always been a gimmick to calm separatist tendencies within India and soften its image in the US and other Western countries while it continues unabated to promote sub-nationalism and proxy wars in Baluchistan, FATA and the Northern Areas (Gilgit-Baltistan).

Why India continues to be a permanent threat to Pakistan remains a major unanswered question. Perhaps, its anti-Pakistan stance is built into the Indian psyche or perhaps it is motivated to further a political agenda of the religious hardliners who dominate India's political elite. I often ask these questions, to many of my well-educated and mature Indian friends and acquaintances, and I find them to be equally confused. Many of them think animosity is just politics that separates the leaders and the people of both countries. Many people openly criticize religious extremists within the Indian body politic for their hostile attitude that embarrasses India internationally. Otherwise, there seems to be no reason for India's hardline stands against Pakistan. Serious soul searching can be in the interest of both countries.

India Found a Space in Afghanistan

How the Indians benefitted from US sponsorship and how they used Afghanistan territory for their operations against Pakistan, especially in Baluchistan and FATA, is a very painful story. RAW's involvement in Baluchistan continued until the very end when they were forced to fly out of Afghanistan on Indian Air Force aircraft during the night after the US withdrawal and President Ashraf Ghani's narrow escape. Unfortunately, they have continued their heinous activities from Afghanistan, even after the US withdrawal, with a different modus operandi. They are likely to continue such operations for quite some time to come.

It is no secret that India's RAW has been operating against Pakistan from Afghan soil with complete impunity and the full support of Afghanistan's intelligence agency, the National Directorate of Security. Such operations from Afghanistan into Pakistan could not occur without US approval.

These operations have taken a massive number of innocent human lives and caused significant property damage. It is an inexcusable situation and a strategic blunder for which both the perpetrator and its supporters remain answerable.

As an example, the mastermind behind the terrorist attack on the Army Public School at Peshawar on 16 December 2014 was an Indian national, resident of Andhra Pradesh, India. He was housed in Kabul under the cover of being a software engineer and was operating from Nangarhar Province on the Afghan side of the Pak-Afghan border. He was being handled by the Indian consulate at Jalalabad.

He used Jamaat ul Ahrar (JuA), a splinter group of TTP to carry out the attack. The TTP is an alliance of militant Taliban networks formed to fight the Pakistani military. A member of the Afghan Parliament was intercepted using his mobile phone to guide the terrorists. The attack killed 120 schoolchildren and their teachers.

The same Indian national was also involved in terrorist strikes on the Warsak Colony in Peshawar on 2 September 2016 and on Lahore Mall Road on 13 February 2017. When Pakistan intelligence identified and was about to capture him, he was hurriedly taken out of Afghanistan.

Another RAW agent handler operated undercover as the President of a Consulting Services Group in Kabul. The position gave him the latitude to move freely in most parts of Afghanistan and the ability to direct terrorist attacks against Pakistan, particularly in Baluchistan. He also worked as a cut-out between RAW and Baluch militants and brought them into Afghanistan where they linked up with the TTP. Reportedly, he was also linked directly with India's national security adviser at that time.

This RAW operative also masterminded the bombing attack in Mastung Baluchistan in July 2018, in which Siraj Raisani, a prominent Baluch patriot and tribal leader, and more than 150 other innocent people lost their lives. Pakistan tried to have both the RAW's handlers put on the list of global terrorists but was prevented from doing so by the powers that be.

Pakistan intelligence continued to work against these RAW's networks, and by the end of 2019, the noose around their necks was tightening. It was then that RAW repatriated quickly most of them back to India. The Afghan government helped them with their narrow escape.

The last nail in the coffin proving RAW's involvement in terrorist operations against Pakistan was ISI's capture of Kulbhushan Jadhav. He was an Indian naval officer working undercover with RAW on its operations in Baluchistan. ISI was able to develop solid evidence of his operations, supported by cell phone data and voice recordings. His case has been internationalized to the extent that it has been debated openly in the International Court of Justice, highlighting the details of his operations inside Pakistan. Unfortunately, most of the world continues to ignore the reality of RAW's fuelling of terrorism inside Pakistan.

The US adopted a policy of supporting India as the sole security provider for the region, despite India's hesitancy to provide any practical support to allied operations in Afghanistan. At the same time, India's intelligence agency RAW acted as a peace spoiler in Afghanistan and freely used Afghan soil as a marshalling area for its terrorist activities inside Pakistan.

The question that must be addressed is how did the Indians manage to gain so much influence in US policymaking circles and in other allied countries in the West? I asked a senior US security professional why the US believes that India is the right choice to bet on as the sole security provider in the region. He just smiled and expressed his disgust at the choice. I sincerely feel that perhaps there is a communication gap between the highest US decision-makers and their commanders in the field. If so, it has cost them a lot in the region. It is hard to imagine that most of the US decisions in the region overlooked the realities on the ground.

I believe that US leaders were aware of India's contradictory and duplicitous policy positions in Afghanistan and the region, but perhaps accepted them as part of the planning for their global strategies during years ahead. For example, President Donald Trump openly scorned the Indian Prime Minister for refusing to provide support to US military operations in Afghanistan while showcasing libraries that India had built in that war-torn country. Indian government took advantage of the situation and dexterously infused compelling influence on the US and other Western allies, through a well-placed network of agents of influence in all areas of its interest.

Indian Chronicles – A Report by EU Disinfo Lab

According to the reports, Indian intelligence has been targeting the European Union and the United Nations with agents of influence and dissemination of orchestrated disinformation under a well-thought-out strategy to mislead their policies in our region. The modus operandi used makes for an intriguing story.

The Indian national security establishment has worked hard to maintain India's relevance and influence in Afghanistan and the region by influencing US policy away from a smooth, peaceful resolution of the Afghan crisis and in favour of continuing the war. Their agents of influence penetrated various levels of decision-making in the US and in other important countries to influence their policies as per the Indian agenda. Their effectiveness has been astonishing, embarrassing, and caused much damage to the perceived global agendas of these countries.

DIRECTION AND INTENSITY OF THE CROSSFIRE

The most shocking case of India's operations to influence global policymaking was unearthed recently by the EU Disinformation Laboratory based in Brussels. In a section of its 2019-2020 annual report entitled "Indian Chronicles", the laboratory claims to have uncovered a vast information network linked to Indian intelligence agencies operating in all important countries in Europe and the US. The network includes the UN Human Rights Council, accredited NGOs, think tanks, and media outlets operating in over 119 countries. The network aims to promote India's global interests using disinformation, fake identities, forged news, and targeted stories.

In April 2020, the Canadian Security and Intelligence Service reportedly busted an Indian undercover network run jointly by RAW and the Indian Intelligence Bureau that had existed since 2009. Canada's political leadership had been manipulated by Indian agents of influence using money and disinformation to support the Indian government's interests at Canada's expense. Germany busted a similar network in 2020. In that case, several undercover RAW agents were apprehended, convicted by the German courts, and sentenced to various terms of imprisonment.

According to reports at the time, the son of an important Indian cabinet member was heading the Washington, D.C. office of a research foundation, operating as a non-government think tank. This think tank was not registered with the US government as required by US laws and was actively lobbying US policymakers to promote Indian national interests. Similarly, an ex-Pakistan Ambassador to the US who had left Pakistan while under investigation for allegedly anti-Pakistan activities, has been the director of a research foundation in Washington, United States. He also was not registered as a lobbyist with the US government but was lobbying for India's national security interests. He is the same person who worked as the middleman between the perpetrators within the country and from outside, to orchestrate the removal of General Pervez Musharraf from the presidency in 2008.

These lobbying efforts by key voices for India in Washington D.C. influenced the US government's policymakers in their pursuit of US regional and global agendas. As a result, besides winning full support from the US administration and other major countries in the West for its international pursuits, India gained access to Afghanistan, with which it shares no history, borders, culture, or economic ties. It was all done with a single goal: destabilize Pakistan with terrorism and create massive infighting, using Afghan soil as the base for operations inside Baluchistan and Khyber Pakhtunkhwa (KPK), one of four provinces in north-western Pakistan. The US provided India with access to Afghanistan, and the Afghan puppet government became the facilitator for Indian operations into Pakistan from Afghan soil.

RAW has been directly involved in most of these operations, although in some cases, it facilitated terrorist attacks carried out by other militant or terrorist organizations. Most of these operations were carried out by underground militant organizations in Baluchistan and FATA and were aimed at government institutions, pro-Pakistan political personalities and military installations. To augment their attacks, RAW sought support from the Pakistani media, some political parties, religious groups and lawyers' communities.

The Indians were facilitated to establish a series of consulates along the Pak-Iran and Pak-Afghan borders at places where the consulate staff outnumbered Indian families living in the areas. At some locations, a hundred per cent of the consulate staff were RAW operatives. This encirclement by Indian intelligence bases, fully supported by the Afghan and US governments, made our jobs much more challenging.

Among India's top priorities has been to create unrest in Baluchistan by promoting the idea of a Greater Baluchistan. It fomented anti-Pakistan feelings in the province of Khyber Pakhtunkhwa (KPK) and instigated demands among anti-Pakistan elements in Afghanistan to establish Pakhtunistan, a new country made up mostly of Pakistani territories. India's aspirations to override its neighbours' interests and dominate the region, Iran's changing position on regional issues, and turmoil in the Arab world are major circumstances that directly affected Pakistan's national security.

The U.S. and its other Western allies mostly remained indifferent towards India's blatant interference inside Pakistan and in some cases, wittingly or unwittingly, provided it with indirect support to operate freely inside Pakistan to destabilise us in one way or the other. Additionally, the U.S. and its allies kept hammering us down with the demands to keep following their policies irrespective of their fallouts on our national interests.

How the world was made to lend deaf ears to all Indian conspiracies and malicious tactical and strategic manoeuvrings against its neighbours and believe in the cover stories hatched to earn support for its illegitimate ambitions, is another intriguing facet of the conspiracies unearthed by EU Disinfo Lab. It will be an interesting research work for those who wish to dig out the modus operandi used by Indian Intelligence to generate and disseminate organised disinformation campaign in all areas of its interest and use it as a strategic weapon.

Orchestrating Disinformation as a Strategic Weapon

It has recently been reported that the Indian government has also built a massive Disinfo lab, with a huge network of its agents spreading orchestrated

My Childhood and the Educational Institutions that I Attended

Semi concrete house where I spent my childhood.

The house under heavy snow.

Left: Sardar Muhammad Ashraf Khan, My father.

Below: Sahib Jaan, My mother

With my siblings and mother.

Above left: In my Landa Coat that changed the world for me

Above right: All set for the new journey.

Eleventh Entry, Cadet College Hasan Abdal, 1964.

Class 10 Cadet College Hassan Abdal, 1967.

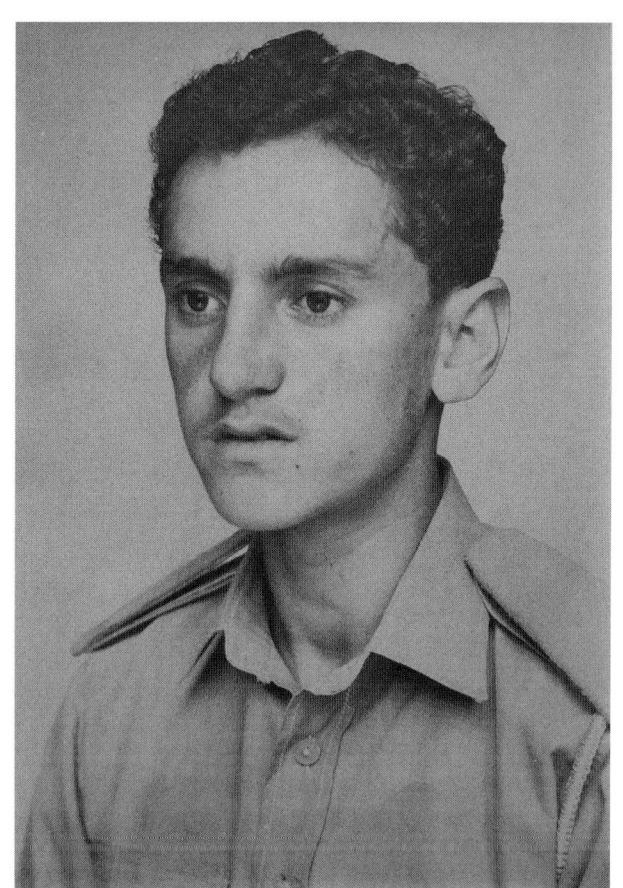

Right: As a Prefect at Cadet College Hassan Abdal, 1967.

Below: Class 12 Cadet College Hasan Abdal, 1969.

Above: College Football Team, 1968 to 69.

Below: The Athletics Team, 1968 to 69.

Right: In my college blazer with colour badges.

Below: The Leading Sportsmen with Lt. Col (Retd) J.D Chapman.

Above left: The Athletics Championship, 1969.

Above right: With college friends.

Below: An outing with college friends.

IN THE KHAKIS (NOVEMBER 1969 TO JULY 2010)

Training at Pakistan Military Academy

As a Gentleman Cadet, 1969.

Sports Sergeant Sala ud din Company 1971.

Above: With my Platoon mate, GC Khalid during EX Initiative.

Right: With a close friend Ijaz Gillani.

Above: With a group of Abdalians then PMA Cadets with Major Nadir Pervez, SJ (Bar).

Below: Reunion of 45th PMA Long Course, 2006.

Amongst the Dashers (16 SP Regiment, Artillery)

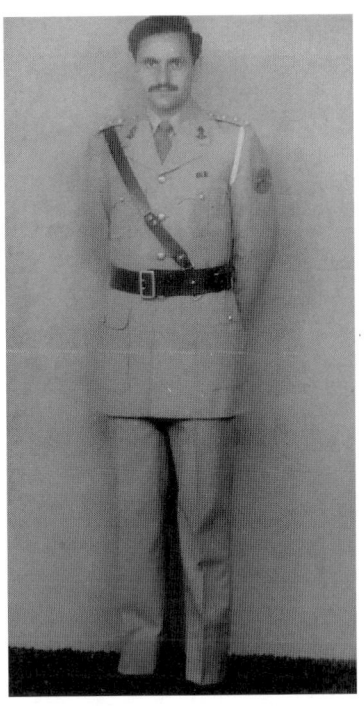

Right: As Adjutant The Dashing 16.

Below: With my team at the OP (Observation Post).

Receiving the degree from Late Gen Musa at Command and Staff College Quetta.

At the Regimental Quarter Guard.

With Lt. Col Muhammed Afzal as 2 IC in the Field.

Commanding the Dashers in the Field.

My Official Residence as Commander, The Dashing Sixteen (1989).

Installation Ceremony of the First Col of the Regiment.

Gen Pervez Musharraf being Installed as Col of the Regiment.

Some memories of my sports diplomacy in Dubai

Nasim, Imran shuttle to title

By Our Sports Reporter

NASIM Khan and Imran Shah won the Pakistan Day Golden Jubilee doubles badminton title with a 21-13 victory over Hamid Khan and Waheed Hamid at the Pakistan Sports and Recreation Club, Dubai on Saturday.

The champions had to work hard in the early parts of the match before wearing down Hamid and Waheed.

In the earlier games, Nasim and Imran defeated Shakil Qaiser and Iqbal wan and, Hameed and Shahab by identical scores of 15-10. The runners-up defeated Altaf and Baber 15-6 to nip into the final.

Waheed, however had some consolation when he won the one-set singles 15-7 against Asim Nasim in the enter the final.

heed downed Amir 15-10 to Pakistan Consul-General Sajjad

• Pakistan Consul-General Sajjad Ashraf presenting the winners trophy to Nasim and Imran.

Ashraf distributed the prizes in the Pakistan Consulate organised tourney.

Finally, some time out to pose with my wife in army uniform

Glimpses of my Post Retirement Ventures

Above left: Soldier turned Entrepreneur.

Above right: Security Managers LLC on its way.

Inaugrating Security Managers Professional Management Trainining Institute (SMPTI).

Gen Musharraf - our first guest speaker.

Dr. Zhiqiang Wu an honourable speaker from China

Des Myers, our cosultant from Australia.

Manuel di Casoli, our cosultant from Italy.

Roberto Zeoli, a cosultant from Italy.

Welcome address to a symposium.

At a training event.

My self, as a Trainer.

Conducting a Training

With training participants.

Group photo (Road Safety Training).

Above: At Intersec, Dubai

Left: As part of International Police Best Practices Symposium

Above: Our team with Director Dubai Police Academy

Below: Introducing the company at an event.

Above: Director Dubai Police Academy at our company event.

Below: Attending an event held at First Security Group, Dubai.

MY MENTORS

The People Who Shaped My Life

My Father.

My Mother.

Above left: Choudhary Khuda Buksh My Father in Law.

Above right: Saeeda Begum My Mother in Law.

Below: Anwar Khan, My Brother.

My Maternal Grandfather – Sardar Sajawal Khan.

PRINCIPAL
A.W.E. WINLAW T.Pk. T.D, M.A.
1959 - 1964

Principal Cadet College Hasan Abdal (1964).

Sitting (from left to right) : Mr. Iftikhar Ahmad Chaudhry - Mr. Sajjad Baloch - Mr. Azhar Ali Jafari - Mr. Qadir Baig - Syed Dilshad Hussain shah - Syed Muhammad Ali Bukhari Maj. Gen. Islam H. Naqvi - Mr. Mehboob ur Rehman - Mr. Moeen ud Din Qureshi

Standing (from Left to right) : Mr. Abdul Qayyum - Brig Hassan Shah - Mr. Misbah ul Hasnain - Mr. Ahmed Hasnain-Prof. Mohammad Asif Malik - Mr. S.M. Zaki - Mr.Talat Tariq Mehmood Mr. Mohammad Yaqoob Abid Chaudhry - Mr. Shahid Shamsi - Mr. Khalid Mehmood - Mr. Faqir Mohammad Chaudhry - Mr. Mehmood Ahmad Mr. Mohammad Anwar Farooqi - Mr. Mohammad Sarwar Shafqat

A recent picture of some of the Faculty Members - Cadet College Hasan Abdal (1964).

General Akhtar Abdul Rehman, Chairman Joint Chiefs of Staff Committee, Pakistan Armed Forces and Ex DG ISI.

General Pervez Musharraf, Ex President, and Chief of Army Staff.

Remembering General Pervez Musharraf

Left: With Mrs and General Musharraf during later years.

Below: At his residence.

At wedding of my son.

At a special event of my company in Dubai.

Presenting him my company shield.

With my family.

disinformation within the country and abroad. The Disinfo Lab has been established in a remote area in New Delhi since mid-2020 and operates under the supervision of career intelligence officers from RAW. Its team leader and his deputies intermingle with social media activists, Western journalists, and commentators under fake identities to perform their responsibilities. Its agents attack their target audience on social media platforms like YouTube, X (Twitter) and Facebook, under the Indian government sponsorship. To suppress the negative news within the country, the propaganda campaign is strictly channelled through internet shutdowns in the targeted areas/states as and when required. Indian province of Punjab and IHK are amongst the most affected areas for the purpose.

Working along the lines of the Atlantic Council's Digital Forensic Research Lab and the EU Disinfo Lab, this Disinfo Lab is aimed at targeting influential organizations and individuals in Washington and other Western countries with planned disinformation, to gain their support. The organizations or the individuals who do not align with the Indian government policies are blackmailed through fabricated stories damaging their creditability. Augmented through pro-Indian influencers, these allegations are subsequently, exploited by Indian officials on television networks and other social media outlets and also formally presented to the US administration to seek its support. The disinformation is mostly spread through high-profile figures with a large following on social media platforms to gain global reach.

The functioning mechanism of this Disinfo Lab is an interesting case of how the country's intelligence agencies are being used for online propaganda campaigns waged by the Indian government to advance its political objectives, much beyond their traditional domestic realm. Shunning the unrest and separatist tendencies in the Indian part of the province of Punjab and covering up Indian atrocities in Indian Occupied Kashmir (IOK) have been among its major pursuits at national and international levels. When the Indian government was coming under intense international criticism for revoking the semi-autonomous status of the State of Jammu and Kashmir in August 2019, the organization remained very active in misguiding foreign correspondents in New Delhi and the international media abroad about India's true perspective. Similarly, how this organization used a carefully scripted narrative to justify an airstrike conducted against Pakistan in 2019, will be useful research work for many who want to know how this Disinfo Lab works to cover up the Indian government's illegitimate offensives in its neighbouring countries. Among the reports it has published so far, the organization has often portrayed India as under attack by collaborators funded by Pakistani intelligence and some other Muslim organizations.

Involvement in Transnational Organized Crime

The June 2023 murder of an alleged Sikh separatist leader in Canada exposed the Indian continuing hegemonic mindset of overriding the diplomatic norms by intruding in foreign countries to further its malicious designs or settle its domestic violence /separatist tendencies on foreign soil. The killing of this well-known Sikh leader Hardeep Singh Nijjar, the elected head of the Guru Nanak Gurudwara, a Sikh place of worship in Surrey, Vancouver, triggered serious diplomatic standoffs between Ottawa and New Delhi. India had officially categorized Mr Singh as a terrorist, attempting to create disharmony amongst different communities in India. RAW's undercover operatives are being blamed for his killing.

Reportedly, India's hard-headedness had been a point of discussion between US President Joe Biden and other leaders with the Indian Prime Minister at the G-20 Summit, held in India on 9 and 10 September 2023. Would there be any effect of these half-hearted sermons on Indian leadership, which has so far been blatantly overriding the international norms and operating in various foreign countries for their illegitimate ambitions? Independent minds have serious reservations. Many believe that powers who matter, have their own priorities and such actions are nothing more than an eyewash. The matter seems to have already met its dead end as the Canadian high-ups as well as the other world leaders have apparently put the issue in the background. This is how it goes, unfortunately.

As per various media reports, in another case, eight ex-Indian Navy officers were sentenced death penalty in Qatar on the charges of espionage. Qatari authorities are being quoted to have confirmed that these former Indian naval officers were spying on Qatar's secret submarine programme for Israel. They were all picked up by Qatar's intelligence agency, the State Security Bureau on 30 August 2022, and remained under detention for over a year before being awarded the death penalty. Some of these individuals had been high-profile Indian naval officers and some were also award winners.

These retired Indian naval officials were working undercover in Al-Dahra Global Technologies and Consultancy Services, a private firm that provided training and various other related services to Qatar's armed forces and security agencies. The officer working undercover as a managing director of the company, had commanded several Indian Naval warships and was also the recipient of the Pravasi Bharatiya Samman award.

All these ex-Indian naval officers working together as a team in Qatar and working for an intelligence agency from a third country raises many eyebrows. Can it be an individual act by a few ex-colleagues from the Indian Navy? Definitely not.

There can hardly be any doubt that it was another RAW's third-country operations, in league with its allied foreign intelligence agency. RAW mostly uses Indian naval personnel for their operations in the Gulf and Middle East. Kulbhushan Jadhav, a serving Indian naval officer arrested by the Pakistani security forces a few years back, had also been working on behalf of RAW, for its subversive and sabotage activities in Karachi and Baluchistan province of Pakistan.

It is high time that the US government and other Western countries understand the true motives behind the Indian malicious game plan that has cost them so much internationally and is likely to adversely affect their interests in our region in future conflicts, as well.

A Feeling of Betrayal Emerges in Pakistan

This was all happening to Pakistan despite the fact the Pakistan Army and ISI played a pivotal role in defeating Russian forces in Afghanistan while the CIA, British MI-6, and other NATO member intelligence agencies were mostly in supporting roles. It would not be wrong to say that Russia's defeat in Afghanistan was mainly due to ISI's meticulously planned operations and its skilful handling of all Afghan factions to maintain a common effort against the fast-advancing Russians. Then, ISI successfully provided strategic support and intelligence to the Taliban against the Northern Alliance and the Taliban prevailed during the Afghan Civil War. Having been personally involved in the Afghan War as a field intelligence operative for decades, to me personally, it seems quite evident that Pakistan was betrayed by its most important allies in the fight. In the end, they not only abandoned Pakistan but also turned their guns on us when they thought it convenient to do so.

Despite all the backstabbing, Pakistan remained the strongest front-line Non-NATO Ally of the US-led occupation forces in Afghanistan following 9/11. We allowed US supplies to flow through our ports, over our roads, and through our airspace to support US and NATO forces in Afghanistan, even though it created deep divisions among our people and destroyed the country's infrastructure.

There are indeed no permanent friends or foes at the strategic level. Instead, it is more of a marriage of convenience. If the interests between the states coincide, their collaboration looks solid and deep, but the moment the priorities of the countries change, so do their partnerships. However, if the change of heart immediately follows a hard-earned victory that was won mainly at the cost of our interests, it pinches more. "It's not the stab in the back that kills you. It's when you turn around and see who's holding the knife." That was our experience in Afghanistan War.

Powerful states understandably have separate, comprehensive long-term strategies prepared for each region and state in the world. They execute their strategies in a time frame and in tune with changing security environments. Sometimes this requires changes to be made at the tactical level to meet different contingencies. Unfortunately, Pakistan has been the victim of this phenomenon, too frequently. Other countries often try to use it as an instrument to support their own international strategic and tactical interests, while ignoring Pakistan's national interests.

In this case, the situation went to the extreme. Our sympathies for the US following the 9/11 attack were exploited, our national interests were damaged, and our adversaries were fully supported in their efforts to take advantage of the situation. India's ingress into Afghanistan was facilitated with multiple objectives.

India was promoted as a regional power to counter China's increasing hegemony. At the same time, it engaged in subversion and sabotage against Pakistan from bases in Afghanistan. India's intent was to weaken Pakistan as a potential nuclear Muslim state, and its close collaboration with the Afghan government made the situation dangerous. Resultantly, transnational terrorism will remain a major security challenge for Pakistan for years.

At home, a significant number of people believe that our involvement in Afghanistan was unwarranted. They term it as fighting the "other's war". But what they fail to realize is that Afghanistan's geo-strategic location vis-à-vis Pakistan and its connection with the US leave us with no options but to continuously keep ourselves relevant and involved in that country. We must remain in a position to influence events in Afghanistan that have a direct bearing on our national security. We must not forget that Afghanistan is our neighbour; we share porous borders; religious, ethnic, and tribal affinities; as well as family linkages. We have many Afghan refugees who fled to Pakistan during the Soviet-Afghan War and settled in our country. Our goal as a country must be to adjust our security strategies as necessary to protect our national interests while avoiding, as much as possible, involvement in Afghanistan's domestic politics.

In summary, Pakistan has made countless sacrifices because of the war in Afghanistan. Its armed forces and its affiliated intelligence agencies have defended Pakistan's national security interests through forty-two years of conflict, and continue to contend with its unending fallout while combating other enemies, internal and external, old, and new. Our adversaries remained critical to Pakistan's transformation into a steady, brave, and confident self-governing sovereign state. The end result is a testament to the hard work and success of many good people who worked for Pakistan through their blood and sweat.

A Retrospective View of the Pakistan-US Relationship

It is worth looking back at the Pakistan-US relationship from a historical perspective. The US was one of the first nations to recognize Pakistan and establish diplomatic relations with it in 1947. The relations between the two countries remained very cordial and friendly for nearly a decade or so. Those who are well versed in the history would remember how grand receptions were always showered on the President of Pakistan General Ayub Khan in Washington and London during his visits to these countries. However, since then, relations between the two countries have been a 'Roller Coaster' ride, with peaks of working together as dependable allies and valleys marked by bilateral estrangements. The relations cooled after India's defeat in the 1962 Sino-India war. The US shipped arms to India without notifying Pakistan and ignored the government's concern that the arms could be used against Pakistan. A few years later in 1965, the US refused to provide military support to Pakistan in its war with India, despite having signed a treaty with Pakistan to do so. This history repeated itself in 1971 when Pakistan again went to war with India and the guaranteed support by the US did not show up until the war was nearly over. The Central Treaty Organization (CENTO) and the Southeast Asia Treaty Organization (SEATO) proved to be paper tigers, useless in times of crisis.

Pakistan received thirty billion US dollars in aid from the US between 1948 and 2017. Half of the money was to be used to provide goods, services, and equipment for the Pakistan military. However, the money was limited to purchasing American products only, and Washington imposed sanctions repeatedly on Pakistan to determine how it would be used. Sanctions were imposed to prevent Pakistan from doing what it thought was needed to protect its people and lifted when Pakistan's actions were seen to further US interests. For example, US sanctions were lifted in 1994 to permit Pakistan to participate in military operations in Somalia and Bosnia but reimposed in 1998 after those operations were completed. The sanctions were lifted again when the US became involved in Afghanistan in 2001 and needed Pakistan's help and reimposed again in 2018 when military assistance was suspended, and civilian aid cut in half.

Relations were at their best during the period 1979-1989 when both countries were fighting Russian forces in Afghanistan. The tide turned; however, the moment Russian forces ended their Afghan War and withdrew from the country. The US began immediately to distance itself from Pakistan.

The US-Pakistan relationship during the war in Afghanistan highlights the difficulties of making foreign policy and exercising diplomacy in a multipolar world. Pakistan is a key player on the subcontinent and an important influencer on US relations with China, Russia, and even India. However, there is significant distrust between the two countries that hinders their successful cooperation against common threats. For the rift to heal, the US must listen and understand the threats Pakistan faces and work with it with an open mind and clear strategic thinking.

Withdrawal of Allied Forces from Afghanistan

The fiasco of the US withdrawal from Afghanistan is being seriously questioned. Was it a massive policy failure, a massive intelligence failure, or both? The fact remains that the withdrawal of the US and its allies from Afghanistan has produced major consequences that have yet to be fully understood. Yet, two things are clear. First, the abrupt withdrawal of allied forces coupled with the Taliban's victory has changed perceptions of security in the region. Second, the allied withdrawal shattered the existing world order, and dealing with its aftermath in our region will be very challenging.

The US war in Afghanistan was, more or less, a replay of the First Anglo-Afghan War of 1842. That war was perhaps the West's most significant military embarrassment in the East. The British Army, then the most powerful military establishment in the world, was utterly defeated by poorly equipped Afghan tribesmen. On Britain's departure from Afghanistan, military chaplain George H. Gleig wrote in his memoir in 1843, shortly after his return from the battlefield of the First Anglo-Afghan war, "A war begun for no wise purpose, carried on with a strange mixture of rashness and timidity, brought to close after sufferings and disaster, without much glory attached either to the government which directed it, or the great body of troops which waged it. No benefit, political or military, has been acquired with this war. Our eventual evacuation of the country resembled the retreat of an army defeated."

Fought about 170 years later, under the guise of a different philosophy, the US experience in Afghanistan replicated the British experience in almost every way. The same tribal affiliations the British used were again exploited but with new ideologies, and political and military theories. The result was virtually the same. The puppet ruler the British tried to install in 1839, Shah Shuja-ul-Mulk, was from the Popalzai sub-tribe, the same tribe as Hamid Karzai. Popalzai's opponents were the Ghilzai, who comprised the bulk of the Taliban's foot soldiers in this war. Mohammad Shah Khan was the Ghilzai leader who led the slaughter of the British Army in 1841. Mullah Omer was also a Ghilzai.

What brought the US Afghanistan campaign to its abrupt and disastrous end was that America did not foresee a peaceful solution, India overestimated its covert operations capabilities, and NATO forces fighting in Afghanistan thought the mujahideen were like the TTP. Afghanistan did not fall to mujahideen by chance. It was the result of the mujahideen's meticulously planned infiltration of various levels of the Afghan government and a well-thought-out effort to expand its political influence in multiple segments of Afghan society. In the end, the mujahideen were better at guerrilla war.

The Taliban managed to infiltrate the Afghan army from top to bottom, enabling the mujahideen in the end to take over the country without much resistance. Unit by unit, the Afghan army started to surrender, and then it started to snowball. Within nineteen days, the army had surrendered almost totally. Key to its collapse was the number of high-ranking Afghan army officers who abandoned their posts. They melted away in the wind as the Taliban took city after city and finally took Kabul. It should be noted that most of the Afghan army's officers were trained at the Indian Military Academy.

Credit goes to the Taliban for widening their political base during twenty years of war. In 2001, the Taliban was overwhelmingly Pushtun, and their politics were mainly Pushtun-centred. By 2021, Taliban fighters were prevalent in Uzbek and Tajik-dominated areas. Many ethnicities were united in a common war against the foreign invader. The war ended quickly because the Taliban were present as a political force in towns and villages throughout the country and were able to take control of these areas without wasting time or military forces. The fact that people chose the Taliban during the war's chaotic ending does not necessarily mean that most Afghans support them. It only means that given the limited choices available, they were probably the best choice because they were the only potent political organization fighting against foreign occupation.

Indo-Pakistan Relations

An Overview

India and Pakistan have had a complex and largely hostile relationship since they parted ways in 1947. The bad relations are rooted in a multitude of historical and political events. The two countries have fought two major wars and there have been multiple skirmishes along the border. The status of Kashmir continues to cause major problems for both countries.

India's instigation of insurgencies and terrorist attacks inside Pakistan in areas such as Baluchistan and the Frontier Provinces is a major source of tension. The operations originate in Afghanistan. They are launched by third-party nationalist groups with India's approval and support at targets inside Pakistan. The modus operandi for these murderous operations takes many forms and they continue to plague Pakistan till today.

Pakistan's Peace Overtures

While standing firmly with the allied forces in the war on terror, Pakistan has continuously been trying to negotiate solutions to its problems with India. In July 2001, General Musharraf reached out directly to Indian Prime Minister Mr Atal Bihari Vajpayee and arranged for a one-on-one meeting. They agreed to work together to develop a working relationship between the two countries. Both sides condemned terrorism, recognized Kashmir as the major dispute between the two countries and resolved to take concrete steps toward its resolution. General Musharraf followed up with a bold step at the SAARC summit held in Nepal in January 2002. After his speech, he went to the Indian prime minister and extended his hand in friendship. The gesture was an open invitation for a serious dialogue to eliminate the impasse that exists between the two countries.

General Pervez continued his interactions with the new Indian prime minister, Manmohan Singh, who followed Mr Vajpayee in office. He made significant progress in his dialogue with India's state machinery. During a one-day visit to India on the pretext of watching a cricket match between the two countries, he met the new Prime Minister and held fruitful discussions with him. They agreed to resolve the Kashmir issue through an 'outside-the-box' solution. Each country would accept the LOC as the permanent international border. They also agreed to identify geographic regions that still needed resolution, demilitarize these areas, take no aggressive action against the other, introduce self-governance in disputed areas and set up a joint management committee with membership consisting of Pakistanis, Indians, and Kashmiris. Both Prime Minister Vajpayee and Prime Minister Singh were very positive towards the negotiations, but unfortunately, the agreement was sabotaged by the Indian bureaucracy before a joint declaration could be made.

The Kargil Operation and its Follow-up

The Indian lobby exploited the Kargil Conflict in Kashmir (May – June 1999) to create distrust between the two sides. The 1999 Kargil incident has been portrayed as the Kargil War, but it was not a major attack on Indian outposts but rather one in a series of small tactical moves and countermoves that both sides were conducting to consolidate their lines of defence along the LOC. At Kargil, the Kashmiri Mujahedeen, with the support of some elements of Pakistan's Northern Light Infantry, occupied a gap in the Indian Army's defensive line. The gap was created when Indian troops left the area due to cold weather and winter snow. It was a replay of what the Indians had done at Siachen where they took advantage of a gap in the Pakistani line to occupy strategically important heights in that area. It must be noted that most of the heights in the Kargil sector captured by Kashmiri mujahedeen, were initially part of Azad Kashmir but had been taken under the Indian Army's control, as had happened in Siachen Glacier.

The Kargil's effort was an attempt to deny the Indians any advantage and to discourage them from launching another misadventure in the area. It caught them completely by surprise. Kashmiri freedom fighters captured about eighty square miles without firing a shot. The result completely unbalanced the Indian Army because it threatened India's line of communication with the Ladakh/ Siachen Glacier in the north. Indian troops made desperate attempts to recapture the area but with only limited success. The loss caused India to move its strategic reserves, leaving them without the capability to attack anywhere else on the Indo-Pak border.

The Indians mobilized an international campaign to create pressure on our civilian leadership. Although our political leadership had been briefed in detail prior to the operation and was totally on board with it, they refused to acknowledge responsibility in the face of international pressure. The hard-won victory at Kargil was given back to the Indians on a silver plate through a US-sponsored ceasefire in July 1999. This is how it goes in Pakistan, unfortunately. Dragging the army into controversies for personal and political gains, even at the cost of critical national interests, has been a long-standing curse in our political culture.

The Indian bureaucracy, faced with a possible agreement between Prime Minister Singh and General Musharraf launched a successful propaganda blitz to discredit the agreement by linking it to the Kargil incident and the damage it caused to India's position in Kashmir.

An obstacle to lowering the tensions between India and Pakistan is India's habit of falsely claiming that Pakistan is about to attack it. The Indians have been doing it for years, and it usually occurs just before a critical military or political event to generate public support for the Indian government.

On 27 February 2019, the Indian Air Force bombed some barren hills in Kashmir near the LOC in the Balakot area of Khyber Pakhtunkhwa Province, in Pakistan. India claimed it was a pre-emptive strike and said that it destroyed a base camp of Jaish-e-Mohammad, a militant Kashmiri mujahideen organization that was responsible for a suicide bombing on the Jammu-Srinagar National Highway in Pulwama District of Jammu & Kashmir on 14 February 2019. The bombing had caused many casualties among members of India's Central Reserve Police Force. Pakistan had condemned the attack and denied any connection to it. Still, India used the attack as a pretext to bomb uninhabited areas near the LOC. Satellite imageries of the attack site revealed no camp in the area, and there were no causalities from the airstrikes.

The day after the bombing in Khyber Province, two attacking Indian Air Force aircraft were shot down by Pakistan's Air Force. Indian Wing Commander Abhinandan Varthanan was piloting one of these two aircraft, a MiG-19 when he was shot down by the Pakistan Air Force and captured. He was released the next day and promptly thanked the Pakistan Army for a "Fantastic cup of tea" before returning to India. His message went viral on social media.

The publicity of this incident reminded me of the time when my ISI field operatives had arrested the RAW Station Chief based in Islamabad while he was meeting and exchanging information about operations in Baluchistan with a Baluch militant. I was a brigadier, heading ISI's counterintelligence section at the time. The RAW Station Chief based in Islamabad was my guest for a few hours in a safe house in Islamabad and he too praised the "fantastic cups of coffee" I had offered him while we talked about his RAW intelligence work.

India's government planned the Balakot bombing to bolster its image with the Indian public before the general election held in April 2019. It had staged a similar drama in the Uri sector on the LOC on 29 September 2016, just before the elections that year. This time Indian forces skirmished with Pakistani troops and claimed it to be a pre-emptive strike on training camps belonging to Kashmiri mujahideen in Azad Kashmir. Indian troops had never crossed the LOC and had been firing at Pakistani troops from their side of the line.

Unrest in Indian Held Kashmir (IHK)

India's effort to blame Pakistan for the Kashmiri mujahedeen's struggle against them carries little weight with people who know and understand Kashmir. It is a place that straddles a disputed border between two countries, with Kashmiris living on both sides of the LOC. Families are separated by the LOC, but they have unbreakable links, and they keep themselves connected, directly and indirectly. They are fighting to stay together.

On the other hand, India has been encouraging and supporting militant Baluchis who are involved in terrorist activities aimed at creating anti-Pakistan feelings amongst them in pursuance of a larger game plan of creating a state of Greater Baluchistan in the region. It has no moral links to the militants and its instigation of violence in Baluchistan cannot be justified by any standards.

Bombay Attacks 1993

The famous Bombay attacks in 1993 is another example of maligning Pakistan in terrorist attacks in India. The incident involved a series of bombings in Bombay, India, on 12 March 1993 that caused a massive loss of life. A Bombay-based international underworld group, known for extortion and gang wars, claimed responsibility. It launched the attacks as revenge for the 1992 riots in Mumbai during which a mob tore down Babri Masjid and turned it into a Hindu Temple.

The Indian police arrested many of the criminals. Some of them were convicted and executed on charges of killing innocent people during the attacks.

Yet, the Indian government blamed Pakistani intelligence for perpetrating the bombings. It claimed that the mastermind was operating from Pakistan, but there is no evidence linking the perpetrators of these attacks to any Pakistani intelligence agency. The mosque's destruction caused religious violence throughout India, and the Indian government sought to exploit the unrest to accuse Pakistan of terrorism and create international pressure against it.

Impact of US Strategies in the Region

Despite India's intrigue and malicious activities, Pakistan has continuously been trying to normalize relations with its neighbour. Unfortunately, India's hegemonic designs for the region have kept relations between the two countries in cold storage, and the situation seems likely to continue for years. US support of India's ambitions enables it to maintain the status quo.

Indian Prime Minister Narendra Modi's visit to the US in June 2023 is a case in point. It featured high-level bilateral talks with US President Joe Biden, an address to US Congress, and a grand state banquet at the White House. For people who understand the intricacies of Modi's dubious game plan in South Asia, the Biden administration's effort to boost its ties with India while soft-pedalling the differences between the two countries was interesting to watch. It was surprising to see the US shower Modi with extensive flattery, overlook the Indian government's crackdown on human rights, and ignore India's double game with Russia in Ukraine and its expansion of trade relations with Moscow. Modi's applauding democratic values during his visit is in sharp contrast with what his government is doing to undermine democratic principles in his own country by oppressing minorities and conducting a war of terror in Kashmir. India's export of terrorism inside Pakistan, which is an open secret in the international community, was completely ignored. Instead, contrary to good diplomacy, Pakistan was accused of promoting terrorism inside IHK during a formal joint press conference by Modi and Biden. The US president's praise for an Indian leader who has been widely accused of overseeing a series of repressive actions in his own country was a surprise for many people in Pakistan.

The arms deals between Modi and Biden aimed at weaning India off arms purchases from Russia stems from India's strategic importance to the US campaign to counter China, as well as American interest in limiting Russian influence among developing nations. The US ignored the democratic values for which it stands in favour of sponsoring India as the sole regional leader. Its abandonment of the interests of the other countries in the region is worrisome and creates serious apprehensions.

Changes in times, titles and political agendas in Washington are quite evident and have certainly raised alarm bells in Pakistan which needs to continuously monitor the situation to adjust its strategies in the region to safeguard its national security concerns.

Pak-China Nexus

The rise of China and its close association with Pakistan, with particular reference to the development of the China-Pakistan Economic Corridor (CPEC) and the Chinese One Belt One Road initiative, are significant developments that appear to threaten the existing world order, particularly with respect to the US and its Western allies. The abrupt withdrawal of allied forces from Afghanistan and the Taliban's subsequent victory is the region's most significant development with far-reaching consequences and suggestions of a new world order. Regional perceptions of security have changed. Pak-China collaboration has gained greater prominence and influence in the region's security considerations. The US withdrawal, Russia's resurgence, and its overtures towards China and Pakistan are causing severe turbulence and weakening existing security arrangements that have already begun to show visible cracks of varying magnitude. The world seems to be heading towards a new international security arrangement.

Considering the US's open tilt towards India, and its willingness to overlook the security concerns of other regional players, Pakistan is left with no option but to look for alternate solutions to safeguard its security interests. China has been Pakistan's most trusted ally since the end of the Cold War and the partnership between the two has deepened significantly over the past few years. Geopolitical shifts in South Asia, particularly the sharpening US-China competition, the swift decline in China-India relations and the withdrawal of US forces from Afghanistan in 2021, have greatly encouraged the Pak-China relationship. The West's blockade of arms sales to Pakistan, and its limited support in other public sectors while concurrently, supporting India with arms and other military hardware have left Pakistan with limited options. As a result, close military ties and the procurement of military hardware from China have grown considerably over the years.

From the reports published by various strategic institutes and think tanks in the West, it appears that the US government and its leading analysts are paying more attention to Pak-China military relations than is generally known. Some of these reports suggest that Pakistan is one of the few countries where China might locate additional military facilities to help its domination of the region and the world. The Port of Gwadar on Pakistan's western coast is mentioned as being more than what it actually is. There is also a question of how China might leverage its relationship with Pakistan for power projection in future and the prospect of China's air and naval bases on Pakistan's western coast. Besides assisting Pakistan advance its strategic capabilities, China may also be assisting Pakistan to develop and acquire hypersonic weapons. The narrative is probably based on what the US approach is in the Indo-Pacific; namely building partnerships, creating access, and putting in place logistical arrangements that can be operationalized in high-end contingencies.

Pakistan always preferred to maintain a balance between the US and Chinese influence, and this remains the key to the enhancements in Pak-China relationships. The US and Pakistan are natural allies. The US officials who worked with us over the years in Afghanistan know this is true. We fought together as loyal allies, and we were forthcoming even during the worst circumstances. What happened is a point to ponder.

If the US decides to maintain a balance in its relationships in our region as Pakistan wishes to maintain, it can win the larger strategic contest. Pakistan, however, has been stabbed in the back too many times to take any more risks. The US debacle in Afghanistan should be an eye-opener for many.

The Emerging Scenario

Afghanistan Situation

The outcome of the three-decades-long Afghan War has jolted the existing world order. US dominance of global affairs may not yet be over, but the tide is turning. A new global arrangement is around the corner. The US military setback is only part of the story. The disastrous outcome of its thirty-year-long campaign in Afghanistan has exposed the dangers of policies characterized by faulty decision-making, overconfidence, and fanaticism. Where it will all end has yet to be determined, but one thing is certain. The outcome of the Afghan campaign is a direct and existential threat to globalization and the present world order as perceived by currently powerful countries.

It is too soon to say much about the Taliban government. There are many ifs and buts about what it may do. Although its leaders and its rank and file have given conciliatory and encouraging signals, many analysts have expressed serious reservations about Afghanistan's future. Moreover, the presence of highly violent factions and splinter groups with uncompromising religious beliefs within the Taliban movement cannot be ignored.

Just as the Afghan Jihad of the 1980s encouraged similar movements in other parts of the world, this Taliban victory may trigger similar movements elsewhere. There will be resistance, pushback, and physical attacks against the new Afghanistan government. There will also be resistance and animosity toward it by other countries that feel threatened by its governance system. We must not forget, however, that the Afghan war of the 1980s, and their subsequent resistance against foreign occupation, are the only Muslim resistance movements that drove out foreign occupation forces and returned victorious from the battlefield in the past 200 years.

It looks like the baton has changed hands. Albeit unceremoniously and unbelievably, the US appears to have chosen an indirect approach to maintain its influence in Afghanistan. That will surely involve an attempt to drag Pakistan into this rot once again. Most of the people in Pakistan consider the prevailing political and economic crisis in the country as a foreign sponsored manoeuvring and part of the same conspiracy theory.

The approach the West will likely take is best described in a story that is said to be narrated by Winston Churchill:

'I took a taxi one day to the BBC office for an interview. When I arrived there, I asked the driver to wait for me for forty minutes until I got back, but the driver apologized and said, "*I can't, because I have to go home to listen to Winston Churchill's speech,*" I was amazed and delighted with the man's desire to listen to my speech! So, I took out ten pounds and gave it to the taxi driver without telling him who I was. When the driver collected the money, he said, "*I'll wait for hours until you come back, sir! And let Churchill go to hell!*"'

The former prime minister's story about how money corrupts people merits thoughtful soul-searching. Pakistan needs to remain aware of the hidden conspiracies. The list of betrayals masked by a cloak of friendship is unending. We have been stabbed in the back time and time again, and I am sure we are not ready to fall into yet another death trap that will expose us to a new 'war on terror'. That is something we cannot afford. Though the US no longer has troops in Afghanistan, its 'war on terror' is seemingly poised to continue.

The world is still in shock at the Americans' hasty withdrawal from Afghanistan, but it is also starting to recognize the crucial role that the Pakistan Army and ISI played during the Afghan fighting. The saner elements have begun to acknowledge the challenges Pakistan faced, particularly the deadly violence and terrorism in Baluchistan and Khyber Pakhtunkhwa (KPK) in northwest Pakistan, and the terrible sacrifices our country had to make to deal with these challenges.

Had there been a comprehensive US victory, India would have established a strong presence in Afghanistan for years to come. It would have been able to push against us from all sides by encouraging nationalist and secessionist forces in Baluchistan, Sindh, and northwest Pakistan. It would have undermined our national unity and cohesion and placed our nuclear assets under constant threat.

India could not do so because it failed to comprehend the real US intent, failed to understand the Taliban, and ignored the weaknesses of the corrupt Afghan government. The outcome of the Afghanistan war is a great setback for the Americans, but it is no less a disaster for the Indians.

What happened in Afghanistan is in the past. Our great concern now is what will happen in the future. Looking over the fence and waiting to see what happens is not an option for us. The fire that started in Afghanistan can jump across the border if we do not have well-thought-out preparations to contend with it. In fact, it has already started. We must take a fresh look at our strategies to counter new emerging threats to the country's peace and prosperity.

Indian Aggression

India's anti-Pakistan game plan is likely to continue unabated. It will continue to exert pressure on Pakistan directly and indirectly. Their terrorist and sabotage activities in Baluchistan and the Frontier Provinces will gain momentum. There will be efforts made to derail or at least retard the development of the CPEC. One scenario that we expect to see is India currying favour with anti-Pakistan factions of the Taliban.

Mounting International Pressure

To keep Pakistan aligned with international game plans, serious efforts will be made to destabilize it politically and economically. We also expect to see the IMF come down on us mercilessly, imposing sanctions on Pakistan through the international organizations it controls. In fact, they have already started tightening the noose around our economic vulnerabilities, while political turmoil in the country has reached its worst level, ever. Keeping it away from China and Russia will be the key factor in Pakistan's relations with the West.

Internal Destabilization

Within Pakistan, anti-state elements will become more active, foreign-sponsored terrorist attacks will pick up momentum, and corrupt elements within our social and political structure will increase their anti-army rhetoric to push state machinery toward managing the country in accordance with the plan of their foreign masters. Ethnicity and sectarianism will be exploited through their agents of influence. Hybrid warfare, a tailor-made mix of conventional and non-conventional war strategies, is likely to gain tremendous momentum throughout the country and across the region. Things have already started to unfold in that manner.

A New Regional Outlook

For some strategists, it is the start of the second Cold War. The Chinese are once again in league with the Russians and showing signs internationally of a resurgence. In a significant development, Russia is rebuilding its relations in the region, with developing nations including Pakistan. That will have profound consequences. The idea of converting Afghanistan into the 'Emirates of Afghanistan,' a confederation of varying entities within the country is another evolving idea with the potential for far-reaching consequences.

As matters stand, Pakistan must be prepared to follow a pragmatic policy that balances relations with major world powers, such as the US, China, and Russia. It will also have to contend with regional challenges, such as those that may arise from India, Iran and some other countries in the Gulf/Middle East.

The Enemies Within

Domestic security challenges remain a significant part of Pakistan's future. In most cases, our internal weaknesses supplement our external security threats. Political partisanship, corrupt leadership, weak governance, sectarian and ethnic divisions, provincialism and regionalism, anaemic government institutions, and a poor economy have been our traditional fault lines. In each instance, foreign players have been able to manipulate these vulnerabilities for their own benefit. A brief look at some of our vulnerabilities will help us to understand what is happening.

Shaky Governance and Non-Supportive Socio-Political Culture

Pakistan has been racked by turbulence mainly because of poor governance and a divisive political culture that enables the country's leaders to put in place plans and programmes that do not benefit the common good. Political parties lack internal democracy and rely on patron-client networks. The political elites have been captured and are controlled by feudalists and industrialists. Their politics revolve around inherited and family privileges.

Religious and Ethnic Exploitation

Religion, tribalism, and ethnicity are used to exploit people's emotions. Our education system has lost its meaning and relevance. Madrassas and other religious seminaries, mostly run by entities linked to foreign countries and foreign money, make our internal security problems worse. They allow so-called religious clerics to misinterpret Islam and exploit the unemployed and uneducated to their advantage. Many terrorist groups and organizations, both domestic and foreign, maintain links with most of our madrassas. Their financial support for these religious schools is a crime that unfortunately persists.

In one such case during the mid-1990s at a foreign airport, I personally witnessed the arrest of a so-called leading Pakistani religious scholar and a politician on money laundering charges involving five million dollars. He had illegally brought the money to Pakistan from a foreign country under the guise of funding his religious madrassas. We have had many other such characters who exploit religion and play with our national interests for personal gain. They threaten both our security and our religious values. Unfortunately, the country's existing multi-ethnic provincial structure creates a tug-of-war for personal and political power among various segments of our society.

Politicized Government Institutions and Un-professional Media Outlets

Most government institutions are politicized, corrupt, and divided. Unfortunately, so is our judicial system, falling short of the proclaimed norms of justice. Some of our irresponsible media outlets misuse treacherous and damaging information to influence our governance systems, derail our culture, and create faulty perceptions to suit their vested interests. They work in unison with each other for their mutual benefit, 'You scratch my back, and I'll scratch yours', and together they are injuring the national interest by spreading despair in society.

Civil-Military Relations—Intriguing Misconceptions

Civil-military relationships have been a persistent challenge in Pakistani politics. They have been successfully manipulated by our adversaries to discredit our armed forces through disinformation and false perception building. Most of these anti-army themes are foreign sponsored while many anti-state elements within the country help them ignite the false allegations against the army which is being considered as the centre of gravity of our national strength and cohesion.

The Pakistan Army is often blamed for derailing democratic governments. It is worth looking at some of Pakistan's history of governance since its independence.

Governor General Ghulam Muhammad's first coup in 1953 was called a 'Constitutional Coup.' In this coup, Ghulam Muhammad dismissed the government of Prime Minister Khawaja Nazimuddin, even though the Nazimuddin Government enjoyed the support of the Constitutional Assembly.

In October 1958, President Iskandar Mirza abolished the 1956 constitution, declared martial law, and appointed General Ayub Khan as chief martial law administrator. Subsequently, he announced a cabinet and named Ayub Khan prime minister. Three other lieutenant generals were given ministerial posts. Zulfikar Ali Bhutto was part of this cabinet. The army viewed these appointments as an attempt by Iskandar Mirza to neutralize Ayub Khan's authority as army chief. In relation to that, Iskandar Mirza was forced to quit, and General Ayub Khan came to power.

General Ayub Khan lifted martial law in 1962 and introduced the second constitution. The country progressed significantly under his rule, making visible economic progress. Unfortunately, the progress did not reach many people. Instead, it concentrated amongst '22 families', who became famous for having accumulated a major portion of the country's wealth. During Ayub Khan's presidential election in 1965, Zulfikar Ali Bhutto, as foreign minister, built a campaign for him, based primarily on resolving the issue of Kashmir. Major promises were made to liberate Kashmir, even if it had to be done by making war. Ayub Khan's election victory was negated by how the 1965 Pak-Indo War ended. Nothing much changed, except Ayub Khan's image and credibility as President were badly damaged.

Subsequent events suggest that Bhutto had anticipated the war's outcome and planned to benefit from its expected damage to Ayub Khan's reputation. The events followed that path. A strong wave of anti-Ayub Khan feelings erupted throughout the country. Bhutto abandoned him to join the opposition and in due course, formed his own political party, Pakistan People's Party. Confronted with rising opposition, Ayub Khan announced his retirement in March 1969, and the country descended into another period of martial law under Gen Yahya Khan.

Yahya Khan reorganized the country and reconstituted the original four provinces of West Pakistan, ending the country's One-Unit system. After the 1971 Pak-Indo War and the loss of Bangladesh, Yahya Khan resigned, and Bhutto assumed the presidency as Pakistan's first civilian chief martial law administrator.

At this point, Zulfiqar Ali Bhutto who had won a majority of seats in the national assembly in West Pakistan in the elections before the war with India that separated East Pakistan, began to amass political power into his own hands, and he continued to do so throughout his tenure in office. Amongst the first victims were the then Chief of the Army Staff Lieutenant General Gul Hassan and Chief of the Air Staff Air Marshal Rahim Khan. Both were prematurely retired from the service by Mr Bhutto for refusing to use military force against the protesting policemen, demanding pay rise in the province of Punjab. Lieutenant General Gul Hassan had taken over the command of the army on 20th December 1971, the same day Mr Bhutto took over the rein of power in the country and was prematurely retired from the service on 3rd March 1972.

The opposition, frustrated by his autocratic, dictatorial, and suppressive rule and his continuous quest for more power, organized large protest rallies that completely disrupted the country's administration. Notwithstanding the unrest, Bhutto ventured into his first election in 1977. Opposition political parties came together and agreed to create a joint opposition movement.

There was massive rigging of the election on Bhutto's behalf and the opposition responded with widespread protests and anti-government rallies. They completely paralyzed the Bhutto government, and the army was called upon to help restore order. The military tried to handle the situation within constitutional boundaries, but the situation grew worse. On one occasion, a massive opposition protest rally was blocking the roads in Lahore cantonment, and its civil authorities asked the army to disperse the crowds with armed force, if necessary. Using firearms for such purposes is very difficult, especially when dealing with political activities. The brigadier in charge of the military forces in Lahore refused to use armed force against civilian protesters and informed the local administration that he would not do so.

After Bhutto had imposed martial law in Sindh, Baluchistan, and the North-West Frontier Province (now KPK), in an effort that failed to end anti-government agitation, Gen Zia had to step in and remove Bhutto's government. The takeover occurred on 4 July 1977.

General Zia died in a mysterious air crash on 17 August 1988. Investigators found potassium, chlorine, antimony, phosphorus, and sodium traces at the crash site. Since these elements are not generally associated with aircraft operations, the inquiry concluded that internal sabotage of the plane caused the crash. It seemed likely that gases were used to disable the pilots. The mysterious presence of the chemicals was never explained, and the case was not pursued further. Unfortunately, this is how it goes sometimes. Pakistan has been the victim of this phenomenon quite often.

The army did not take over after General Zia's death. Instead, the Chairman of the Senate, Ghulam Ishaq Khan, became the acting president. Benazir Bhutto formed a coalition government in November 1988 in accordance with the constitution and continued the journey from where her father left off. She challenged the army and removed Lieutenant General Hameed Gul, then the head of ISI, and replaced him with retired Army General, Shams Ur Rahman Kalu.

The situation reached a point where government institutions were being undermined, and President Ishaq Khan had no option but to use his constitutional powers to sack Benazir Bhutto's government. Nawaz Sharif was elected prime minister. The change did not stop the tug of war for power between the new prime minister and President Khan. Eventually, the situation stabilized when the prime minister and the president, each unable to prevail over the other, both had to resign from office under a deal brokered by the then COAS General Abdul Waheed Kakar. An uneasy relationship between the new President and the new Prime Minister continued due to treasonously prepared plans to dominate the country's governance system resulting in another sacking of the government.

During the period from November 1988 to October 1999, no national or provincial assembly completed its term in office. There were four Prime Ministers and three Presidents. Tussles between the Presidents and Prime Ministers were constant, with the former using the office's constitutional powers to repeatedly sack the latter. Relations between the Prime Ministers and the Army Chiefs also remained strained most of the time.

During the government of Mr Nawaz Sharif the presidential powers under section 58, 2 B of Pakistan's Constitution that empowered the president to dissolve the government in adverse situations were defused. Efforts were also made to pass constitutional amendments that would have allowed the prime minister's complete monopoly over his party and the judiciary, thereby, allowing him a free run with no checks and balances. Somehow, that plan could not materialize.

Subsequently, the Prime Minister forced Army Chief General Jehangir Karamat to resign and replaced him with General Pervez Musharraf. General Jehangir Karamat, speaking at the Naval War College at Lahore, had suggested forming a potent National Security Council to brainstorm national security issues and recommend remedial strategies to the government in power. In his opinion, this would help to prevent the army from taking over the government even under the worst of conditions. The Prime Minister of that time considered the suggestion to be an intrusion into his domain and asked General Jehangir Karamat to either publicly retract from the suggestion or resign. Gen Jehangir Karamat opted to resign.

His resignation, however, was not taken well within the army and it adversely affected the civil-military relationship.

The Kargil Conflict in Kashmir in mid-1999 brought yet another testing time for the civilian government. Faced with US pressure, the Prime Minister completely distanced himself from the operation although he had been fully briefed about the operation prior to its launching and had personally approved the plan in a meeting between the Prime Minister, the army chief, and relevant commanders. The operation had forced the Indian Army to move its strategic reserves to control the damage, thereby, putting itself in a complete strategic imbalance along the Indo-Pak border. As a backlash, Pakistan came under tremendous pressure from the US government which had continuously, been sponsoring India as the sole manipulator of its policies in South East Asia. Unfortunately, the civilian government could not face the US pressure and completely disassociated itself from this operation and started criticizing the army's hard-won victory and downgrading the Pakistan Army's operational efforts during these clashes. The army, from top to bottom, felt let down and humiliated. Differences between the Prime Minister and the army's leadership increased. A plan was hatched to use General Pervez Musharraf as a scapegoat by removing him from the post of the army chief.

I was in ISI at that time and was in charge of the counterintelligence section of the organization. We had picked up certain leads indicating the government's plan to unceremoniously remove General Pervez Musharraf from the post of the COAS, a few months prior to the actual attempt made to do so. General Zia ud Din, then the DG ISI, was treasonously, lured into the trap by offering him the appointment of the COAS as the replacement of General Musharraf. After several secret meetings with the political elite, General Zia ud Din agreed to play his part in their favour.

It was only when the plot against General Musharraf was being executed, that the army reacted. On the fateful day when General Musharraf was returning to the country from abroad on a Pakistan International Airlines' flight, the aircraft was not allowed to land at Karachi airport or any other place inside Pakistan. Despite the pilot's warning about very limited fuel available in the aircraft, he was directed to fly over to India or any other foreign country. The Karachi army corps headquarters reacted. Major General Iftikhar, the General Officer Commanding the local army division, personally took control of the airport and enabled General Musharraf's aeroplane to land under the army's protection. General Musharraf was escorted to the corps headquarters with the full protocol due the Pakistan Army's chief of staff.

In Islamabad, while the badges of the rank of the COAS, were being put on Gen Zia ud Din's uniform at the Prime Minister's house, even then the secretary of defence, Lieutenant General (Retd) Iftikhar Ali Khan, who had also been called to the Prime Minister's house to issue the official notification about his appointment, refused to oblige and left the Prime Minister's house. The attempt by the civilian government to remove General Musharraf unceremoniously failed and the army took over.

General Pervez Musharraf held an online conference with the corps commanders and principal staff officers at the General Headquarters at Rawalpindi. Arrangements were made for Gen Pervez to take control of the government as the country's Chief Executive till subsequent constitutional provisions were put in place.

Unfortunately, the impression in the West is of the Pakistan Army's repeated unwarranted interference in civilian rule. It is probably due to the West's ignorance about Pakistani political affairs. In fact, it is always the governments and the political parties that push the army to play a role in resolving their political issues. The same does not happen in Western countries because their militaries are not dragged into politics.

The sacking of General Jahangir Karamat also created tremendous resentment within the army, which became a major reason for its strong reaction when the then prime minister tried to do the same to General Pervez Musharraf. It was an unconstitutional attempt to gain more power over the army and it brought about the end of the civilian government of that time.

Despite a brilliant start, General Musharraf's government also got bogged down in politicking, which caused it to lose creditability. Intriguing politics in the country and its foreign manipulation worsened the situation. The environment became even more unpleasant when General Musharraf declined to accept foreign agendas being imposed in our country that ignored our national interests. Taking advantage of Pakistan's delicate political situation, international power brokers used their paid Pakistani politicians to embark upon a regime change operation to force General Musharraf out of office. One of the major Pakistani political players who was later used to play the key role in the removal of General Musharraf from the Presidency, had also been spotted hobnobbing abroad with the sponsors of the regime change. Interestingly, in one of the ISI counterintelligence operations we were able to identify a foreign non-government organization (NGO) that played a significant role in discrediting General Musharraf publicly. My field operatives uncovered and traced direct linkages between this NGO and a foreign intelligence agency. The foreign agency had launched the NGO inside Pakistan for the specific purpose of discrediting General Musharraf and paving the way for his downfall.

Subsequent political governments have been a replay of the political drama that, unfortunately, has gone on in our country since its creation. Pakistan's governance has experienced continuous turbulence with adverse consequences, mainly because its political structures are mostly controlled by an elite within the society with mala-fide intentions.

Numerous malicious propaganda themes were generated to defame the armed forces. Our adversaries have paid much attention to discrediting the Pakistan Army by hiring moles in different segments of our society to exploit misconceptions about its perks and privileges. Officers of the rank of brigadier and above are targeted and criticized for their so-called lavish lifestyle. The critics forget to mention that in the army no more than ten to fifteen per cent of officers reach the rank of brigadier, while in the Pakistani civil services about seventy per cent of the officers reach the equivalent rank and pay of a brigadier. About three to four per cent of army officers become major generals and less than a single digit of officers become lieutenant generals. General officer promotions are based purely on the officer's professional skills and dedication to service.

The individual career profile of each officer being considered for promotion is placed in front of a board of officers, discussed and final action taken. For promotion to the rank of major general, all formation commanders under the chairmanship of the COAS sit together and review the candidates. For promotion to the rank of lieutenant general, all relevant principal staff officers sit with the COAS and discuss the merits of each candidate.

Promotions in Pakistan's army have nothing to do with the officer's background. The general perception is that the son of a general will also become a general, but that is not true. The sons of ordinary middle- and lower-middle-class civilians and the lower ranks of society have become generals and even achieved the rank of chief of staff of the army. As I mentioned before, during my selection process for the PMA, there were five candidates from CCH and four of us with a middle-class civilian background were selected. The only one who was not selected was the son of a serving major general.

On the financial side, the pay structure of Pakistan army personnel from COAS down to a sepoy is accessible on the internet. Officers become members of the army housing programme upon entering service, and a dedicated amount is deducted automatically and regularly from their pay slips as instalments to cover the cost of the house. Similarly, the rent for their official residential accommodation, utilities, and income tax throughout their time in the army is also deducted from their pay on a monthly basis. The amount deducted for utilities, and income tax alone amounts to almost two months of the officer's total pay for one year.

No officer below the rank of brigadier is authorized an official vehicle. Use of such vehicles is limited to official duties, and in certain specific situations to immediate family members only.

The Defence Housing Authority allots a plot of land as a service benefit to retiring officers and JCOs with good professional records of service and to the families of soldiers who have sacrificed their lives for the country. Others have to pay the cost of the land in instalments even after their retirement. Agricultural land is given only to the families of those who have sacrificed their lives, to officers and soldiers who have suffered serious injuries during operations, such as amputated limbs, and to a few senior officers in recognition of their extraordinary services to the country.

Under the army housing scheme, officers pay for a three-bedroom apartment in instalments during their service. Retiring officers pay a large chunk of their pensions to clear off the balance due before they acquire possession of the three-bedroom apartment.

Pakistan's armed forces have established several industrial and commercial organizations that employ ex-servicemen and create job opportunities in the communities where they are located. Prominent among these organizations are the Army Welfare Trust (AWT) and the Fauji Foundation. The AWT is a diverse organization that was created to employ ninety per cent of the officers who retire between the ages of forty-four and forty-nine. It makes money through a variety of businesses in areas such as insurance, aviation, agriculture, manufacturing, and real estate. Presently, it employs more than twenty-eight thousand people directly and indirectly, and it is among the country's largest taxpayers. The Fauji Foundation is another organization that operates under strict financial controls and is particularly supportive of retired military personnel and their families. Financial accountability in all these institutions is ensured by regular audits by general headquarters. The foundation's taxes are also paid regularly into the government treasury. Pakistan's per capita expenditure on every soldier in the army is among the lowest in the world.

Ironically, many people who criticize the army still prefer to live in Defence Housing Authority managed housing and cantonment areas, get medical treatment from Combined Military Hospitals, and educate their children in the army public school system. It is all about promoting their own self-interests.

A common misconception among Pakistan's youth is that most army officers possess only a high school education. In reality, every officer undergoes two years of academic studies at the PMA and has to pass an examination held by a recognized civilian university to get their bachelor's degree. Officers from the Corps of Engineers, Signals, and Electrical and Mechanical Engineering have engineering degrees from the National Defence University. Besides these qualifications, various domestic and foreign staff course qualified officers obtain Master of Science degrees also from the National Defence University. Officers with the potential for promotion to the higher ranks attend War College Courses, and some go on to complete doctorates in strategic studies.

Occasionally, one hears complaints that army officers often ridicule and disrespect civilians with their behaviour and language. It should be noted that ninety per cent of officers and soldiers do not come from army families. Their relatives, close and distant, are purely civilians. The remaining ten per cent are also connected to the civilian world through relatives and friends.

There could always be exceptions. Some officers may behave immaturely and beneath their dignity. There can be misunderstandings, but bad behaviour toward civilians is never condoned at any level. There is a system in place to address such incidents as and when necessary. The army is an inward-looking institution and does not seek to interact with the public about actions taken against its wrongdoers. Portraying army officers as arrogant and condescending is a method used to ignite anti-army feelings among the public, particularly among our youth.

It is fair to say that the army too has cases of ill-discipline and misappropriation, though it is very rare. These are dealt with severely whenever they arise. Brigadiers, major generals, and lieutenant generals have been convicted, lost their benefits, and imprisoned for misconduct.

In contrast, some of Pakistan's civilian institutions are untouchable despite limitless nepotism and corruption at various levels of management. Politicians enjoy a special status. The courts hand down verdicts against them for society's ills, but they not only manage to escape punishment but also usually succeed at getting back into power. Unfortunately, the relief comes through the same judicial system but with the sitting judges possessing different mind set and being influenced by their political leanings. The trend set starts from the lowest level of the judiciary and climbs to its top tier.

The army is probably the only institution in our country that enforces our laws strictly. The difference is the army's willingness to set standards and adhere to them. Army cantonments are green and beautiful because a lot of attention and effort goes into making them that way. The same is true for educational facilities and other welfare projects run by the army. Municipal corporations are supposed to do the same thing for civilian communities, but they deliver less because of corruption, mismanagement, and lack of accountability.

We need to understand that the army belongs to all of us. It cannot be separated from the civilian population. It faces the same issues and challenges as the civilian institutions do. Each of us is trying to contribute toward a better and more secure tomorrow so that our next generation can prosper and live a peaceful life. No profession is better than another; no one has the right to look down on another. We all contribute toward our common undisputable cause—the well-being of Pakistan.

Cynicism in our Approach

Unfortunately, a general trend of negativity prevails in our society, and there is cynicism in our approach to tackling the challenges we face. Many people are dissatisfied with their lives. Barring the few who are willing to explain themselves, most people fail to communicate the reasons for their dissatisfaction. They become negative and this negativity adversely affects every aspect of their lives, and results in pessimistic responses to life's challenges. Instead of facing problems boldly, they start looking for shortcuts, and that is when social evils begin to corrupt individual character, and gradually find their way into the community. The result is disjointed communities, divided institutions and widening gaps between various segments of our society. Our inability to resist these social evils adversely affects our capabilities to manage crises and provides our enemies with opportunities they can exploit for their own benefit.

Ongoing Political and Economic Crisis

The current situation in Pakistan is worrisome. Since the U.S. and its allies left Afghanistan and adopted a new approach towards our region, Pakistan has experienced increasing political unrest and economic uncertainty. Power-hungry feudalists and business tycoons' control most of the country's political parties. They maintain their power by undermining the public's trust in key government institutions, come what may! The army has been one of the main targets for vested interests, within the country and abroad.

Pakistani politicians have made a mockery of our democracy, our parliament, and our constitution. The country's population, heavily influenced by its youth, is bitterly polarized, and divided. Entrenched power centres have created false political narratives that promote divisiveness and support personal or partisan self-interest. Corrupt office holders and their influential sponsors ignore or dismiss the people's legitimate concerns to loot and plunder of the public coffers. All of this is weakening Pakistan's social, political, and economic cohesion at a time of increased great power geostrategic maneuvering, in the region.

The current problems began in April 2022, when an alliance of opposition parties introduced a resolution of "No Confidence" in the National assembly, claiming the government was oppressing its opponents and restricting the people's freedom of expression. Government officials argued that the resolution was the work of foreign powers designed to bring about regime change because Pakistan's government had rejected U.S. demands for military bases in Pakistan to continue its ventures in the region. As proof, they revealed a warning note from Pakistan's ambassador in Washington that claimed the Americans were upset about Pakistan's close relations with China and its growing reproachment with Russia.

Notwithstanding the government's arguments, the National Assembly approved the opposition's "No Confidence" resolution, and the existing government was removed from power. It was the region's first major political development following the U.S. departure from Afghanistan in August 2021.

Some politicians and a few other pseudo-intellectuals amongst various other segments of the society, misleadingly accused Pakistan's army as an institution, of having helped bring about the government's downfall. The speculative accusation created a false perception of a divide between the people of Pakistan and its army. The opposition used this misperception to blame the ousted government officials and its affiliated politicians for attacking the army, to help win the resolution's approval and gain advantage during the subsequent political activities in the country.

Many strategists predicted that the U.S. strategic retreat from Afghanistan would produce serious political and security turmoil throughout the region. In Pakistan's case, increased economic crisis was expected, triggering the International Monetary Fund to impose harsh austerity measures, aggravating the situation further. Things moved in that direction shortly after the U.S. pulled out of Afghanistan and the security situation in Pakistan began to deteriorate each day.

A new government, composed of political parties that passed the "No Confidence" resolution, remained in office until new elections were held on February 8, 2024. It was a period of great upheaval with the new government accused of coming down heavily on its opponents, by-passing all the norms of justice and good governance. Subsequently, the caretaker government set up to hold the elections, also seemingly, did everything in its power to prevent the ousted party from participating in the elections. It apparently became a one-sided show. However, with popular support from the frustrated masses, irrespective of their political affiliations, the members of the aggrieved political party were able to circumvent the effort to disenfranchise them. By running as candidates not affiliated with any political party, they succeeded in winning the largest number of seats in the new National Assembly, although it was not a majority. Their victory mainly reflected the frustration of the people with the feudalist mafia that has ruled the country for most of its history. Many people cast their ballots against what they described as a "mock democratic culture" that has given safe haven to the corrupt who exploit the masses.

The election resulted in a deadlocked parliament. No political party had enough seats to form a stable government. A popular consensus formed that the elections had been rigged to deprive the ousted political party from gaining a majority to form the new government. The resulting public discontent put pressure on the interim administration and the judiciary to do something about it. Unfortunately, nothing worked and instead, several competing political parties were facilitated to set aside their differences, joined together, and formed an alliance to seize the reins of power. A combination of politicians and technocrats began to run the government. Most observers believe this ad hoc arrangement will benefit the country's existing power brokers temporarily, but that it will not last long. In the meantime, while it exists, the country will suffer, perhaps irreparably.

A U.S. Congressional committee conducted hearings in March 2024 to address concerns about alleged U.S. Government involvement in the passage of Pakistan's "No confidence" resolution and in the subsequent elections that produced the new Pakistan government. The hearings attracted a great deal of interest. Their results were mixed.

The U.S. Assistant Secretary of State for South and Central Asian Affairs bluntly denied any U.S. Government involvement in Pakistan's internal affairs relating to the "No confidence" resolution or the subsequent elections, but he failed to explain the purpose of his meeting with Pakistan's ambassador to the United States two days before the resolution was introduced in Pakistan's National Assembly. He also failed to address the question of the demarche that was handed over to the U.S. Ambassador in Islamabad, by the Pakistan government against the U.S. interference in the internal affairs of the country. The note had been issued after the meeting of the National Security Committee of the government of Pakistan. The U.S. Assistant Secretary's failure to answer these questions weakened his credibility as a witness.

Many members of Pakistan's intelligentsia watched the U.S. congressional hearings carefully, hoping that this senior US government official would signal a new direction in U.S. – Pakistan relations. It didn't happen. Instead, while he was claiming that the U.S. was not interfering in Pakistan's internal affairs, the Assistant Secretary pledged to stop a joint initiative by Pakistan and Iran to build a gas pipeline! His contradictory statements caused confusion and distrust of U.S. intentions toward Islamabad.

The prevailing political uncertainty in Pakistan is threatening the country's national security. Pakistani society is polarized, and there is distrust and disharmony among and within its key institutions and social organizations. The turmoil has apparently created a gap between the people and the country's armed forces with far-reaching consequences for the nation. The army is being blamed for Pakistan's political problems. The criticism of these professional warriors who have enjoyed widespread and unconditional public support for their integrity and commitment to the country's well-being has reached the point of becoming destructive.

Unfortunately, dragging the army into policy disputes among Pakistan's political parties has become a common practice. Politicians are quick to offer political conspiracy theories involving the army, and repeat them over and over again, if they perceive that it will benefit them to do so. Inaccurate or false accusations are an unnecessary and sometimes dangerous burden that the army has had to carry for most of its history. Politicians dragging army into the governance to suite their agendas and attacking it when it benefits their way of politicking, is one of the root causes of problems in our country's system of governance because it undermines public trust in the nation's military forces. Our goal must be to create a national governance system that promotes trust in government institutions, pairs well with the country's socio-political culture and is supported by a strong National Security Council instead of a National Security Committee with hardly any powers to make a difference, even within the domain of the security of the country.

Our adversaries and their agents of influence are working hard to achieve their objectives in the region at our expense. We are well aware of their plans, but blaming others or the army for our failures is not a good option. We must look at our problems realistically, with a clear eye and a cool head, and take action to solve them based on our national priorities.

We have not done this because historically feudalists and business tycoons have dominated Pakistan's politics and pursued their own personal and party interests while ignoring our democratic values. The elite capture in Pakistani politics and governance emerge very early in our history and became well known with the appearance of Twenty-two families accumulating 99% of the country's wealth. Their descendants have continued to accumulate wealth and political power and have made a mockery of democracy by creating a system of governance that permits the few to manage the many for their own benefit. The result is a governance structure ill-suited to meet the Pakistani people's needs and concerns.

The system's failures reverberate far beyond Pakistan's borders, and present foreign powers with opportunities to pursue their agendas by meddling in our country's internal affairs. Unfortunately, too many of our politicians are prepared to help foreign powers with their meddling, for their own personal or political benefit. It has been this way for decades. The willingness of our politicians to promote foreign interests has been a major source of political instability.

In recent years, there has been a visible decline in the performance of many important government institutions. Among those is the Police Service of Pakistan, the agency primarily responsible for maintaining the country's internal security. Involvement in political maneuvering under the garb of maintaining law and order due to pressure from political mafia, has badly damaged its credibility, and caused it to move away from its mission. It has become a tool of the country's ruling elites to oppress their political opponents.

The organization's morale becomes low, the result of pursuing politics over professionalism and the leadership's failure to maintain the organization's honor and worthiness as a law enforcement agency.

The sharpest decline, however, has occurred in the institutional performance of our judicial system. It poses the greatest threat to Pakistan because of its impact on the nation's economic and social institutions. Many people have lost confidence that disputes will be resolved fairly and according to law. Today, many Pakistan judges are known not for their morals and competence but rather for the vested interests they favor. "Might makes right," not justice and the law, has become the way it goes in Pakistan's courts.

Pakistan's army has also been affected by the country's political uncertainty. There is a saying that if you stand next to a pond of muddy water, the slightest disturbance in its surface will splash you with muck. Unfortunately, Pakistan's army finds itself in such a situation. It has no choice but to remain near the pond to protect the people and their leaders but at the same time, some of the politicians who disturb the water's surface, do so deliberately to splash muck on the army.

They try to lure the army into political controversy to gain personal advantage or to promote their own political agendas. Interactions between the army and politicians, even when done with the best intentions, create opportunities for other politicians to criticize and disparage the army if they disagree with what is being done. Senior military officers who meet with foreign government officials in the normal performance of their duties and in furtherance of Pakistan's interests often become the subject of conspiracy theories and are condemned unnecessarily for what they have done. Efforts by the army to publicly deny false accusations or to set the record straight only draw it deeper into the controversy. Every instance of army-politician interaction requires careful calculation to avoid unwarranted criticism of the army.

It has been that way for some time. It was that way during General Ayub Khan's time, General Zia's era and it was that way during General Musharaff's time. Despite its strengths and good work, the army's involvement in partisan political maneuvering has given it a bad name. The toxic mix of military force and political intrigue has been one of Pakistan's major problems.

Notwithstanding its challenges, the army remains the country's best hope for a prosperous and peaceful future. It is Pakistan's strongest force for stability and the rule of law. Time and again, it has provided the leadership that has enabled us to weather dangerous storms. Many people believe that it will do so again at this critical juncture in our history. Prolonged political chaos in the country, however, is creating anxiety for the future among our friends and determination to exploit our weaknesses among our enemies.

The powerful political groups in our country have divided people into special interest groups based on ethnicity and religious beliefs for many years. It is a common practice to control the population. Unfortunately, it has been a practice during the military regimes as well. Besides, playing political games in tune with their creators, these special interest groups are vulnerable to manipulation by foreign intelligence agencies who seek to deepen societal divisiveness and promote anti-state activities.

When I was in charge of Pakistan's counterintelligence effort during General Pervez Musharraf's era, we were in contact with Nawab Akbar Bugti who was a major tribal leader in Baluchistan. He opposed certain government policies that were causing much public unrest in his area. The purpose of our efforts was to address and resolve his grievances. It was a difficult assignment because our enemies have traditionally tried to create civil unrest and promote separatist sentiment in Baluchistan.

I found Nawab Akbar Bugti to be a patriotic Pakistani, who was ready to do anything for his country. We worked out an acceptable agreement that addressed his concerns, and a final meeting was scheduled between Bugti and President Musharraf to mark the end of civil unrest in the province. While the information was being processed to the president, several politicians learned of the agreement and decided to cash in on it. They approached Nawab Akbar Bugti and, in the government's name, tried to extract undue benefits from him. The personal trust that we had worked very hard to establish with Bugti was broken and the agreement collapsed. Subsequently, killing of Nawab Bugti along with some senior military officers in a cave where he was hiding, was fully exploited by enemy's intelligence agencies depicting it as a clash with the law enforcement agencies. These army officers had been called in the cave by Nawab Bugti personally, to agree upon certain modalities for his surrender. The entrances to the cave got blocked due to mine blasts either incidentally or as part of the enemy's plan.

As a result, civil unrest continued for years in Baluchistan, and was deftly exploited by our enemies, causing great damage to Pakistan and to the people of Baluchistan. Later, during one of our meetings when General Musharraf was living in Dubai, he told me that he miscalculated when he made politicians part of his administration because they misused his name to enrich themselves and gave both him and the army a bad name. The missed opportunity to end the civil strife in Baluchistan was just one of many instances when self-promoting politicians brought discredit upon the army with their schemes to benefit themselves personally and politically. General Zia ul Haq had the same experience with politicians when he served as Pakistan's president.

The U.S. withdrawal from Afghanistan has brought about major political and strategic changes throughout the region with far reaching security implications for Pakistan. While its security services are able to handle the country's immediate security challenges, greater domestic political stability is needed for Pakistan to achieve long term success. Public confidence and trust in the army is critical to building such stability. The army must not become the captive of any political party, and it must not be used as a tool for political oppression. The country's leaders, military and civilian, must find the ways and means to reverse the current trend of using the army as a mean to resolve partisan political disagreements because the current practice is weakening the ability of the nation's military forces to defend the country.

There is a need to act quickly. Our adversaries are working diligently to exploit the public's growing distrust of our army. Ad hoc arrangements to create temporary solutions are not an answer. We must not exchange temporary short-term gains for long term chaos and confusion.

Our enemies are already actively fomenting hatred and separatist sentiments in Baluchistan and Khyber Pakhtunkhwa. We need to ensure that it does not spread to Azad Kashmir and Gilgit-Baltistan. The history of Gilgit-Baltistan is very similar to that of Jammu and Kashmir. The people of these areas had to fight for their independence and their right to join Pakistan in 1947. Among the great warriors in this struggle were Mujahid Bakhtawar Shah and Colonel Hassan Khan, two well-known freedom fighters who fought against a company of 26 Dogra Regiment at Bunji Pass near Skardu on 4th November 1947. That battle dealt a fatal blow to India's occupying troops and enabled local freedom fighters to win their independence to join Pakistan.

The people of Azad Jammu and Kashmir and the Northern Areas love Pakistan, but they have been subjected to much propaganda and subversion by our enemies. All of Pakistan's major political parties have, very rightly, established their political presence in these areas. All these setups must be allowed to participate fully and fairly in the democratic processes. Any move to restrict their efforts undemocratically will create much public discontent that our enemies will exploit. In the recent unrest in Azad Kashmir during the month of May 2024, local population had to protest against certain restrictive policies of the central government in Pakistan. It is a very damaging development in the area with far reaching consequences. Minor issues of governance were exploited to create a major upset, which later thankfully got settled. However, igniting the sentiments of the local people by imposing political governance against their will is a treasonous act that can create rippling effects in the state and will also give the Indian government a leverage to cover up its atrocities in Indian Held Kashmir. Reportedly, the Indian Intelligence has been active in exploiting the situation to their advantage and is likely to boost its efforts in the future. The same had previously happened in Gilgit and Baltistan, creating a lot of discontent and anti-centre feelings amongst the people of the area.

Greater political stability is also important to give support to our deteriorating economy. The International Monetary Fund (IMF) is poised to take actions that will likely create more economic stress on a population that has already suffered greatly. People find it difficult to make ends meet. More pressure may increase rather than reduce the country's political instability and make it easier for the IMF to implement its agenda at the expense of the Pakistani people.

A Treasonous Interplay with Staggering Consequences

Our foreign adversaries have taken advantage of Pakistan's internal vulnerabilities to promote their agenda by developing strong inroads among various segments of our society. Creating anti-army feelings is part of their strategy. As a result, we are engaged in a two-front war. In addition to hostile foreign actors, we have a problem with internal enemies. Unfortunately, it is due, in part, to a gradual decline in our core values and strengths. Over the years, patriotism has lost its meaning and corruption and nepotism disguised as so-called democracy, have become a way of life.

Our adversaries have brutally exploited our failure to distinguish between personal benefit and national interest. They use this weakness to undermine our governance system, create ethnic and religious divides, and damage inter-organizational harmony. Hostile covert intelligence operations deployed against us from within and abroad support anti-state movements inside Pakistan. Several non-government organizations and international organizations have successfully created strong lobbies to promote agendas that are not in Pakistan's best interests.

The internal threat, coupled with the external threat, has created a complex national security challenge for Pakistan. To meet this challenge, we must first and foremost protect our borders and bridge our internal divides. There is a dire need to reorient our strategic thinking to focus on these two areas. If we are to continue to exist and develop, we must learn to adapt.

CHAPTER 8

EMERGING SECURITY CHALLENGES AND THE WAY FORWARD

An Overview of Regional Security Challenges

South Asia, with almost a quarter of the world's population, a complex historical background, massive regional diversity, and disputed international borders, confronts some of the toughest conventional and non-conventional security challenges in the world. Disputes between India and Pakistan top the list. There has been a rise in ethnic and communal strife in some parts of the region, the outbreak of Hindu versus Muslim riots in India being one example.

The situation in Afghanistan continues to be unstable. Increasing oppression and the Taliban's unpredictable policies have paused its international recognition and support. Bloody brawls over power and governance rack the country and there is a growing threat of renewed chaos and bloodshed, putting the region back to the turmoil that it has been through during the past four decades. Pakistan will be the worst affected in this case.

The growing Chinese influence throughout South Asia adds a visible layer of stress on Indian hegemonic ambitions and for the US for its perceived new world order. The 1962 Sino-Indian war signalled the beginning of a developing rivalry between the two regional giants. Recent border skirmishes between the two with Indian troops getting visible bashing, have sent alarming signals for anti-Chinese forces in the region about what they may face in any future war scenario.

The shift in US policies toward India to counter China's growing power is accelerating the Indo-China rivalry and pushing Pakistan to embrace Chinese initiatives such as the CPEC and some other mutually supportive enterprises. Most of the region's countries are developing closer military and economic relations with Pakistan, but Pakistan is having a tough time trying to navigate its relations between China and the US. With India counterbalancing China on behalf of the US there is great danger that Pakistan will once again get sucked into a US dispute in the region.

An analysis of the current political and international security landscape indicates that chronic and growing violence will remain part of the security landscape for the foreseeable future. We have already entered an era where emerging conflicts and endemic violence are changing the nature of human social fabric and political governance systems. The lines are increasingly blurred between conflict and non-conflict zones, with pockets of vulnerability co-existing alongside pockets of progress. The lines are also blurred between criminal and politically motivated violence.

The emerging scenario demands that all the regional states work together to better address mounting security issues and develop their economic potential. Mutual suspicion and the pursuit of parochial agendas weaken the prospects for such cooperation with the result that external powers will continue to manipulate the region in pursuit of strategic dominance.

Major Security Concerns for Pakistan

Regional conspiracies to destabilize Pakistan have long been a staple of our history, but there have also been international conspiracies involving the superpowers attracted by Pakistan's geo-strategic location and ready to exploit it to further their regional and global ambitions. Under the circumstances, we need to have a clear understanding of the issues and come together in a unified effort to thwart the mischievous designs of our adversaries.

Recent transformative shifts in global political, economic, and military power are having profound effects on the existing global security paradigm. The fiasco of the US withdrawal from Afghanistan and the fallout on global security patterns, particularly with respect to how it affects Pakistan, is a case in point.

Two developments in the prevailing international security landscape influence how Pakistan must proceed. First, weakening states have created a power vacuum that opens space for the rise of armed non-state actors. The presence of these actors globally and in the region complicates our national security planning because they represent an alternative to traditional state-based security threats. Second, strategic competition between the world's strongest states has resumed to levels seen formerly during the Cold War. Such resurgence poses a unique threat to weaker states because they are subject to being manipulated by stronger powers in ways that are outside the mandate and capabilities of current global security arrangements. As a result, we are facing the rise of hybrid warfare with no distinction between friend and foe or between military combatants, non-state adversaries, and civilians. We have a more serious task at hand in this context.

In some parts of the world, nations are directing violence against their own citizens or supporting terrorist activities abroad to achieve or promote their interests. Nations themselves are becoming drivers of insecurity rather than guarantors of peace and stability. What happened in Afghanistan and a few other Muslim states and what India is now doing in Kashmir are clear examples of this trend. The problem is exacerbated by forced migration and refugee flows in many parts of the world that wittingly or unwittingly have provided cover for insurgent groups to move back and forth between safe havens and their target countries. We are a major victim in this case.

Mobilization of ideologically motivated special interest groups after the Russian withdrawal from Afghanistan has posed a new challenge for Pakistan. We expected the Taliban to make positive changes vis a vis Pakistan, but that did not happen. Instead, we became a target for the worst kind of extremist terror, and a battleground for competing proxies and intolerant interpretations of radical theories and philosophies. Unfortunately, our inconsistent approach to the problem of these special interest groups has contributed to their development of terrorism in the region and has made us the target of criticism within the international community.

One of Pakistan's main challenges is to fashion diplomatic and strategic options to counter terrorist violence. We have been focused on targeting specific terrorist groups when we need to focus on the root causes of terrorism itself. The fiasco of the US withdrawal from Afghanistan and its fallout on global security patterns, particularly with respect to Pakistan, suggests that it is an area that needs immediate attention.

Unfortunately, most of Pakistan's national security issues are an outgrowth of our internal sensitivities. We have many pseudointellectuals with vested interests within our society who offer routinely a distorted image of our country, the armed forces, and the ISI. In most cases, foreign sponsors are behind their efforts, using our own people to promote their anti-Pakistan agendas. Their manipulation of public perceptions against our armed forces weakens the country's centre of gravity and therefore its national strength. Some of our other hereditary internal sensitivities provide them with ample opportunities to exploit. These adverse manipulations, therefore, need to be seriously handled.

Role of Pakistan Armed Forces

A country's national security infrastructure must be competent enough to handle the complexity of the overt and covert threats against it, and generally, it must do both at the same time. Intelligence agencies have a dual role to play. On the one hand, security forces are required to gather information about all kinds of threats, analyze them to determine the most dangerous and provide the state with forewarning in time for it to plan countermeasures. Intelligence agencies must also actively identify and destroy enemy intelligence operations inside the country. Having participated in these operations both in the army and in ISI for nearly four decades, it is fair to say that Pakistan's armed forces and intelligence agencies have served and protected the nation well and have succeeded in protecting it against a deadly combination of internal and external threats.

Their achievements remain mostly off stage, behind the scenes for most people at home and abroad. Pakistanis need to be made aware of just how well they have served the country, and how the misrepresentation of their achievements is being exploited to discredit our national institutions and undermine our national unity. The armed forces and their affiliated intelligence agencies are the country's main strength and that makes them the enemy's priority target.

ISI is the country's premier intelligence agency. It is responsible for gathering intelligence from around the globe and processing it for relevant authorities to formulate our national strategies. It consists primarily of serving military officers from all three services; army, air force, and navy, and civilian cadre recruited through competitive examination and interviews.

The agency has made many important contributions toward keeping the country's physical and ideological frontiers safe, and its history bespeaks invaluable accomplishments. It played a pivotal role in supporting the Afghan mujahideen against the Soviet invasion between 1979 and 1989 earning global recognition for its competence and professionalism. The fallout from this war posed grave challenges to our national security and kept ISI very busy after the Soviets left. For a while, that battle worsened with each passing day as the stakeholders and their interests kept changing. Tremors from it are still felt even today, but through it all ISI managed to keep the country safe.

Pakistan's adversaries have had many opportunities to penetrate its civil society during the past few years and have used them to exploit for their own benefit what they see as opportunities born of geopolitical turmoil in the region.

Hostile intelligence agencies have made significant inroads by manipulating social divisions over politics, ethnicity, and religion, expanding their networks among various segments of our society, and increasing their capabilities to undermine our national sovereignty. Corrupt mafias with partisan and personal agendas are ready to work with them for mutual benefit. However, ISI's handling of this onslaught by the country's external and internal enemies has been commendable.

In addition to combating hostile forces, Pakistan's army provides immeasurable support to the people during natural disasters. Nobody can forget what our armed forces did during the 2005 earthquake that struck the Northern Areas, Frontier Province, and Azad Kashmir, registering 7.6 on the Richter scale. This massive disaster affected twelve thousand square miles, killed seventy-three thousand people, destroyed five hundred thousand homes and buildings, and made homeless three and a half million Pakistanis.

The army deployed about ten brigades and fifty battalions throughout the affected area, dividing it into "Army Nodes." Each node had an officer in charge whose name and telephone number were published by the media for easy public access. Relief bases were organized and needed supplies were brought to them with helicopters, airdrops, and animal transport systems. The army began immediately to do reconstruction and rehabilitation work on a vast scale.

Army relief operations are done routinely to support civil administrations during torrential rains and heavy snowfalls that cause flooding in different parts of the country. Army battalions have repeatedly removed massive amounts of mud and debris during heavy rainfalls that shut down huge networks of roads and canals and destroy villages. The army's contribution to relief operations during heavy floods in the recent past has again been outstanding. During the recent coronavirus pandemic, the army established an effective National Command and Operational Centre to support the national response. Its effectiveness in fighting the pandemic has been recognized and commended internationally.

Pakistan's army has a long and cherished history since 1960 of participating in peacekeeping operations under the auspices of the United Nations. It has been the UN's most significant and consistent contributor to peacekeeping forces, serving in more than forty-one Peacekeeping Missions worldwide, including some very challenging ones. Many officers and men have lost their lives performing these duties. In Somalia, a Pakistani battalion tasked with performing a rear-guard mission threw a security cordon around Mogadishu and protected UN forces while they executed a tactical withdrawal under fire. The outstanding performance of Pakistani troops who faced very dangerous conditions during this mission is well known at the UN. Regrettably, the film 'Black Hawk Down' ignored their role in that fight. Our soldiers operating in

Somalia, Sierra Leone, Libera, Congo, Ivory Coast, and Bosnia have suffered a high number of casualties.

Pakistan's contribution to UN peacekeeping has been flexible, as varied as our country's cultural, geographic, political, and security conditions. More than two hundred thousand troops have been sent to twenty-three countries on almost all the continents and won recognition for their hard work and devotion to duty. Pakistan has been consistently one of the UN's largest troop-contributing countries for many years.

The Pakistan Army's affiliation with almost all national sports federations in the country and its promotion of sports is well known and admired. Apart from organizing, planning, and conducting its own sports, the Army Sports Directorate works with sister services to organize events at the inter-service level. It sponsors national events, takes part in all national championships on a regular basis, and is one of the recognized and affiliated services organizations of the Pakistan Olympic Association.

It is the backbone of the country's national sports teams and provides many athletes who compete at that level. Mountaineering is one of the sports it promotes every year, and it is known for routinely rescuing mountaineers, mainly from foreign countries, who become stuck in its high snow-covered mountains. Similarly, it regularly promotes hockey, football, and cricket. Pakistan's Air Force is a pioneer in promoting squash throughout the country. Pakistan's Navy has been actively involved in yachting.

The role of Pakistan's army in safeguarding our national security and integrity is an unending story. Their services in the social sector have been immeasurable. Unfortunately, "No one loves a warrior until the enemy is at the gate." We all need to think carefully about that.

The Way Forward

Establishment of a National Security Council

The army remains the mainstay of our national strength and cohesion. Its proactive role under the prevailing security configurations is of paramount importance. The most challenging task is to keep it away from internal controversies while strengthening its ability to defend the country. The most compelling need is to establish a potent National Security Council of civil-military leadership, one that works in unison to handle the country's security challenges and one that understands how our internal issues are harbingers of future external threats. This idea has been in discussion at various levels in the past but could not get into any shape due to opposition by vested interests.

Rebuilding National Institutions and Creating Inter-Organizational Harmony

Major reforms need to be brought to the police department. It is a difficult proposition. The prevailing system that has been working over the years, has become a way how the organization is tuned to operate. Unfortunately, it remained amongst the major root causes for many ills in our society. There had been several attempts in the past, to bring in necessary changes in the induction system and operational procedures in the department but the vested interests never allowed that to happen. Similarly, major judicial reforms need to be put in place in the judicial system that works in the country. Induction of judges at senior as well as at junior level, needs a re-look. Induction of judges at senior positions from various lawyer's associations that are politically aligned to various political parties, should be re-examined. It is most annoying to see visible division amongst the judiciary based on political leanings and other self-motivated factors. The net result is the complete loss of confidence in our judicial system, paving the way for a revolutionary approach amongst the youth, which is fully charged to take on the challenges on their own rather than to suffer from one-sided justice. A purposeful scrutiny of many other important government departments can make a lot of difference to the standards of governance in the country.

Visible steps need to be taken to improve inter-organizational coherence. The system's re-orientation, joint training events for senior officials, and increased interactions at the appropriate levels of management will increase the nation's inter-institutional prudence and collective wisdom.

The current situation is one of geopolitical uncertainty, with no signs of it changing in the near term. New crises crop up unexpectedly and long-term conflicts remain unresolved. It is imperative that these geopolitical and international security risks be given serious consideration by executives at all levels with complete coordination and cohesion, to avoid further destabilization.

Aligning Governance with National Ideology

Conflict mismanagement, poor governance, and corruption erode economic growth and development, particularly in low and middle-class-income countries. International economic relations and security policies are now intertwined. Harmonious relations among states produce trade and investment patterns driven by economic considerations. During times of tense relations, economic considerations are overshadowed by the politics of national security.

The combination of complex external security challenges and the fragile state of our internal political and social systems poses an existential threat to the nation. There is nothing but crisis after crisis, one after the other, with no let-up. We need to set aside the political blame game and adopt realistic approaches that will bring solutions and stability. We must realize that in most cases a crisis is caused by faulty political and economic systems. The challenge is to candidly recognize this reality, identify the flaws in our governance systems and make needed changes to address our problems.

It is in the interest of our governance system to be flexible to accommodate changes that can minimize the failings and sufferings of the people. Unfortunately, some beneficiaries of the current system have persistently maintained the status quo for their own benefit, while the challenges continue to grow. That approach is short-sighted because the worsening problems can endanger the complete systems in vogue. We must not forget that eventually, people will choose their own ways to solve their problems and sufferings, which can create unmanageable lawlessness in the country and destroy its governance structure.

Our prevailing governance system tends to showcase the illusion of democracy. It has deteriorated to the point where a corrupt political and economic elite dominates every aspect of our socio-political culture. As a result, decisions relating to our national security and societal cohesion are being made by people who do not represent the common good. At times, it is hard to imagine what kind of decisions they will make.

Just talking about an ideology based on our country's founding values is not enough. We need to understand what goes into making an ideology and how the doctrine for creating a separate homeland for Muslims on the Indian subcontinent was conceived by Quaid-e-Azam Muhammad Ali Jinnah. The word 'ideology' comes from the word 'idea'. Taking the idea of our country and building a whole narrative around it based on personal agendas will not bring us the fruits of our founding values. Unfortunately, that is what we are doing. As a result, we have a system of governance that is contradictory to the original ideology as described by our founding leader. It does not support the country's socio-political welfare and it is incapable of solving the challenges we confront. For Pakistan, we must put our house in order so that we have a system of governance that aligns with our social and political culture and is also capable of addressing our challenges. This is especially important as the world adjusts to the crumbling effect on the existing international order of the US withdrawal from Afghanistan.

We must remember that we chose our system of governance based on the true principles of a social welfare state as envisioned by our religious beliefs. The ideology of Pakistan is to shape our individual and collective lives according to the teachings of Islam and safeguard our society against all ideologies that are against Islam. It should be a state where every citizen enjoys equal rights irrespective of religion, creed, and social status. Even our national flag represents these values through different colour codes. For example, the white portion of the flag represents the country's minorities. Quaid-e-Azam said, "Pakistan not only means freedom and independence but the Muslim ideology which has to be preserved, which has come to us as a precious gift and treasure and which, we hope others will share with us."

We need to create a state which is run by the best people and find a methodology that identifies the best who will lead us. Our country's existing method of governance is not competent enough to provide a sustainable platform upon which to confront our national challenges. We must understand that democracy is more than a set of globally identical government institutions and practices. There are common, well-understood norms, values, attitudes, and practices, but the interpretation and implementation of these common characteristics may vary from society to society based on diverse cultures and traditions. Pakistan's current system of governance has created disharmony and frustration within the society.

The most democratically elected leaders often choose to become dictators after assuming office. In contrast, military officers who replace civilian leaders tend to become democrats after taking over, often losing their grip on government institutions in the process. The solution to this problem is a system that is free of the contradictory and undemocratic behaviours of the country's current political elite. How and who will be able to do it is the big question. If we cannot find a solution from within, then perhaps a look at the history of how other nations in similar distressing situations fought their way back and rose to positions of influence. While democracy remains the baseline for sustainable governance in Pakistan, the parliamentary system is definitely not a workable option for a society like ours. A tailor-made infrastructure within democratic norms may be a solution for most of our problems. China's governance system, with suitable modifications, would make an interesting case study, for example.

Emerging Role of Leadership

The current situation is one of geopolitical uncertainty, with no signs of it changing in the near term. New crises crop up unexpectedly and long-term conflicts remain unresolved. It is imperative that these geopolitical and international security risks be given serious consideration by executives at all levels, to avoid further destabilization.

The situation demands leadership that correctly identifies and understands the most pressing transformations that need to be made and the trends that are driving them. Strategic forecasting, based on carefully researched and authenticated scenarios, will help leaders assess what the future might look like. A well-coordinated process of developing and using these scenarios can generate the relationships necessary to drive needed change. Geopolitical risks and global realignments of power around interests rather than values demand greater participation by a wider range of stakeholders in creating global mechanisms to handle emerging security challenges.

To confront these challenges, our leadership at all levels needs to modify and reshape their roles and responsibilities. They need to develop good crisis leadership skills, and the ability to identify challenges and mobilize the most relevant and trustworthy expertise to resolve them in a system of governance that integrates risk management and multi-stakeholder partnerships.

Understanding geopolitics and the emerging international and regional security paradigms is central to mitigating future challenges and building the capabilities needed to confront them. We must remain aware of what is happening around us and ensure that it does not disturb the peace and tranquillity in our country. On the one hand, we need to understand what drives emerging global risks and how they are adversely impacting fragile and weaker states that are already under great stress. On the other hand, we also need to understand how we can counter these threats successfully through efficient governance and public-private collaborations.

Business leaders, with better understanding of international security and geopolitical trends that influence global economies, must become more involved in resetting the strategic landscape. The private sector can be a constructive partner in addressing many security challenges and neutralizing the forces that seek to manipulate vulnerabilities. Security agencies at the organizational and governmental levels need to modify their organizational frameworks and processes to build more public-private partnerships. Building greater flexibility by using genuinely forward-looking multi-stakeholder processes and strategies is the best way to meet the collective global challenges.

Re-Streaming Educational System

One of the core elements that makes a democracy, or any other system work, is education. Unfortunately, our education system has lost its core values and its relevance to our socio-cultural environments. Unless our ruling class learns to exercise wisdom and what is required to rule the people, Pakistan will continue to lurch from crisis to crisis.

Our educational system needs revamping. The existing system has negatively affected our progress and efficiency in all walks of life, whether political, cultural, ethnic, or even religious. It is laughable that our political elites emphasize the importance of education while a few years back eliminating our constitution's requirement that members of Parliament possess a college bachelor's degree.

Reforming our education system to place a greater emphasis on character-building and moral values is needed. Religious education should be an integral part of the curriculum. At the national level, an educational training course on 'Self-discipline and Character Building' should be developed jointly by the Ministry of Education and the National Defence University (NDU). People from different segments of society and public officials should be able to participate in these short courses like the national security workshops, already conducted regularly by NDU. Cadet colleges and other well-respected educational institutions can help provide the training base that will be needed to establish such a venture.

Religious radicalization and its exploitation by people for partisan gain is a serious security challenge in Pakistan. The manipulation of religion for politics is the country's biggest betrayal. Madrassas, mostly with foreign links and foreign funding, play a significant role in weakening our country's national security. We should immediately halt foreign involvement in religious education and reverse the damage that has already been done through well-thought-out strategies and the strict imposition of the state's writ where necessary. The selection and appointment of religious scholars to manage the country's mosques and make them a part of our civil service system would be a significant step forward in creating a true and authentic interpretation of Islam that would lead to religious harmony.

Finally, the national trend toward cynicism about everything we see, which has become almost embedded into our national psyche, must cease. Our pessimistic attitude toward life leads us to embrace social evils and causes us to lose our way when faced with new challenges. A reformed educational system, from top to bottom, that incorporates character-building and self-discipline as an essential part of the academic curriculum will be a great help in this regard.

Ultimately, we all must never forget that unity is strength. We are like a fist when we stay together. No army can win if the public does not support it. The people's continuous moral support is essential to keep the army strong. We should not fall prey to those who would split us apart by manipulating the facts and vilifying our security forces. We, as a nation, need to stand together against all odds. Together we stand, divided we fall.

A word for International Community

An accurate narrative based on real-time information and experiences will help analysts and strategists ponder the military history of this region based on facts and ground realities. By connecting the dots, the international community, will hopefully realize the necessity to have a re-look at the tailor-made hypothesis presented to them about Pakistan, by the vested interests. It has already cost them a lot. The picture presented to them needs to be seen in its correct perspective. A well-calculated interpretation of the developments in the region will help members of the international community suitably align their relationships and cooperation in the region based on ground realities.

The US government was amongst the first few countries in the world which recognized Pakistan as an independent nation in 1947. A look back to General Ayub's era during 60's will be interesting to know how both countries and a few in Europe, worked together for the benefit of their people. Recent history of jointly defeating Russia in Afghanistan and their successes during subsequent operations, despite certain reservations on some of the US policy decisions, are testimony of their sustaining partnership. Unfortunately, how Pakistan was betrayed by its partners after decades of partnership, is the other side of the same story for which there seems to be no plausible excuse to offer. On the other hand, the Pakistan-China friendship is another example that proves my point emphatically. How these two countries have been working hand-in-glove since 1970, while, Pakistan continuously maintains a close relationship with the West, is a point to ponder.

In the backdrop of its experiences, the Pakistani nation actually feels frustrated for having been let down time and again, and even at times, betrayed at critical junctures in our country's history.

As a seasoned Pakistani intelligence operative, with decades of experience collaborating with our allies, particularly during our operations related to the Afghan War since the Russian invasion of that country, I maintain the belief that Pakistani and the US combatants in the field have consistently proven to be crucial allies. Together we were able to produce positive results. Identifying the prevailing gaps within the partnership will be very beneficial for both ends.

An understanding of the Pakistan Army, based on ground truth and how it responded to different historical junctures, is essential for peace and stability in the region. Sacrifices rendered by Pakistan's armed forces due to four decades of turmoil in Afghanistan need to be recognized. Although we entered that war mainly to protect our own security interests, we played a pivotal role in Russia's defeat and many other US-sponsored pursuits in the region. Pakistan remains a natural ally of the West and all it requires is mutual trust, confidence, and loyal partnership.

We do understand that international relationships at the strategic level are developed and maintained based on changing situations and interests. Irrespective of who has been using whom, however, betrayal at the expense of each other's critical national interest is not a sustainable course of action.

PART 4

FAREWELL TO ARMS AND POST-RETIREMENT VENTURES

CHAPTER 9

RETIREMENT FROM THE ARMY AND A JERKY RE-START

Transition to Civvies

No matter how good or bad it is, everything has an end. The sigh of relief enjoyed after a period of hard work, stress, and struggle, is balanced by memories of the great moments we no longer have. After thirty-two years of regular service with the army and ISI and about seven years of additional contractual service with ISI, the day finally came when I, too, had to say goodbye to those great institutions.

What the army gave me over all these long years is much more than I was able to give back. I had tremendous opportunities to serve as a field soldier and taste war on Pakistan's borders. I was given the honour of commanding Pakistani soldiers at various levels. It is a unique trust that I enjoyed thoroughly.

Serving in ISI exposed me to a unique kind of warfare. How these men remain continuously battling against internal and external enemies and the endless sacrifices they make in the country's defence is a story that unfortunately remains unknown to the public. It is painful and frustrating to watch the clueless pseudointellectuals in our society, especially some politicians and some members of the media, malign our defence organizations with baseless accusations, whether on purpose or out of ignorance.

My goal, in whatever capacity I served, was to perform the task at hand to the best of my ability and in the process to train my subordinates to excel and make a difference within the service. It is not about who we are but what we can do for the people and the institutions we serve. My three guiding principles were, to always honour my oath, always take care of my men, and always stay mission-focused.

I lost many of my comrades during my time in the Khakis. I remember each one of them and pray for their departed souls. I wish to pay special homage to those warriors who lost their lives while safeguarding the integrity and sovereignty of our motherland.

Amongst those fallen warriors is my brother-in-law, Captain Umar Farooq Amir Moin, an artillery officer who sacrificed his life at the age of twenty-four at Siachen Glacier, the longest glacier in the Karakorum Mountain range where the LOC between India and Pakistan ends. Amir was a highly patriotic young man. He had earlier, rejected the opportunity to join his brother in Canada in favour of joining the Pakistani army. Subsequently, he volunteered to serve on the highest battlefield in the world.

We do not know how God chooses martyrs. We do know that such people give us the most precious possession they have, their very lives. That is the gift Amir gave to Pakistan. It is the cause, not the death that makes the martyr. Not all of us are here to die a martyr's death, but we all need to have the same spirit of self-sacrifice and love for the country.

Transitioning to civilian life is just another part of military life. Like any other activity in the army, the more preparations one makes, the more smoothly the transition goes, irrespective of how many years we served. It takes a lot to bring one's army career to a close. We must work out meticulously our post-retirement requirements and learn as much as possible about the environments we are likely to live in after we retire.

The Close Circuit Routine

Service in the army teaches us to face life's challenges and recognize our mistakes. I failed to transition smoothly from the military to civilian life because I could not recognize what awaited me outside the closed-circuit routine of army life. The army provides a form of immunity to deceitful financial dealings. Our salaries are directly credited into our accounts, with duplicate pay slips distributed to others. Expenditures are deducted automatically. There is no way to conceal the burdens on a soldier's salary. Mess and canteen, utility bills, school fees for the kids, and other routine expenditures are systematically managed and paid in accordance with well-known procedures. We are left with a limited amount to pay for household expenditures. All of it is done transparently leaving us without the hassle of paying bills and no room for concern about our financial decisions. It is only upon retirement that we are exposed to the realities of civilian life, the deceptive arts by which some people obtain money, and the task of personally managing our finances. We are not used to it, and consequently, some of us stumble. I was one of those unfortunate ones who fell prey to some fraudulent entanglements created by a few unscrupulous characters.

Adjusting to the social settings of civilian society is the most challenging job for most of us who are tuned into military life. I did not foresee the challenges that I would be facing once I retired, and I too became a victim of the ills prevalent in society. Had I done so it would have spared me much frustration before my life settled down in civvies.

Soldiering Through a Patch of Turbulence

Nothing hits us harder than life itself. It does not matter how hard we hit back. It is about how much we can take and keep fighting; how much we can suffer and keep moving forward. That is how we win! That is how things went for me immediately after my retirement. Thank God that my army background gave me strength, and reminded me as a soldier to stand fast, keep fighting, and never give up. I did stumble and fall at times, but I always got up to fight another battle on another day. It took a little longer time, but in the end, Alhamdulillah, I was on my feet again and ready to continue my life's journey honourably.

When I retired, I went to work as an administrator of an army-affiliated educational institution and served there for about a year. While I was there, an old friend and businessman approached me for help finding some investors for his company in South Africa. Since I had known him well for several years, I shared this opportunity with three of my other friends, two civilians and an ex-colleague from the army, a major. I had known these three men for a very long time. All of them decided to take advantage of the opportunity and invested some money with my businessman friend.

A few months after receiving their money, the businessman left Pakistan and stopped communicating with me. I kept trying to reach him but was unsuccessful. My three investor friends became nervous. Then they began demanding that I give them back their money plus the amount of interest they expected to earn.

I felt certain that my businessman friend would contact me eventually and that only a little patience was needed before the matter would sort itself out. I told them to wait, be patient, that the man with their money would surely call me. They agreed but asked me to give them surety cheques in case he did not call. I was very confident that my businessman friend would do nothing wrong and that he would contact me. So, I gave a security cheque to each of them.

I had no legal paperwork describing my duties and responsibilities in connection with these actions. Likewise, I had nothing in writing concerning the security cheques. It was a terrible mistake. My intentions were honest, but

I had naively undertaken responsibility for paying back the three investments plus the agreed-upon profits.

The two civilians tried to cash their security cheques and get me into legal trouble, but my bank refused to have me charged with fraud. Before it was over, I had to sell the home I received as part of my retirement under the army officer's housing programme and borrow additional money to pay them off and save myself from further embarrassment.

The third investor, the army major, started threatening to report me to my ex-bosses and ruin my hard-won reputation for honesty, respect, and honour. He also began calling my family and friends to discredit me with baseless allegations of misconduct.

The year following my retirement was a firefighting exercise, getting money from one source to pay another, and not hearing from my businessman friend although I still thought he would. I waited too long to confront the issue head-on, and it trapped me into an unmanageable bog. In the end, I lost most of my assets and went into heavy debt.

That year was a terrible period of great personal embarrassment and suffering that lingered on many years later. It brought me down from the highest point in my life to the lowest. It shattered me financially, mentally, and even socially. The worst of all was when I saw the fake masks fall from the faces of many who I had thought were friends, who had hovered around me during all the good years when I was well known and was in a position to help them in one way or the other. Suddenly it became clear that people I had known for years had changed their attitudes towards me. I was no longer someone they wished to be seen with. It was so painful when the people for whom I thought I had been a source of inspiration, and a mentor suddenly started to doubt my character and my intentions.

But the experience made me wiser. With respect to the retired army officer involved in the case, I learnt that a professional background does not guarantee that one will be honourable. Unfortunately, there are such people in the armed forces as well as elsewhere in society and that is to be expected. After all, the army is part of the same society as civilians, and it is equally affected by that society's prevailing social evils. Black sheep exist everywhere.

Sometime later, when the pressure on me had eased, I learnt that my businessman friend had died of cancer. Perhaps, his illness was why he never called me.

I was also contacted by the son of one of the civilian investors who had tried to cash his surety cheque and then have me charged with fraud. Unfortunately, this investor had died, and his son requested me to pardon his late father for having wrongfully pressured me into paying him money. He wanted my forgiveness so that his father would not suffer in the afterlife. He knew his father had extorted the money and offered to pay it back to me. He apologized for the trouble his father had caused me and my family.

    I refused to take his money, but his plea on behalf of his father did change my heart and helped me to understand that for me forgiveness was the best way forward. I decided not to expose his father publicly for what he had done to me and to my family, and I prayed the lesson I had learnt would serve me well in the future. I think it was the right decision. Now three of those involved in this terrible part of my life have passed away. May God guide us all to live a life with honesty, grace and dignity.

    Though the episode happened many years ago, I still wonder why these people did this to me. I find it hard to accept that just passing along a proposal from one friend to another could have cost me so much in life. Still, looking back my conscience is clear. I know that my intentions were good, and I did not attempt to avoid any responsibility that I may have had. I made sure that their money was returned but at a great personal cost. Had I been more careful in managing my affairs, more cautious in choosing my friends and less naive in my judgements, I could have saved myself and my family much agonizing pain and very heavy financial losses.

CHAPTER 10

QUESTIONING LIFE IS NEVER AN OPTION

Getting into Warrior's Mode

Perhaps, the biggest lesson I learnt after having gone through a small patch of turbulence in my life is that starting to question your life or blaming fate does not pay. The only option is to face your difficulties and tackle them head on. See yourself as a warrior and fight back.

In the army, we plan to deal with any situation we encounter and execute any task we are given. For example, suppose we are told to defend a chunk of territory. First, we assess the situation. What does the terrain look like? What is the enemy's troop strength? What is our troop strength? What will the weather be like, etc? We identify possible options for how to accomplish our tasks and prioritize them. Depending on what we learn during our analysis, we select a course of action and plan for its implementation.

Our effort is still not complete, however, until we have developed contingency plans in case our original battle plan does not go as we expected. Taken together, the original battle plan and the contingency plans become the master plan of action.

In most cases, our plans work, but there are times when the battle takes a turn that we do not foresee. That is when the commander must rise to the occasion and use to the best of his ability whatever resources he has at his disposal to win the fight. Timely decisions save lives and prevent damage.

The same is true for a personal crisis. We all plan out our lives in ways that suit the environment in which we are living. We also consider contingency plans in case we confront unexpected scenarios. But sometimes events pop up that we did not think about and for which there are no contingency plans. That is our testing time when we must react swiftly with whatever resources we have at our disposal to neutralize the adverse effects of the unexpected challenge. It is easy to write a thesis recommending ways to confront such situations, but when it happens, it is easy to become confused and overwhelmed.

The Fightback

That is what happened to me. I had never planned to owe large amounts of money I did not have. The first year, after my business friend disappeared, was a period of firefighting and nothing else, handling one setback after another with whatever strength I could muster. To pay back the investments, I started borrowing loans wherever possible. The strategy was an absolute disaster. I ended up taking out loans to pay other loans. Instead of improving my situation, I kept sinking deeper and deeper into debt with each passing day. Had I had a close, trustworthy friend, with experience in managing money, I probably would not have made that mistake, but unfortunately, I did not have such a friend and that made my situation worse.

The friends and relatives from whom I had borrowed money began to panic. They were losing hope in me. Some of them demanded their money back. I had no choice but to sell almost everything I had to pay off most of my debt.

With the situation worsening, I decided to rent a small portion of a house in Islamabad, leave my wife and three daughters, and go to Dubai to see if there was anything I could do there. I chose Dubai because I had lived there for nearly three and a half years as a diplomat and because my eldest son also worked there in a senior position in one of the banks. I stayed in Dubai for about a month, exploring possible opportunities. There were some, but I would need a substantial investment to take advantage of them and I did not have the money. During my stay, I attended an international security exhibition to learn more about the private security sector and about what future opportunities might exist in that field.

From Dubai, I went to the United Kingdom to meet some of my old colleagues who had retired there. I stayed in England for nearly three months. With the help of an acquaintance, I formed a private security company, 'Security Managers International,' in Kent. My elder brother, Muhammad Anwar Khan, who was a UK citizen, was a great help to me. Knowing what I was going through, he was extra kind and caring and treated me like a father. Unfortunately, he passed away about three years ago. May Allah bless his soul.

The UK was a good place to be in the private security business. I tried to kick-start my company, but the lack of money to invest in its growth prevented much forward movement. We did manage to get some exciting opportunities, but without adequate working capital, I could not make them work. With my family back in Islamabad and no hope of obtaining the money I needed to build the company in England, I decided to move back to Dubai and see what I could do with the company there.

This time I connected with some of my acquaintances in the Dubai Police Department and was successful in registering my private security company under the name, Security Managers LLC. My children arranged an initial investment and paid the company's bills until I was in the position to take it on myself. It was very hard going but with perseverance, we were finally able to make a foothold.

The uncertainty was almost over. I had entered a new phase of my life, this time as part of the private security industry in Dubai. I did not look back and instead took advantage of the opportunity to continue my decades-long work in the field of security and intelligence. Since June 2014, when I launched my first private security project, I have kept moving forward and my company has kept growing. The Security Managers' network is expanding, and I am back on my feet. By the grace of Allah, I now find myself in a very stable situation, my family is with me, and I have earned a good name in the industry. I am reborn and pursuing my professional future with confidence and motivation.

After battling hard for nearly a decade to come back from where I was, I sincerely said goodbye to the mental torture of that experience; the sleepless nights, the embarrassment, the betrayal, and the rejection of people I thought were my friends, and the heartbreak. I consciously put it all behind me. Now what is left are the lessons.

Lessons Learnt

Letting Go

The great basketball player Michael Jordan said, "Obstacles don't have to stop you. If you run into a wall, don't turn around and give up. Figure out how to climb it, go through it, or work around it" I tried to follow what he said. I too, had no option but to start over from wherever I was, use whatever I had, and do all I could to avoid total disaster. I went all out and learnt my way through it. My personal flaws and imperfections surfaced quickly but they helped me to understand what had happened, regroup, and move forward more powerfully. I had to stay composed and focused to fight back.

An important step was that I decided to let go and say goodbye to the people who betrayed me and left me circling in confusion, spending sleepless nights thinking about their broken promises. Instead of focusing on them, I accepted the change and began to focus on making my life better. I found out that with practice, effort, and thoughtful management of our aspirations, we can turn our lives around. Time, hard work, and a positive attitude have a way of letting things unfold and work themselves out for the better. It also reaffirmed for me what old soldiers say, "Tough times never last, but tough people do."

The worst is over, and I am on the road to recovery. Alhumdulillah. God has been very kind to me. My close relatives and a few devoted friends came to my rescue with solid support. My wife and children stood by me and guided me through stormy seas back to safe waters. Though the times were tough, they taught me some other very important lessons.

Recognize Mistakes and Accept Responsibility

We all make mistakes. Sometimes, they are minor; sometimes not. When the consequences are serious, we often prefer to make excuses for what happened and why. The best course of action is to admit the mistake, own it, make amends, and move on. Making mistakes is not desirable, but if we fail to handle the situation well, they can become much worse, and the consequences become much greater. Punishing oneself for a mistake will make it harder to put the mistake behind us. We might even lose our self-confidence, which can prevent us from moving forward.

On the other hand, owning a mistake demonstrates integrity and responsibility. Such actions earn respect and bestow credibility. So, do not make assumptions about what happened. Clearly understand the facts and start with zero expectations. Then, admit the mistake, talk about it with the people involved or who can help, devise a solution, and follow it through with confidence and perseverance. Nobody is perfect. It is not the mistakes, but what we do about them that will help us to become more respected, dependable, and possibly even admired as willing to fight against the odds.

Perseverance and Self-belief

Life has a way of kicking us when we are down, and just when we think we cannot fall any lower, we get kicked again. But it is important to remember that setbacks, failures, and tragedies are part of life, no matter how painful they may be. Whether we overcome difficult times largely depends on our ability to persevere through adversity without giving up. Persistence can change failure into extraordinary achievements.

Perseverance and persistence mean finding even during the roughest of times something that makes us understand that life is not all bad. That the seemingly endless stretches of fear, disappointments, pain, and headaches will pass. Life's meaning comes from the continuous reframing of our mindsets to tell ourselves to keep going. Hope makes the present moment less difficult to bear, and a problem becomes the chance for us to do our best. If we believe tomorrow will be better, we can face the hardship at hand with more courage and confidence. We must remember, "It is in our darkest hours that we may discover the true strength of a brilliant light within ourselves that can never be dimmed". It depends upon whether we see our difficulties as stumbling blocks or stepping stones. Anything that does not move is dead. 'Win or die' is what makes warriors great. We need to keep moving forward no matter what. Believing in oneself is the key to success.

Management of Relationships

Understand and manage one's relationships carefully. The best things in life to hold on to are family and friends. Relationships are how we connect with society and maintain the social structure. Understanding our different relationships and the role each one plays in our lives is essential. If our expectations of others are too high or too low, it can cost us heavily. Failure to measure our relationships accurately is where we generally go wrong and get ourselves into trouble. The nature of our connection to another person, whether a family member or close friend, does not necessarily determine if we can rely on that person. A person's reliability is better judged based on clear and transparent communication, commitment, and compromise.

Family is not all about blood linkages. My experience taught me it is something much more than what I had thought. 'True family' are the people who chose us in their life and will remain with us, no matter what. It is unmeasurable when compared with social standing, worldly gains, or any other kind of advantage. It is not about how much financial, or material support one family member can give to another; rather it is about the love, affection and emotional support provided when one needs it. The relationship is based purely on genuine feelings for one another.

I know this definition of 'true family' may sound unrealistic, perhaps even absurd to some people, but I think that is where we get it wrong. 'True family' is much deeper than what we normally think of it on the surface. It is something more than just connections by blood. It can include friends and acquaintances. The relationships that show one's 'true family' members emerge only during times of testing. They reveal the people who stand by us and believe in us, irrespective of whether they are blood relatives, friends, or acquaintances. Once we identify them, they become part of our families to value until the end.

During my time of testing, my wife and the children stood steadfast with me like rocks with all the physical, mental, and financial resources at their disposal. The extra amount of love and care they gave me when I needed it most can never be repaid. Each of them made me feel strong and motivated. Their sacrifices for me were immeasurable.

I received unconditional love and support from some other close relatives and friends who stood by my side until the end. My younger brother Shamim sold his house to give me money. My elder brothers were also very kind and supportive. My sisters gave me unwavering support and love, boosted my morale, and offered everything they owned to help my problem.

The fatherly care and concern for me by Dr Mazhar Saeed Choudhary, my wife's elder brother, was immense. Dr Mazhar is a Fellow of the Royal College of Surgeons in the United Kingdom, a professor of surgery, and now retired. Other people would tell him of problems I was having, and he would solve them without telling me about it. I am indebted to Khaula Jabeen, my wife's elder sister. She is a very kind and selfless person who stood with us through thick and thin.

Another couple that remained with us was my wife's cousin Kamal Uddin Tipu and his wife, Dr Khola Iram. Dr Khola's unwavering support throughout this period was reassuring. She called me frequently to check on my welfare and vowed repeatedly to stand by me through thick and thin.

My story of 'true family' is incomplete unless I mention an unknown warrior who helped me in my struggles by taking it upon himself to fight half of my battles. Sardar Zaheer Zaufran is a colleague of my daughter Madiha and shares ownership with her of an advertising company in Pakistan. He was with me the whole way, like an old-time buddy. He was the kind of comrade I would expect to find among army warriors while I was facing challenging circumstances. During my year of firefighting, he was there, day or night, to represent me whenever and wherever I needed him. There are no others like him. A wonderful soul with a very kind and loving heart. He remains an essential pillar of my 'true family'.

Ups and downs are part of life and things must go on. Succumbing to the odds is not a solution to problems; we must stand and fight back until we succeed. I will end this chapter by penning down a famous quote by C.S. Lewis, 'You cannot go back and change the beginning, but you can start where you are and change the ending.' It is not the mistakes that matter. It is how we interpret failures and heed the lessons we learn from them.

Private Security Sector, My New Playground

C.J. Lewis's words were hammering my mind 24/7. I needed a restart from where I was. What could be the options that I could exploit? Getting into any private business venture after such a horrifying experience earlier on, was a frightening deal. Getting a job in any private sector at an age where I was, was also not a viable option. While I was in a state of uncertainty, I got an opportunity to visit Dubai, a place where I had spent some very enjoyable and productive years while I was serving there as a diplomat. As they say, destiny takes you where you should be and that's what happened with me as well. My visit to Dubai coincided with an international security exhibition (Intersec), a yearly event that is organized in Dubai for security professionals from across the world. The visit to the event and exchanging notes on my lifetime experiences and listening to theirs initiated a new thought process in my mind. Why not make private security as my new playground? The idea seemed practical and encouragement from a few of my ex-colleagues paved my way into this field.

Within a few days I was an entrepreneur in the private security sector and owner of a private security company, 'Security Managers LLC', providing security services in both public and private sectors. Though I had managed to establish the company, my lack of experience in the private sector held me back for quite some time and it took me two to three years to overcome the initial hitches. The company finally started to gain momentum and secure reasonable contracts for security work.

In a year and half, in parallel with Security Managers LLC, I established a training institute, named 'Security Manger's Professional Management Training Institute'. I used my old contacts and recruited some well-known international security management experts from around the world to staff the company. Many of them were ex-military and former intelligence professionals who had extensive training, knowledge, and experience in national and international security matters. Besides helping me with the training institute, they provided me with valuable insight into the prevailing international security rigmaroles hunting the security issues all over the globe.

Within a month or two, I had a team of about thirty-three instructors from thirteen different countries who were ready to help us, including some very senior internationally known security professionals with decades of practical experience in professional management. In quick succession, we were able to organize several important professional management courses for senior level managers and executives in the United Arab Emirates, other Gulf countries, and some countries in Africa.

Everything was going well but managing two companies at the same time with a small number of full-time staff and limited financial resources became a difficult proposition. In retrospect, I could have made things much easier by limiting our initial effort to one company.

Both companies had the potential to grow, but to keep my financial situation under control, I thought it best to concentrate on just one and leave the other for later. So, I decided to temporarily close the training institute as it was much more expensive to run and the logistics of arranging trainers and students from all over the world was complicated and very time-consuming. The plan to focus on one company was the right decision. Security Managers, LLC is doing very well and getting better every day, Alhumdulillah.

The company has built a good reputation, operating in Dubai, and providing security solutions to both public and private sector clients. My security background and that of my partner Mr. Mukhtar Hussain have enabled us to organize well-trained operational security teams that are widely recognized for providing high quality security services.

From my time in security and intelligence while serving in the army, and my post-retirement security work in the private sector, I have been a witness to several fast-changing developments in this field. The experience helped me to forecast emerging trends in the field of security and to share my experiences and opinions through written articles, lectures, and seminars on hot security topics. The print media at home and abroad has been particularly helpful by publishing my articles in a timely fashion. The Security Industry Regulatory Authority, Dubai (SIRA) has also helped to publicize my thoughts about security related matters.

The prevailing international security framework, which is linked directly to regional and global security patterns, sets the parameters for public and private security needs. The international security perspective is changing and by doing so is transforming and expanding the roles and responsibilities of public and private security professionals. Realizing the need to share my thoughts on how the key trends in the international security outlines are affecting the private security sector, I thought of dealing with the subject as a separate chapter in this book.

CHAPTER 11

GLOBAL SECURITY PATTERNS: TRENDS RESHAPING PRIVATE SECURITY PROTOCOLS

The private security sector evolved through a very interesting development process. As the burden of protecting humans and property shifted gradually away from governments to the citizenry, private sector security companies began to appear. They grew substantially during the late 1960s and early 1970s, creating a private sector industry. The industry became more prominent and powerful in our region during the Russian invasion in Afghanistan in the late 1970s and grew even more following the attack in New York City on 9/11. Globalization, shifting balance of power, rise of non-state actors in few parts of the world, terrorism, transnational organized crime, forced migration, geopolitical shifts, and increasing access to technological and social resources, have raised the world's vulnerabilities to a new level and are changing the security paradigm significantly.

The worsening global security environment increased the need for private protection and many companies developed capabilities to meet it. Governments began to augment their public security capabilities with private security arrangements.

Today, private security dominates the field of personal and private property protection. With each passing year, the demand is growing, and the private security industry is expanding, and gaining prominence around the globe. The biggest challenge to the industry is to keep itself relevant to the changing global order and keep modifying and upgrading its operational capabilities to meet the challenges at hand.

The Prevailing Security Framework

The evolution of international geopolitical and strategic factors creates the road map that shows what organizations operating at regional and international levels will need to protect their people and their assets. The geo-strategic and geo-political developments during the last two to three decades have radically changed the perceptions, concerns, policies, and mechanisms of these organizations. Among these significant developments are economic disparity, political polarization, extremism, malicious exploitation of technology, and the abandonment of a globalized world view in favor of a nationalistic inward-looking stance. From the private security standpoint, these developments have been highly disruptive. Moreover, large-scale involuntary migrations, resulting from violence, conflict, environmental, or economic reasons, have added to perceptions of insecurity. Some of these immigrants are criminals; others fall prey to vested interests who use them mercilessly to further their own political and military objectives.

Changes in the geo-political and geo-strategic environment have brought about changes in the nature of security threats. Unfortunately, we now have criminals and other hostile actors or offenders who are much better trained, operate under well-conceived cover, and in some cases, are part of organized gangs. In many cases, they are controlled from remote secure bases of operations and fully supported by the latest technology. Barring a few criminals who continue to operate individually, we now confront transnational crime organizations with well-planned and well-funded command, communications, and logistic capabilities.

There are ordinary societal problems to contend with, in addition to geo-strategic and geo-political developments. Among them are poverty, unemployment, drug traffickers, money launderers and illegal migration.

Globalization, with its positives and its negatives, is unfortunately the root cause for most of the security challenges that we face today. The fallout from a problem created in one corner of the world travels quickly throughout the globe, and it creates ripple effects in places far from its origins without regard to limits in space and time.

Cyber-crime is the biggest challenge the private security industry faces today. Technology is being used to steal, expose, alter, disable, or destroy information through unauthorized access to computer systems. Employers face a significant insider threat. Malicious or incompetent employees, deliberately or by accident, can cause significant damage to a company's assets and reputation. This trend is likely to increase over time.

The recent Covid-19 global pandemic, with its negative social, economic, and political consequences, has reminded us that health security is an indispensable part of national security, depending on the scale of the disease, the urgency for action, and the depth and extent of its impact on society. It too must now be prioritized among other security challenges.

Private sector security threats often employ a mix of conventional and unconventional means to attack their victims. Sometimes tailored and complicated security management procedures are required to be used to counter them. It has caused the job of a private security provider to become quite technical and complicated.

The net effect of all these changes is more insecurity for individuals and for their businesses. In this context, our goal as professionals is to maintain reliable security services, protect the well-being of our clients and community, and maintain the safety of our staff. It is a complex task that requires us to be mindful about our contractual obligations, safety, the strategies, tactics, and protocols we have adopted, and the intricacies of current threats.

Emerging Trends in Private Security

Like all other businesses, the security industry has had its ups and downs in recent years. Traditional security firms and corporate security teams have undergone dramatic changes. To meet the evolving threats, they have had to improve the training of their people, modernize their processes, and acquire more modern technology.

Traditional security firms have a unique challenge because personal security threats are tailored to the targeted victim and because there is always the question of how much security is too much, and how much is not enough. Many people who fall victim to breaches of personal security are high profile figures. They are targeted with information attacks to steal their personal and/or financial information, and at times, they are also exposed to physical attacks. State-of-the-art electronic counter-surveillance and security measures can protect them from cyber-attacks. Bodyguard services and trained security advisors can help to protect them and members of their families from physical attacks.

A new type of security professional has come into being – the personal protection officer - who focuses on technology and secures the protected from online information attacks. These specialists deal specifically with online hackers who may be trying to steal personal and/or financial information. Their goal is to harden cyber protections and thwart possible cyber-attacks.

The role of traditional bodyguards has also changed. Most of their work is done 'behind the scenes'. In cases of danger, they must be ready to step in and protect their clients. Previously, the job used to be mostly about reacting to an immediate physical threat to the client. Now it involves much more planning and proactive work to identify and counter potential threats.

For example, terrorism in public places has seen an alarming increase over the last decade, making public and private security more of a necessity for targeted individuals and riskier for security officers. Bodyguards protecting high risk clients must be proactive rather than reactive, checking cars for improvised explosive devices or watching for potential shooters or suicide attackers, instead of waiting until someone approaches the victim. Their goal has changed from reaction to prevention.

There is also the problem of social media. Criminals and terrorists gather from the internet most of the information they need to attack their victims, and they use the internet to publicize how they have damaged their targets. If an attack is successful, it will be publicized widely on social media, a lasting reminder of the private security company's failure to protect its client.

Corporate security professionals also face some other unique challenges. Chief Security Officers (CSOs) often use the Enterprise Security Risk Management (ESRM) approach to prepare holistic security programs for their companies. They face significant challenges, including flaws in the alignment of people and processes, workforce training and innovative strategic planning. Last but not least, security considerations have become such an important part of all corporate operations that security officials must now function as an integral part of the company's business management team. That requires them to possess skills not normally found in the realm of traditional security consultants.

Expanding Horizons of the Security Professionals

Two important challenges facing security operations today are reactive threat management and intuitive decision-making based on preconceived notions about the nature of a potential problem. They make it difficult for organizations to practice proactive security, thereby putting the people, the brand, and the organization at risk. The security professionals are under obligation to keep themselves updated with the ever-increasing demands of the industry and equip themselves with the capabilities that enable them to react spontaneously to the emerging challenges.

When people, processes and technologies are connected and working together across an organization, it improves not only security but also business performance. The private security industry must follow the demands of its customers to ensure tailor made security solutions, embrace information technology, and learn to employ countermeasures that will protect its clients from digital abuse. Security professionals who are not proficient in digital matters are rapidly becoming irrelevant.

Digital transformation has revamped risk management. As technological improvements continue to evolve, new capabilities such as artificial intelligence (AI) and data analytics must be incorporated into and complementary of physical security measures. Areas of special focus should include identity management, threat detection and investigation and enhanced physical security. By challenging conventional thinking and re-examining current practices, security professionals can take the private security industry to the next level of performance, improve client safety, and create value in organizations beyond traditional security upgrades.

With external environments changing rapidly, security planners often find it challenging to develop long-range plans that remain relevant because they have no ability to control the operating environment. Senior executives crafting organizational strategy need as much certainty as possible to plan for unexpected events. In such an environment, the security program is a continuous work in progress and needs to be very flexible. Security planners must constantly monitor the current and future operating environment as it relates to the work envisioned by the company based on its mission, priorities, targets, and objectives. As the operating environments change, security planners will have to adapt and refine their strategies to meet future challenges.

Security staff are now seen as first responders in the event of an emergency. That means that security officials must broaden their focus beyond the office or the building they are protecting, beyond just employees and facilities, to include areas surrounding client locations. With the help of police and other public officials, they should keep track of what is happening in areas that could adversely impact their clients. For example, the number and types of crimes in surrounding areas, changes in traffic patterns, or an increase in public discontent should be noted and factored into the client's current safety and security assessment.

The implementation of security modifications to meet changes in the operating environment is the most challenging part of the strategic planning process. Close coordination with clients is essential. Security professionals, of necessity, must be part of business management teams. Likewise, client involvement in planning and implementing security measures has become critical to success.

The bottom line is that effective security requires close interaction between security professionals and business leaders. The security sector must adjust its framework and processes to promote a culture of integrated risk management, and businesses must be open to work closely with the security sector.

Higher education for security staff has become a critical requirement to work in today's security environment. Clients want security professionals who improve their reputation and brand. A security staff that carries out their duties by meaningfully interacting with the company's management, other service providers, and its customer base is a strong indicator of good corporate management.

Continuing education is part of higher education. Routine security staff education and training that addresses specific current threats and more general industry-wide threats is essential. Specialized training tailored to fit the needs of security officials with unique or specialized responsibilities is also very important. The effort must focus on crime prevention, intelligence, procedural knowledge, innovation, and critical thinking.

CHAPTER 12

BEYOND THE FRONTLINES: A SILENT TRIUMPH

Before I conclude my story of life 'In the Khakis', I thought it appropriate to pen a few words about my 'battle at the home front' which has been the most satisfying experience of my life.

The family members of soldiers, especially officers, are known as half-soldiers because they too become part of the army. While living in well-organized cantonments with convenient amenities and reasonably good schooling can be comfortable; the challenging and busy work schedules of officers and men deprive family members of their care and affection. The situation becomes even more difficult for them when they are forced to endure long separations because army personnel move to field areas or are assigned to non-family stations.

The story of my army career, therefore, is also the story of my family. I was a major when my wife and I were married, and a brigadier when I retired. All my children grew up in army culture and have embarked upon professional lives of their choosing. All of them were and are an equal part of my army life.

The Base of Fire

In military terminology, 'the base of fire' is a supporting force that provides overwatch and covering fire to the advancing forces while they are executing fire and movement tactics to reach up to their objectives for the final blow. In the context of the personal life of the army officers, their wives play the role of a potent and well-placed 'base of fire' to win their battles while they are in the field or off the field under all circumstances. The wife of an army officer has a crucial role to play. An anonymous poem about a soldier's wife best describes it.

CAUGHT IN THE CROSSFIRE

I wear no uniforms, no blues or army greens,
But I am in the Army in the ranks rarely seen.
I have no rank upon my shoulders, Salutes I do not give,
But the military world is the world where I live and am rarely seen.
I'm not in the chain of command, orders I do not give or get,
But my husband is the one who does; this I cannot forget.
I'm not the one who fires a weapon, which puts my life on the line,
But my job is just as tough; I'm the one who is always left behind.
My husband is a patriot, a brave and prideful man,
And the call to serve his country not all can understand.
Behind the lines, I see the things needed to keep this country free,
My husband makes the sacrifice, but so do our kids and me.
I love the man I married; The military is his life,
So I pledge to support my hero,
And stand among the silent ranks known as "THE ARMY WIFE".

I married Khansa Shaheen at the age of twenty-nine when I was in charge of the ISI field detachment in Islamabad. Khansa was a professional educator, a lecturer in History at Government Girls Degree College in Rawalakot, my native town. She was a colleague of my elder sister. It was an arranged marriage. I had never seen her before the day we got married. I saw her for the first time after the marriage ceremony and welcomed her into my life. Since then, we have been in happily married life for the last forty-three years. It has been a wonderful experience, the one I cherish most. Khansa has stood by me like a rock all these years, and we have faced all the good and the bad that came our way together.

Her contribution to the upbringing of our children has been incalculable. She always provided the family with a clean and neat home, but more than that she has been an educator. In addition to teaching at various prominent academic institutions, she became our children's tutor and educational mentor. She guided and instilled high moral values in each one of them. She maintained ties with our extended families on both sides, which has earned her great honour and respect. She actively supported the army welfare schemes while I was serving. She ran the Children Welfare Centre at various cantonments where we were posted and made a significant difference in the lives of the families living there.

Mine and Khansa's parents have been our role models in raising our children. My father-in-law, Chaudhry Khuda Buksh came from a background like that of my father. His pursuit of higher education was the hallmark of his life, and he overcame financial and administrative obstacles to make a very successful career in the field of education. At the time of the partition in 1947, he migrated to Pakistan, leaving behind everything he possessed. He lost more than half of his extended family to the violence between Hindus, Sikhs, and Muslims that followed the break-up. After a small part of Kashmir was liberated, he was among a very small number of professional educators who helped establish a new government in Azad Kashmir. He worked day and night to kick start an interim education department, travelling on foot throughout the state, organizing schools, authoring textbooks, and motivating people to educate their children and raise them to live better lives. He was one of the role models for me in raising my children and giving them the best possible education, I could manage.

My mother-in-law, Saeeda Begum, likewise made sure that her children had the best possible education and mentoring at home. She also became a role model for my family to make us a well-knit team. She was a very loving and kind person. Unfortunately, she passed away too early in life, but she remains close in our hearts.

The Infinite Gain

Khansa and I had six children to raise: two sons, three daughters, and the son of my eldest sister.

The environments in our home and at their schools helped all my children to become part of a well-knit team and to excel in their studies. Despite limited financial resources, we provided them with the best possible education opportunities, selling whatever we needed to sell to support their schooling. Fortunately, a small period of turbulence that confronted me in my life, badly affecting me financially, came after I had supported them to complete their education. Had it come prior to this; things would have been really tough for me.

The most notable aspect of their growing up was their mutual support and care for each other. My sister's son, Asif was admitted to Lawrence College in Murree, and after his intermediate examination, he left for Australia where he earned college and post-graduate degrees in business administration from Bond University. He returned to Pakistan and prospered in his business. He has always considered himself and been considered by us to be part of our family. He loves and cares for all his brothers and sisters. Seeing him doing well in his life is a matter of great joy and personal satisfaction for us. He has a devoted wife, Nadia, who is a Professor in Psychiatry, and a pair of twins, Zunair and Mahrosh. Both their children are doing very well in their educational pursuits.

My eldest son Asim, after his intermediate exams, went to the United Kingdom to pursue his higher education. He earned a master's degree in computer sciences at the University of Oxford. Over the years, he has grown into a thriving and successful information technology consultant, working in senior positions in various international banks and other important organizations. Besides his professional success in the field of computer sciences, he is also a programme leader for Landmark Worldwide, a global personal and professional growth, training, and development company. His wife, Tamreez is a graduate of McGill University in Canada and a post-graduate from Oxford University in Global Governance and Diplomacy. Their son, Elhaan is also an up-and-coming intellectual with far-reaching ambitions.

After completing her bachelor's degree in management of information systems from the London School of Economics and Political Science as a part of their external programmes, my eldest daughter, Maryia earned her post-graduate degree, in analysis, design and management of information systems also from LSE, in the UK. She has also earned project management certifications from the United Kingdom and the United States. She has worked successfully in various managerial positions at leading multinational companies and in the economic development sector. She has built an international reputation for her knowledge and professionalism and is currently working as a subject matter expert and instructor in project/program management.

The chain of family success continued with our younger daughter, Mehwish who, after completing her bachelor's and master's degrees from Bahria University, Islamabad, joined my other children in London. There, she obtained her second master's degree in management, organization, and governance from the London School of Economics and became an international human resource professional. She managed the human resources department of a leading multinational oil and gas company for several years, and now she works as an independent human resource consultant. Her husband, Fawad is an accountancy consultant and possesses a bachelor's degree in applied accountancy from Oxford Brookes University, in the UK. They have two wonderful daughters, Manal and Aaima.

Our youngest daughter, Madiha received her bachelor's degree with honours from Bahria University Islamabad and later earned her master's degree with a gold medal from the same University. She worked as the marketing manager for a leading advertising company for several years and now runs her own advertising agency. Madiha is very innovative, continuously adds new ideas and designs to her advertising, and is well-thought of within her professional field.

My youngest son Ammar received his bachelor's degree in mechanical engineering from Middle East Technical University in Ankara, Turkey. It is one of the world's leading schools for engineering. He has also completed a Diploma in Digital Business from Columbia Business School in the United

States, under their external programmes and is presently working as a Lead Engineer/Product Owner for a well-known global enterprise. He has already experienced much success and is on track to go a long way in his profession. His fiancée, Esra is also an accomplished engineer with far-reaching ambitions.

By the grace of Allah, my wife and I had the opportunity to attend the graduation ceremonies of all our children at these prestigious universities. Each time that I saw them given their degrees, I thought of my *'taat'* school in Azad Kashmir where I had my first opportunity to learn. I think of my *taat* school as the mother of all these great educational institutions that gave my children the opportunity to learn. It would not be fair if I did not mention the institution of the Pakistan Army which provided the best environment for the education and upbringing of my children while I was in service. That became a solid base for each child to grow further and reach so far.

Bridging the Realms: From Guns to Books

As a retired warrior, I find myself in the most conducive living envronments at my home in Dubai, where I am presently anchored. The entrance of the house is decorated with some army mementos, gallery walls filled with pictures of my children receiving their degrees from various universities around the globe, and a small bookshelf with some books on geo-strategic/political and security rundowns at regional and international levels. These elements keep me upbeat to continue my journey with the same zeal and enthusiasm. My active involvement in the private security industry in Dubai helps me to remain in contact with renowned security professionals from almost all corners of the world and keep myself current with ever-changing scenarios at regional and international levels.

With a mind stockpiled with so much stuff from the days when I was an active machinist in the field of security and intelligence and now living under the ideal environments that any retired warrior can wish for, what could be my next target? Maybe writing another book? Who knows!

God be praised for all His blessings.

CONCLUSION

Understanding the security challenges confronting Pakistan from their correct perspective, was among the most valued accomplishments that I was able to achieve during my almost four decades of service with the Pakistan Army and ISI. Additionally, a golden opportunity to serve my country as a diplomat abroad for almost three and a half years helped me broaden my outlook on emerging geo-strategic and geopolitical developments at regional and international levels and understand their fallouts on our national security, more realistically.

An uproar in the security horizon at the international level during the past few decades, with major stakeholders playing their malicious games in our region overriding our national interests, multiple issues with India, and some of our inherited internal sensitivities, have continuously been haunting our national security with increased intensity. In most cases, our adversaries have been manipulating the vulnerabilities in our domestic realm for their own benefit. Creating a wedge between various segments of our society and amongst sensitive government institutions by our adversaries is, unfortunately, a threat that is a much more serious challenge for our security agencies to handle than most of us perceive. Under the prevailing scenario, neutralizing the intriguing nexus between foreign and domestic enemies is probably among the most serious challenges we confront.

Comprehending the threat perception to our national security in its correct perspective, by all the stakeholders within the country, is of vital importance to plan and undertake appropriate counter strategies. Serious efforts are needed at all ends to dilute the misconceptions and make people at home and abroad aware of the realities on the ground. We all need to realize our responsibilities to ensure national solidarity and cohesion under these trying conditions. Considering my prolonged experience in the field of security and intelligence, a virtuous material for the people, particularly, the analysts to ponder history through an authentic premise and predict futuristic security scenarios based on

CONCLUSION

a realistic viewpoint, I decided to share my thoughts on the subject by writing this book.

To make my viewpoint more conclusive, I thought it appropriate to organize the contents of the book in the shape of a memoir of my lifelong experiences in a cohesive manner, to help the readers comprehend the intricacies that drive the life of a Pakistani soldier. My life story has been an interplay of events in a manner that each phase prepared me for the new role that I had to perform subsequently and a new opportunity upon which to accomplish. That makes the story easy to follow and comprehend the life of a Pakistani soldier in its true perspective.

My story begins at a very young age in a remote village with limited education opportunities. It jumps amazingly to a cadet college, bringing me to the noble profession of arms, and after having served in various important positions in ISI for more than two decades, handling sensitive security challenges to the country, finally anchored in retired life in Dubai.

Each part of the narrative has a purpose. The first part highlights the importance of good parenting and a quality education. My education is a tribute to the hard work and determination of my parents, who, despite limited financial resources and inadequate schooling, provided me with access to the country's best educational institutions. I am at a loss for words to express my appreciation and gratitude to them for all that they did for me, and I feel a great responsibility to share their hard work and resolve with all other parents who face similar challenges in life. It is also a reminder to the younger generation to honour their parents' sacrifices by working hard to make them proud.

The second part is an effort to help people to understand Pakistan's army and its inherent culture. I have tried to highlight the critical elements of its innate strengths, the principles that govern its actions, and dynamic mentoring processes at all levels that produce quality officers and men, making Pakistan's army one of the best in the world. I hope it will help people at large, to have a clearer picture of our armed forces than the one often portrayed inaccurately by our internal and external adversaries.

Besides a traditional threat from the east, I have tried to identify multi-directional security threats to our national security from a cleverly orchestrated nexus of international power brokers in our region. Based on personal experiences and authentic/undeniable information, I have elaborated upon most of the significant developments in the region during these testing times, particularly related to Pakistan which many may find absolutely in contrast to what is portrayed to them through malicious propaganda themes by the vested interests. A message for the international community based on ground realities has been made part of the narrative for international strategists/analysts to plan their international relationships and strategies based on authentic premise.

Unfortunately, Pakistan also suffers from susceptible internal divisions that make it more vulnerable to its enemy's exploitation to their benefit. Some of these divergences in our society are inherent in our social structures while many of these are the result of past policies. Prominently among our internal fault lines are weak political culture and our ethnic and sectarian strife that presents significant challenges to our national security. By exploiting our domestic vulnerabilities and our failure to differentiate between personal gains and national interests, our adversaries have successfully created many dissidents within various segments of our society who support their agenda. They exist among the clergy, politicians, lawyers, and the media. Through these moles, the enemies target our strengths, weaken our governance system, create ethnic and religious divisions and damage inter-organizational harmony. Virtually, we are facing a two-front war, one internal and one external.

Based on my experiences in the field of intelligence and security and access to some hidden aspects of the international conspiracies, an effort has been made to present a conclusive national security hypothesis, emerging out of an intriguing interplay between our external adversaries and internal vulnerabilities, as a separate part of the book.

While, presenting an overview of the emerging security challenges to our national security, an effort has also been made to suggest certain way outs of our domestic turmoil through revamping our political culture, the governance system, realigning our educational pursuits and restructuring of democratic values in line with our social fabric. The disconnect between the governing elite and the people is producing poor governance and aggravating our security problems. We must harmonize the people and their leaders to create a political culture and a governance system that works well with each other.

We need to emphasize moral values and character building amongst our youth in an organized manner. Unfortunately, a general trend of cynicism in our approach towards everything that we confront is the most damaging aspect of our social behavior. This attitude adversely affects our approach toward life in general and results in negative and pessimistic responses to the challenges confronting us. Instead of admitting and facing our problems boldly, we start looking for shortcut solutions and begin to embrace social evils to avoid responsibility, giving our enemies another vulnerability to exploit.

We need to understand that for life to be valuable or meaningful, it does not have to be unique. A problem is an opportunity for us to do our best. We must never allow adversity to overwhelm us. We must never hang our heads. There was a phase of my life during which I also faced significant challenges and

CONCLUSION

suffered distress and pain. Instead of succumbing to the pressure during these pressing times, I tried to emphasize my fight to make a comeback, maintain a positive attitude, and move forward despite the odds. Hard times in life also fetch us some priceless lessons which if comprehended intelligently, become a pathfinder to a successful life. Few that I was able to collate while negotiating these difficult times, have been narrated in the last part of the book and would be a useful read for many to benefit at my cost.

The high point of the lessons that I learnt while passing through a turbulent period was that blaming life is never an option to meet the challenges at hand, under any circumstances. We must remember that time and patience are our greatest weapons. Challenging situations demand more mature and positive responses from us. We must be patient, and tolerant, accept what life has given us and live with it. We must learn to face the testing times boldly, with courage, motivation, and self-discipline. Whether we succeed depends largely on our ability to persevere regardless of the pressure. A positive approach and thoughtfully maintained relationships are two powerful assets that we can control and bring to the fight. No one saves us but ourselves. We must fight our battle to the very end to succeed or wear ourselves out completely while trying. It is not what happens to us but how we react to it. The door to sanctuary and peace is inside us. We must believe that in the end, 'our character is our fate'.

The book as a whole, should be a thought-provoking read for the parents who wish to nourish their children to grow them as responsible individuals in society, and educational institutions to plan their formative processes to produce rich nurseries that can provide a suitable workforce for the institutions to meet the challenges at hand. An insight into the 'Khakis' will greatly help people at home and abroad to understand the Pakistan Army and ISI in their correct perspective. Their hard-won successes in guarding the country's security during these challenging times need to be recognized. A realistic assessment of national and regional security challenges should be valuable food for thought for strategists and military historians at home and abroad to base their work themes on a realistic premise. The study concludes with some thought-provoking arguments for people to contemplate.

THANK YOU NOTE

The word 'Thank you' is a very simple and short response, most frequently used to express gratitude, and appreciation to those who have helped us when we needed it. Yet, it is a word that is under-utilized, and its strength, power, and significance to personal relationships remain largely undervalued.

I wish to thank all who have mattered in my life. I want to say 'thank you' to everyone who provided me with extraordinary love, affection, and care in the initial stages of my life and who were instrumental in developing the qualities that kept moving me ahead successfully during the later years of life. My special 'thank you' to all my able mentors who helped me grow stronger and complete a long army career with honour and dignity. Their coaching and guidance were key to making my post-army retirement a purposeful and enjoyable experience.

On this occasion, I also wish to say 'thank you' to all those who chose not to stay with me during my time of testing. Their departure made me realize that not everything in life is permanent and that we need to learn how to deal with loss. The pain of losing them taught me how to stand on my feet and deal with the prospect of disaster on my own.

Ultimately, I want to express my heartfelt gratitude to the '*Pakistan Army*' as the institution that provided me with the capability to pursue my professional goals and continue my pursuits unhindered. An opportunity to discover my 'true family' at a time when I needed someone to hold my hand, has been a blessing. Being a veteran with an inbuilt capacity to face the challenges at hand and unflinching support from my family, I am continuing with my life, looking forward to what comes next.

GLOSSARY

22 families	These were the families which managed to accumulate the major chunk of the country's wealth during early history of the country.
5th G Warfare	Crafting strategies to exploit the weakness of the enemy by using asymmetrical methods such as social engineering, misinformation, cyberattacks etc.
6th G Warfare	Is the doctrine of countervailing war through deterrence.
Abdalian	Students who are studying or have studied in Cadet College, Hasan Abdal.
Adjutant General	Chief administrative officer of the army.
Agent handler	The intelligent operative who cultivates, recruits, and manages the agents under his network.
Agents of influence	Is the description of people whose activities support foreign powers at the cost of national interests. They do so for their personal benefits.
Alhamdulillah	All praises to God Almighty.
Assault Across	Army troops crossing an obstacle in a tactical movement to capture the other end of the obstacle for further operations.
Baluchistan Liberation Army (BLA)	It is a militant organisation in Baluchistan involved in terrorist activities in the province and is being funded by the enemies of the country.

Batman	An individual who used to be provided to Pakistan military officers to help them maintain their uniform etc. This practice has now been discontinued and the officers are paid a fix amount to hire a private helper as per their requirement.
Battery Commander	Commander of artillery gun battery.
Battle Inoculation	It is a training exercise in PMA for cadets to put them through live firing conditions.
Bismillah	Making the start with Allah's name.
Breakout Battle	It is the tactical maneuvering by the troops out of the bridgehead to capture the objective.
Bridgehead Battle	It is a battle to take control of an area on the far end of an obstacle from which the troops can move forward to make attacking maneuvers to capture the objectives.
CCH	Abbreviation used for Cadet College Hasan Abdal.
Central Intelligence Agency (CIA)	The U.S. premier intelligence agency.
CJSC	Chairman Joint Chiefs of Staff Committee, Pakistan Armed Forces.
Chief of the Army Staff (COAS)	The commander-in-Chief of Pakistan Army.
College Adjutant	A military officer who acts as an administrative assistant to the head of the institution.
College squadron	A college club for basic military related training.
Colonel of the Regiment	It is an honorary appointment given to one of the senior regimental officers, serving or retired, to help the incumbent commanding officer in organizing the welfare of unit personnel and their families.
Corporals/Sergeants	Ranks given to PMA cadets to manage their junior cadets.
Counterintelligence	Gathering of information to counter enemy's espionage, sabotage, and other intelligence activities.

GLOSSARY

Dasher's Den   The word is commonly used by 16 SP Regiment to depict the regiment as a 'den' for their officers and men.

Dashers   A word chosen by 16 SP Regiment (Dashing Sixteen) for its officers and men.

Director General of Inter-Services Intelligence (DG ISI)   Head of ISI.

Double agent   An intelligence operative pretending to serve one country while actually serving another.

Embassy-based intelligence setups   Are the intelligence operations where the agent handler is based in a diplomatic mission and operating under cover of a diplomat/staff member.

Federally Administered Tribal Areas (FATA)   These are the areas in Pakistan along Pakistan-Afghan border which have now been amalgamated in Kyber Pakhtunkhwa (KPK) province of the country.

Full-Service Marching Orders (FSMO)   It is a complete dress combination for soldiers to carry their equipment, rations, and personal weapon during combat operations.

General Headquarters (GHQ)   Used for Army Headquarters.

Gentleman Cadet (GC)   Cadets undergoing training at Pakistan military academy.

Gun Position Officer (GPO)   Officer Commanding the Gun position in an artillery battery.

Hannibal   Was a Carthaginian general who commanded the forces of Carthage in their battle against the Roman Republic during the Second Punic War.

Hilal-e-Imtiaz (HI (M))   Second highest award given to civilian and military officers for meritorious services.

Hindutva   A concept of Indian cultural and national/religious identity.

Honorary Lieutenant   It is an honorary rank of Lieutenant given to a Junior Commissioned Officers (JCO).

In the Khakis	'Khaki' is the colour of Pakistan army uniform and army people are generally known as 'men in Khakis'.
Indian Held Kashmir (IHK)	Part of Kashmir under Indian occupation.
'Initiative'	It is the name of an exercise for PMA cadets.
Inter Services Selection Board (ISSB)	Is an army institution for selection of cadets for the three services academies i.e., Army, Navy, and Airforce.
Internal fault lines	Are the domestic vulnerabilities that are exploited by our adversaries to their advantage.
Inter-Services Intelligence (ISI)	Is the primer Intelligence Agency of Pakistan Armed Forces.
Invisible warrior	Army personnel engaged in intelligence activities.
Junior Commissioned Officers (JCOs)	Army rank below officers' ranks.
KGB (Russian Committee for State Security)	Russian Intelligence agency.
Khakis to civvies	Retirement from the army.
LAD, the electrical, mechanical, and engineering section	It is a section from formation's Electrical, Mechanical and Engineering (EME) battalion/ company attached with units from other arms.
Line of Control (LOC)	It is the line that separates Azad Kashmir and Indian Held Kashmir.
Manoeuvring	Movement of troops in a tactical formation.
Martial Law	Military rule.
National Defence Day	Pakistan celebrates its Defence Day on 6 September each year in remembrance of its war with India in 1965.
Non-Commissioned Officers (NCOs)	Army ranks below the rank of junior commissioned officers.
Non-Embassy based operations	The intelligence operations where the agent handler is based in an undercover organisation.

GLOSSARY

Operational intelligence	It is the intelligence effort for acquisition of information/intelligence.
Pakistan Military Academy (PMA)	Academy to train cadets to become officers in Pakistan army.
Paradigm	Pattern or a model.
Prefect	Senior student who is authorized to enforce discipline.
Princely States	These were the states with nominally sovereign entity of British Indian empire during British rule in Indian Sub-continent.
Red clay castle	Is a personalized term used by me for the mud-house in my village where I spent my childhood.
Resident agents	The agents working in the country where they reside.
Right of self-determination	Entitlement of people to have control over their destiny and to be treated respectfully.
Safe house	The houses maintained by intelligence agencies for their intelligence operations.
Sanskrit	An ancient Indo-European language of India.
Self-Propelled artillery regiment	Artillery guns mounted on tanks.
Sepoy Mutiny	A rebellion in form of a mutiny by soldiers of Indian origin in the army against inequality compared to British soldiers in Meerut, India in 1857.
Sergeant Major (SM)	Senior most Junior Commissioned Officer (JCO).
Shalwar-kameez	Pakistani national dress.
Sherwani (jacket)	Part of Pakistani dress.
Silent War Zone	Term used to exhibit intelligence operations.
Sitara-e-Basalat	Gallantry award of Pakistan army given to individuals for distinguished acts of valor, courage, and bravery.

Sitara-e-Imtiaz SI(M)	Third highest award given to military officers for meritorious contribution to security of the country.
Sitara-e-Jurat (Bar)	Recipient of Sitara-e-Jurat (SJ) award twice.
Sitara-e-Jurat (SJ)	Third highest Pakistan military award for distinguished services in combat.
Spy Networks	A group of agents and intelligence officers working for an intelligence agency.
Standing Operating Procedures (SOPs)	Is a set of instructions compiled to help the members of an organisation to carry out their duties according to the specific orders.
Surveillance	Shadowing some person to know his activities.
Taat	Is a mat used in village schools for the students to sit and attend the classes.
Taliban	Afghan religious students turned militants.
Tamgha-e-Basalat (Tbt)	Military award for acts of valor, courage, and devotion to duty.
Tamgha-e-Imtiaz TI (M)	Military award based on self-achievements.
Tamgha-e-Jurat (TJ)	Fourth highest military award for extraordinary heroism during armed combat.
The Bridgehead Operation	Is a military operation to secure an important area across an obstacle for crossing over of a body of troops to launch further operations into the enemy territory.
The Dashing Sixteen	It is the name that the 16 SP Artillery regiment has adopted for themselves based on some dashing actions during 1965 war against India.
Third country intelligence operations	Intelligence operations against a country using the soil of a third country.
Under diplomatic and non-diplomatic cover	Intelligence operative working in foreign countries under cover of a diplomat or in other companies outside the embassy.

INDEX

1. **People with Military Background**

Air Marshal Rahim Khan, 123
Brig (Retd) Riaz Ahmad Qureshi, 68, 70
Brig Arshad Mahmood SJ, 63
British Field Marshal Bernard Law Montgomery, 59
Captain Kirmani, 51, 52
Captain Sikandar Ghumman, 45
Captain Umar Farooq Amir Moin, 153
Director General of the Intelligence Bureau, Brig (Retired) Ijaz Ahmed Shah, 99
Fazal Hussain, 67
General Ashfaq Pervez Kayani, 35
General Ayub Khan, 21, 24, 109, 122, 134
General Yahya Khan, 122
General Abdul Waheed Kakar, 124
General Akhtar Abdul Rehman, 2, 3, 4, 36, 50, 52, 63
General Jahangir Karamat, 92, 126
General Pervez Musharraf, 36, 54, 55, 56, 65, 68, 69, 80, 85, 92, 95, 96, 97, 98, 99, 103, 112, 113, 124, 125, 126, 135
General Shams Ur Rahman Kalu, 123
General Zia ud Din, 125
General Zia ul Haq, 3, 7, 49, 51, 52, 53, 56, 85, 123, 134, 135
Lieutenant Colonel Inayat, 66, 67
Lieutenant Colonel Mughni, 70
Lieutenant Colonel Mumtaz Ahmad Khan Niazi, 39
Lieutenant Colonel Rashid Ahmed, 37, 43, 44
Lieutenant General (Retd) Iftikhar Ali Khan, 125
Lieutenant General Ahsan Saleem Hayat, 97
Lieutenant General Assad Ahmad Durrani, 71
Lieutenant General Gul Hassan, 122, 123
Lieutenant General Hameed Gul, 123
Lieutenant General Khalid Latif Moghul, 70
Major (Retd) Shamim Khan, 70
Major (Retired) Muhammad Farooq Malik, 40, 45
Major Akhtar, 41
Major General Iftikhar, 125
Major Makhdoom Hussain, 49, 53
Major Nadar Pervez, 32
Major Shabbir Sharif (Shaheed), 34
Naik Fiaz, 42, 43

Sepoy Abdul Rehman, 69
Sergeant Major Ibrahim, 39, 40
Sergeant Mohammad Hussain, 66

2. The Politicians
Ashraf Ghani, 100
Atal Bihari Vajpayee, 112
Benazir Bhutto, 123, 124
Donald Trump, 102
Fatima Jinnah, 13
Ghulam Ishaq Khan, 123
Ghulam Muhammad, 122
Gulbuddin Hekmatyar, 50
Hamid Karzai, 110
Iskandar Mirza, 122
Joe Biden, 106, 115
Khawaja Nazimuddin, 122
Maharaja Gulab Singh, 6
Manmohan Singh, 112
Murtaza Bhutto, 49
Narendra Modi, 115
Nawaz Sharif, 124
Quaid-e-Azam Muhammad Ali Jinnah, 145, 146
Siraj Raisani, 101
Zulfiqar Ali Bhutto, 122, 123

3. Other Important Personalities
A.W.E. Winlaw, 21
Arnold Lewis Raphel, 56
Bokhari Sahib, 22
Chaudhry Khuda Buksh, 172
Colin Powell, 95
Dr Abdul Qadeer Khan, 92
J.D.H. Chapman, 25
Jassi Khan, 4, 5
Khawaja Khurshid, 24, 25
Malika-e-Taranum Noor Jahan, 44
Muhammad Anwar Khan, 14, 25, 158
Richard Armitage, 94
Saeeda Begum, 173
Sahib Jan, 7, 11
Sardar Muhammad Ameer Khan, 7
Sardar Muhammad Ashraf Khan, 10
Sardar Muhammad Bulour Khan, 7
Sardar Sajawal Khan, 7, 15

4. People associated with Ethnic/Religious (Militants) Outfits
Brahumdagh Bugti, 80
Harbahyar Mari, 80
Hardeep Singh Nijjar, 106
Kulbhushan Jadhav, 101, 107
Maulana Masood Azhar, 96
Mohammad Shah Khan, 110
Mullah Fazlullah, 90
Mullah Omar, 94
Nawab Akbar Khan Bugti, 80, 135
Osama Bin Laden, 90, 98, 99, 100
Shah Shuja-ul-Mulk, 110

5. Military/Intelligence Organisations
16 SP Regiment (The Dashing Sixteen), 37, 38, 39, 40, 41, 42, 54, 56, 62, 63, 64, 65, 67, 68, 69, 70, 72
1 SP Regiment, 37
46 Mountain Artillery Regiment, 60
Allied foreign intelligence agencies, 99
Artillery Centre at Attock, 68
Atlantic Council's Digital Forensic Research Lab, 105
British Army Command and Staff College at Camberley, 59
British MI-6, 107
Canadian Security, and Intelligence Service, 103

INDEX

CIA, 2, 92, 93, 98, 107
Command and Staff College Quetta, 53, 54, 56, 59, 62, 71
Combined Military Hospitals (CMH) 128
Defence Housing Authority 127, 128
Disinfo Lab in New Delhi, 104, 105
EU Disinfo Lab 102, 104, 105
First Frontier Force Regiment (1FF), 45
Fauji Foundation 128
Indian Intelligence Bureau, 103
Intelligence Bureau, Pakistan's civilian intelligence agency, 99
Inter-Services Selection Board (ISSB), 28, 30
Inter-Services Intelligence (ISI), 2, 3, 4, 46, 47, 49, 50, 51, 52, 53, 54, 60, 63, 71, 72, 73, 75, 76, 78, 79, 80, 81, 82, 83, 85, 89, 90, 92, 94, 95, 98, 99, 100, 101, 107, 114, 118, 123, 125, 126, 140, 141, 142, 152, 172, 176, 177, 179
ISI Detachment Islamabad, 47, 50, 82
ISI Detachment Rawalpindi, 71, 72
ISI Detachment, Sargodha, 47
ISI Sector Headquarter, Lahore, 72

Military Operations Directorate, 71
Military Training Directorate, 71
National Command and Operational Centre (NCOC), 142
National Defence University, 128, 148
National Directorate of Security (NDS), 100
NATO forces, 107, 110
Naval War College at Lahore, 124
Pakistan Military Academy, 28

Pakistan Ordinance Factory (POF), Wah, 16
Qatar's intelligence agency, the State Security Bureau, 106
Research and Analysis Wing (RAW), 79, 80, 92, 93, 95, 100, 101, 102, 103, 104, 105, 106, 107, 114
School of Artillery at Nowshera, 41
US Army Command and Staff College at Leavenworth, 59

6. Civilian Organisations/ Institutions

Army Public School at Peshawar, 101
Bahria University Islamabad, 174
Bond University, 173
Cadet College Hasan Abdal, 16, 19, 20, 21, 25, 29, 30, 38, 41, 47, 64, 127
Columbia Business School, 174
Engineering University Lahore, 29, 30
Fatima Jinnah Medical College, 13
Government Girls Degree College, Rawalakot, 172
Landmark Worldwide, 174
Lawrence College, 13, 173
London School of Economics & Political Science (LSE), 174
Mc Gill University, 174
Middle East Technical University in Ankara, Turkey, 174
Middle School Rawalakot, 15
Military College Jhelum, 38
Oxford Brookes University, 174
Oxford University, 174
PAF Public School Lower Topa, 16, 19
Security Managers, LLC, 159, 163, 164
University of Baluchistan, 60

7. Ethnic/Sectarian Groups
Dogras, 5
Ghilzai, 110
Maharaja, 5, 6
Pashtuns, 4
Popalzai Sub-Tribe, 110
Sikhs, 5, 7, 173
Sudhan, 4, 5
Sudhozais, 4

8. Militant Groups
Afghan mujahideen, 90, 141
Afghan resistance groups, 2
Al-Qaeda, 92, 95, 97
Al-Zulfiqar, 49
Baluch militants, 101
Baluchistan Liberation Army (BLA), 79

Hezb-e-Islami Gulbuddin political party, 50
Jaish-e-Mohammad, 96
Jamaat ul Ahrar (JuA), 101
Northern Alliance, 95, 107
Pashtun tribal lashkars, 5
Taliban fighters, 90, 111
Tehrik-e Taliban Pakistan (TTP), 95, 105

9. The Countries and Places of Relevance
Abbottabad, 98, 99
Andhra Pradesh, India, 101
Arabian sea, 88, 90
Azad Jammu and Kashmir (AJK), 15, 17, 60, 136
Babri Masjid, 114
Balakot, 113, 114
Baluchistan, 79, 80, 91, 95, 100, 101, 103, 104, 107, 111, 114, 118, 119, 123, 135, 136
Central Asian Republics, 88
Changa Manga Forest, 42
Danna in the Village Pothi Balla, 4
Dina, Jhelum, 57
Dubai, 47, 55, 76, 77, 78, 135, 158, 159, 163, 164, 175, 177
East Pakistan, 34, 35, 41, 42, 122
Germany, 103
Indian Held Kashmir (IHK), 5, 75, 105, 114, 115, 136
Indian sub-continent, 5, 145
Israel, 106
Jammu and Kashmir, 5, 6, 105, 136
Jammu-Srinagar National Highway, 113
Jhanda Chichi, 96
Kanganpur, 42
Kharian cantonment, 55, 60, 62
Khyber and Waziristan tribal agencies, 5
Khyber Pakhtunkhwa (KPK), 103, 104, 113, 118, 136
Kohala, 17
Kotari in the Village Pothi Makwalan, 4
Kotli, Azad Kashmir, 97
Ladakh/ Siachen Glacier, 113
Margalla Hills, 51
Murree, 13, 16, 17, 18, 19, 62, 173
Muzaffarabad, 17
Nangarhar Province, 101
Northern Areas (Gilgit-Baltistan), 100, 136, 142
North-West Frontier Province (now KPK), 123
Pir Sohawa, 51
Poonch District, Kashmir, 4
Pyrenees and the Alps, 62
River Jhelum, 17
Saguntum, 62

INDEX

South Asian Subcontinent, 6
The Port of Gwadar, 117
Tilla ranges near Jhelum, 56
Ukraine, 115
United Arab Emirates, 13, 78, 163
United Kingdom, 12, 13, 14, 18, 93, 158, 162 173, 174

10. Strategical/Political Manoeuvrings and References to Wars/Battles

1965 Indo-Pak War, 37
1971 Pak-Indo War, 122
9/11 and its Aftermath, 94-100
A Retrospective View of Pakistan US Relations, 109-110
Afghan Civil War (1989–2001) and US-Pakistan Relations, 90-94
Afghan Jihad (1979-1989), 89
Communal civil war, 6
Hindu-Muslim conflict, 6
Impact of US Strategies in the Region, 115-116
India Found a Space in Afghanistan, 100, 101, 102
Indian Army aggression in 1986/87, 63
Indian Chronicles-A Report by EU Disinfo Lab, 102-104
Indian Involvement in Transnational Crime, 106-107
Indo-Afghan-US Nexus, 100-107

Jammu and Kashmir dispute, 5, 6
Joint operations in Afghanistan with allied intelligence agencies, 48
Liberation of Azad Kashmir in 1948, 6
Orchestrating Disinformation as a Strategic Weapon, 104-107
Withdrawal of Allied Forces from Afghanistan, 110-111

11. The Take-Aways

The Emerging Scenario, 117-120
Domestic Security Challenges, 120-130
On-Going Political and Economic Crisis, 130-137
Major Security Concerns for Pakistan, 139-140
The Way Forward, 143-149
A Message for International Community, 149-150

12. Quotations

C.S. Lewis, 162
Richard Armitage, 94
Michael Jordan, 159
George H Gleig, 110
Quaid-e-Azam Muhammad Ali Jinnah, 146
General Colin Powell, 95
William Shakespeare, 7
Winston Churchill, 118